Given Time

Given Time: I. Counterfeit Money

Jacques Derrida

Translated by Peggy Kamuf

The University of Chicago Press ı Chicago and London

The University of Chicago Press, Chicago 60637
The University of Chicago Press, Ltd., London
© 1992 by The University of Chicago
All rights reserved. Published 1992
Paperback edition 1994
Printed in the United States of America

01 00 99 98 97 96 95 94   5 4 3 2

ISBN (cloth): 0-226-14313-9
ISBN (paper): 0-226-14314-7

Originally published as *Donner le temps,* © Editions Galilée,
1991

Library of Congress Cataloging-in-Publication Data

Derrida, Jacques.
    [Donner le temps.   1. La fausse monnaie.   English]
    Given time.   I. Counterfeit money / Jacques Derrida.
        p.   cm.
    Translation of: Donner le temps.   1. La fausse monnaie.
    Includes bibliographical references.
    1. Baudelaire, Charles, 1821–1867. Spleen de Paris.   2. Mauss,
Marcel, 1872–1950. Essai sur le don.   3. Gifts in literature.
4.   Gifts.   I.   Title
PQ2191.S63D4713   1992
841'.8—dc20   92-7091

Contents

Note on References

Titles of other works by Jacques Derrida that are frequently referred to in the notes will be cited in the form listed below. Where possible, the citation will list page references to both the original edition and the English translation, in that order.

Dissemination: La Dissémination (Paris: Le Seuil, 1972); *Dissemination,* trans. Barbara Johnson (Chicago: University of Chicago Press, 1981).

Glas: Glas (Paris: Galilée, 1974); *Glas,* trans. by John P. Leavey, Jr., and Richard Rand (Lincoln: University of Nebraska Press, 1986).

Grammatology: De la grammatologie (Paris: Minuit, 1967); *Of Grammatology,* trans. Gayatri Chakravorty Spivak (Baltimore: Johns Hopkins University Press, 1976).

Margins: Marges—de la philosophie (Paris: Minuit, 1972); *Margins of Philosophy,* trans. Alan Bass (Chicago: University of Chicago Press, 1982).

Mémoires: Mémoires—pour Paul de Man (Paris: Galilée, 1988); *Mémoires—for Paul de Man,* 2d ed., trans. Cecile Lindsay, Jonathan Culler, Eduardo Cadava, and Peggy Kamuf (New York: Columbia University Press, 1989).

Parages: Parages (Paris: Galilée, 1986).

The Post Card: La Carte postale: de Socrate à Freud et au-delà (Paris: Galilée, 1980); *The Post Card: From Socrates to Freud and Beyond,* trans. Alan Bass (Chicago: University of Chicago Press, 1987).

Psyché: Psyché, Inventions de l'autre (Paris: Galilée, 1987).

Spurs: Eperons, les styles de Nietzsche (Paris: Flammarion, 1972); *Spurs:*

Nietzsche's Styles, trans. Barbara Harlow (Chicago: University of Chicago Press, 1979)

Truth in Painting: *La Vérité en peinture* (Paris: Flammarion, 1978); *The Truth in Painting*, trans. Geoffrey Bennington and Ian McLeod (Chicago: University of Chicago Press, 1987).

Writing and Difference: *L'Ecriture et la différence* (Paris: Le Seuil, 1967); *Writing and Difference*, trans. Alan Bass (Chicago: University of Chicago Press, 1978).

Foreword

Whether one considers the texts it analyzes or its "logical" procedure—I should say *aporia*—this work follows a trajectory that corresponds faithfully to the one I followed in the first five sessions of a seminar given under the same title in 1977–78 at the Ecole Normale Supérieure in Paris and the next year at Yale University. Also, with the exception of certain notes and a few developments, the distribution of the four chapters reproduces the rhythm of the Frederick Ives Carpenter Lectures delivered at the University of Chicago in April 1991. On that occasion, I in fact attempted to formalize the discourse first proposed in 1977–78 and which still had a particular significance for me. It was in the course of this seminar that I gave more thematic figuration to a set of questions which for a long time had organized themselves around that of the gift. Was an explicit formalization of this question possible? What might be its limit? The problematic of the gift, such as it had signaled itself to me or imposed itself on me up to that point[1] reached there, precisely at the limit of its formaliza-

---

1. Cf. wherever it is a question of the *proper* (appropriation, expropriation, exappropriation), economy, the trace, the name, and especially the *rest*, of course, which is to say more or less constantly, but also more expressly and in the vocabulary of the gift, notably in *Writing and Difference*, pp. 127 ff., 133, 151, 219, 395 ff., 423 ff./85 ff., 89, 102, 148, 269 ff.; *Grammatology* pp. 157 ff./107 ff.; *Dissemination*, p. 150/131–32; *Margins* pp. 27 ff./26 ff.; *Spurs*, pp. 89 ff./108 ff.; "Economimesis" (in *Mimesis: des articulations*, edited by Sylviane Agacinski et al. [Paris: Aubier-Flammarion, 1975]; trans. Richard Klein, *Diacritics*, vol. 11, no. 2 [1981]), p. 71/11. But it is especially in *Glas*, pp. 269 ff./242 ff. and passim, and in *Truth in Painting*, pp. 32, 57, 313, 320, 333, 398/27, 48, 274, 281, 291–92, 348–49, that this theme played a more organizing role.

tion, a sort of intermediary stage, a moment of passage. The premises of this unpublished seminar remained implied, in one way or another, in later works that were all devoted, if one may put it that way, to the question of the gift,[2] whether it appeared in its own name, as was often the case, or by means of the indissociable motifs of speculation, destination, or the promise, of sacrifice, the "yes," or originary affirmation, of the event, invention, the coming or the "come."

2. As this problematic then became invasive, I will not give any determined reference here. In the course of the chapters that follow, I will take the liberty of specifying certain of these references, sometimes in order to spare myself a development already proposed elsewhere. Oriented or disoriented by the themes of speculation, destination, or the promise, *The Post Card* referred to the seminar "Given Time" and signaled its forthcoming publication (p. 430/403). See as well "Comment ne pas parler: Dénégations" in *Psyché* ("How To Avoid Speaking: Denials," trans. Ken Frieden, in *Languages of the Unsayable: The Play of Negativity in Literature and Literary Theory*, ed. Sanford Budick and Wolfgang Iser [New York: Columbia University Press, 1989]), p. 587/69, n. 27; and "La main de Heidegger (*Geschlecht* II)," also in *Psyché* ("*Geschlecht* II: Heidegger's Hand," trans. John P. Leavey, Jr., in *Deconstruction and Philosophy: The Texts of Jacques Derrida*, ed. John Sallis [Chicago: University of Chicago Press, 1987]), pp. 587/175–76.

1

The Time of the King

Epigraph

> The King takes all my time; I give the rest to Saint-Cyr, to whom I would like to give all.

It is a woman who signs.

For this is a letter, and from a woman to a woman. Madame de Maintenon is writing to Madame Brinon. This woman says, in effect, that to the King she gives all. For in giving all one's time, one gives all or the all, if all one gives is in time and one gives all one's time.

It is true that she who is known to have been the influential mistress and even the morganatic wife of the Sun King[1] (the Sun and the King, the Sun-

---

1. Madame de Maintenon's sentence is remarkable enough to have attracted the attention of the *Littré*. There are those who will be surprised, perhaps, to see me evoke the secret wife of a great king at the beginning of such a lecture. However, Madame de Maintenon seems to me to be exemplary not only because, from her position as woman and "grande dame," she poses the question of the gift, time—and the rest. She who played the role of Louis XIV's "sultan of conscience" was at the same time—and this configuration is rarely fortuitous—an outlaw and the very figure of the law. Before she became, upon the death of the Queen, the morganatic wife of the King (and thus excluded from all noble titles and rights; the word morganatic says something of the gift and the gift of the origin: it is from low Latin *morganegiba*, gift of the morning), she had led the Sun King back to his duties as husband (by estranging him from Madame de Montespan whose protégée she had been) and as Catholic king (by restoring austerity to the court, by encouraging the persecution of the Protestants—even though

1

King will be the subjects of these lectures), Madame de Maintenon, then, did not say, in her letter, literally, that she was *giving* all her time but rather that the King *was taking* it from her ("the King takes all my time"). Even if, in her mind, that means the same thing, one word does not equal the other. What she *gives*, for her part, is not time but the *rest*, the rest of the time: "I give the rest to Saint-Cyr, to whom I would like to give all." But as the King *takes* it all from her, then the rest, by all good logic and good economics, is nothing. She can no longer *take* her time. She has none left, and yet she gives it. Lacan says of love: It gives what it does not have, a formula whose variations are ordered by the *Ecrits* according to the final and transcendental modality of the woman inasmuch as she is, supposedly, deprived of the phallus.[2]

---

she herself was raised a Calvinist—and by lending her support to the revocation of the Edict of Nantes). She who took so much trouble over what one had to *give* and *take*, over the law, over the name of the King, over legitimacy in general was also the governess of the royal bastards, a promotion she no doubt owed to the protection of Madame de Montespan. Let us stop where we should have begun: When she was a child, she experienced exile in Martinique and her father, Constant, was arrested as a counterfeiter. Everything in her life seems to bear the most austere, the most rigorous, and the most authentic stamp of counterfeit money.

2. "For if love is to give what one does not have . . ." ("La direction de la cure," in *Ecrits* [Paris: Le Seuil, 1966], p. 618); "What is thus given to the Other to fill and which is properly what he/she does not have, since for him/her as well Being is lacking, is what is called love, but it is also hatred and ignorance" (ibid., p. 627); "This privilege of the Other thus sketches out the radical form of the gift of something which it does not have, namely, what is called its love" ("La signification du phallus," ibid., p. 691; "The Meaning of the Phallus," trans. Jacqueline Rose, *Feminine Sexuality: Jacques Lacan and the "école freudienne,"* ed. Rose and Juliet Mitchell [New York: Norton, 1985], p. 80). The symmetry of these formulae, which seem to concern love *in general*, is interrupted when the truth of this "not-having-it" appears, namely, the woman *quoad matrem* and the man *quoad castrationem* (*Encore*, vol. 20 of *Le Séminaire de Jacques Lacan*, ed. Jacques-Alain Miller [Paris: Le Seuil, 1975], p. 36), to use a later formula but one which draws together very well this whole economy. Returning, then, to the *Ecrits:*

> If it is the case that man manages to satisfy his demand for love in his relationship to the woman to the extent that the signifier of the phallus constitutes her precisely as giving in love what she does not have—conversely, his own desire for the phallus will throw up its signifier in the form of a persistent divergence towards "another woman" who can signify this phallus on several counts, whether as a virgin or a prostitute. . . . We should not, however, think that the type of infidelity which then appears to be constitutive of the masculine function is exclusive to the man. For if one looks more closely, the same redoubling is to be found in the woman, the only difference being that in her case, the

Here Madame de Maintenon is *writing*, and she says *in writing* that she gives the rest. What is the rest? *Is* it, the rest? She gives the rest which is nothing, since it is the rest of a time concerning which she has just informed her correspondent she has nothing of it left since the King takes it all from her. And yet, we must underscore this paradox, even though the King takes all *her* time, she seems to have some left, as if she could return the change. "The King takes all *my* time," she says, a time that belongs to her therefore. But how can a time belong? What is it *to have time*? If a time belongs, it is because the word *time* designates metonymically less time itself than the things with which one fills it, with which one fills the form of time, time *as form*. It is a matter, then, of the things one does *in the meantime* [cependant] or the things one has at one's disposal *during* [pendant] this time. Therefore, as time does not belong to anyone as such, one can no more *take* it, itself, than *give* it. Time already begins to appear as that which undoes this distinction between taking and giving, therefore also between receiving and giving, perhaps between receptivity and activity, or even between the being affected and the affecting of any affection. Apparently and according to common logic or economics, one can only exchange, one can only take or give, by way of metonymy, what is *in* time. That is indeed what Madame de Maintenon seems to *want to say* on a certain surface of her letter. And yet, even though the King takes it all from her, altogether, this time or whatever fills up the time, she has some left, a remainder that is not nothing since it is beyond everything, a remainder that is nothing but that *there is* since she *gives it*. And it is even essentially what she gives, *that very thing*. The King takes all, she gives the rest. The rest is not, there is the rest that is given or that gives itself. It does not give itself to someone, because, as everyone knows, Saint-Cyr is not her lover, and it is above all not masculine. Saint-Cyr is a—very femi-

---

Other of Love as such, that is to say, the Other as deprived of that which it gives, is difficult to perceive in the withdrawal whereby it is substituted for the being of the same man whose attributes she cherishes.

The difference of "the only difference being" organizes all the dissymmetries analyzed on this page, which, let us remember, concludes as follows: "Correlatively, one can glimpse the reason for a feature which has never been elucidated and which again gives a measure of the depth of Freud's intuition: namely, why he advances the view that there is only one libido, his text clearly indicating that he conceives of it as masculine in nature" (p. 695/84–85; trans. modified).

The expression "to give what one does not have" is found in Heidegger (in particular in "The Anaximander Fragment" ["Der Spruch des Anaximander" in *Holzwege*] but also elsewhere); see below, chap. 4, n. 28.

nine—place, a charity, an institution, more exactly a *foundation* of Madame de Maintenon's. Saint-Cyr is the name of a charitable institution for the education of impoverished young ladies of good families. Its founder retired there and no doubt was able to devote all her time to it, in accordance with her declared wish, after *the death of the King* in 1715. Would we say, then, that the question of the rest, and of the rest of given time, is secretly linked to a death of the king?

Thus the rest, which *is* nothing but which *there is* nevertheless, does not give itself to someone but to a foundation of young virgins. *And it never gives itself enough, the rest:* "I give the rest to Saint-Cyr, to whom I would like to give all." She never gets enough of giving this rest that she does not have. And when she writes, Madame de Maintenon, that she would like to give all, one must pay attention to the *literal* writing of her *letter, to the letter of her letter.* This letter is almost untranslatable; it defies exchange from language to language. Let us underscore the fact that we are dealing with a letter since things would not be said in the same way in a different context. So when she writes that she would like to give *all* [*elle voudrait* le tout *donner*], she allows two equivocations to be installed: *le* can be a personal pronoun (in an inverted position: *je voudrais tout le donner,* I would like to give it all, that is, all of it) or it can be an *article* (before the word *tout,* which is thus nominalized: I would like to give *all,* that is, everything). That would be the first equivocation. The second equivocation: *tout* or *le tout* can be understood to refer to *time* (all of which the King takes from her) as well as to the *rest* of time: of the time and of what presents itself there, occupying it thus, or of the rest and of what presents itself there, likewise occupying it. This phrase lets one hear the infinite sigh of unsatisfied desire. Madame de Maintenon says to her correspondent that everything leaves her something to be desired. Her wish is not fulfilled or attained either by what she allows herself to take from the King nor even by the rest that she gives—in order to *make a present* of it, if you will, to her young virgins.

Her desire would be there where she *would like,* in the conditional, to give what she cannot give, the all, that rest of the rest of which she cannot make a present. Nobody takes it all from her, neither the King nor Saint-Cyr. This rest of the rest of time of which she cannot make a present, that is what Madame de Maintenant (as one might call her) desires, that is in truth what she would desire, not for herself but so as to be able to give it [*pour le pouvoir donner*]—for the power of giving [*pour le pouvoir de donner*], perhaps, so as to give herself this power of giving. She lacks not lacking time, she lacks not giving enough. She lacks this leftover time that is left to her and that she cannot give—that she doesn't know what to do with. But this rest of the rest of time, of a time that moreover is nothing and that belongs properly to no one, this rest of the rest of time, that is the whole of her desire. Desire and the desire to give would be the same thing, a sort of tautology. But maybe as well the tautological designation of the impossible. Maybe the impossible. The impossible may be—if giving and taking are also the same—the same, the same thing, which would certainly not be a thing.

One could accuse me here of making a big deal and a whole *history* out of words and gestures that remain very clear. When Madame de Maintenon says that the King takes her time, it is because she is glad to give it to him and takes pleasure from it: the King takes nothing from her and gives as much as he takes. And when she says "I give the rest to Saint-Cyr to whom I would like to give all," she opens herself up to her correspondent about a *daily* economy concerning the leisures and charities, the works and days of a "grande dame" somewhat overwhelmed by her obligations. None of the words she writes has the sense of the unthinkable and the impossible toward which my reading would have pulled them, in the direction of giving-taking, of time and the rest. She did not mean to say that, you will say.

What if . . . yes she did [*Et si*].

And if [*Et si*] what she wrote meant to say that, then what would that have to suppose? How, where, on the basis of what and when can we read this letter fragment as I have done? How could we even divert it as I have done, while still respecting its literality and its language?

Let us begin by the impossible.

To join together, in a title, time and the gift may seem to be a laborious artifice. What can time have to do with the gift? We mean: what would there be to see in that? What would they have to do with each other, or more literally, to see together, *qu'est-ce qu'ils auraient à voir ensemble,* one would say in French. Of course, they have nothing to *see* together and first of all because both of them have a singular relation to the visible. Time, in any case, gives nothing to see. It is at the very least the element of invisibility itself. It withdraws whatever could give itself to be seen. It itself withdraws itself from visibility. One can only be blind to time, to the essential *disappearance* of time even as, nevertheless, in a certain manner nothing *appears* that does not require and take time. Nothing sees the light of day, no phenomenon, that is not on the measure of day, in other words, of the *revolution* that is the rhythm of a sun's course. And that orients this course from its endpoint: from the rising in the east to the setting in the west. The works and days, as we said a moment ago.

We will let ourselves be carried away by this word *revolution.* At stake is a certain *circle* whose figure precipitates both time and the gift toward the possibility of their impossibility.

To join together, in a title, at once time and the gift may seem to be a laborious artifice, as if, for the sake of economy, one sought to treat two subjects at once. And that is in fact the case, for reasons of economy. But economy is here the subject. What is economy? Among its irreducible predicates or semantic values, economy no doubt includes the values of law (*nomos*) and of home (*oikos,* home, property, family, the hearth, the fire indoors). *Nomos* does not only signify the law in general, but also the law of distribution (*nemein*), the law of sharing or partition [*partage*], the law as partition (*moira*), the given or assigned part, participation. Another sort of tautology already implies the economic within the nomic as such. As soon as there is law, there is partition: as soon as there is *nomy,* there is economy. Besides the values of law and home, of distribution and partition, economy implies the idea of exchange, of circulation, of return. The figure of the circle is obviously *at the center,* if that can still be said of a circle. It stands at the center of any problematic of *oikonomia,* as it does of any economic field: circular exchange, circulation of goods, products, monetary signs or merchandise, amortization of expenditures, revenues, substitution of use values and exchange values. This motif of circulation can lead one to think that the law of economy is the—circular—return to the point of departure, to the origin, also to the home. So one would have to follow the *odyssean* structure of the economic narrative. *Oikonomia* would always follow the path of Ulysses. The latter returns to the side of his loved ones or to himself; he goes away only in view of *repatriating* himself, in order to return to the home from which [*à partir duquel*] the signal for departure is given and the part assigned, the side chosen [*le parti pris*], the lot divided, destiny commanded (*moira*). The being-next-to-self of the Idea in Absolute Knowledge would be odyssean in this sense, that of an *economy* and a *nostalgia*, a "homesickness," a provisional exile longing for reappropriation.

Now the gift, *if there is any*, would no doubt be related to economy. One cannot treat the gift, this goes without saying, without treating this relation to economy, even to the money economy. But is not the gift, if there is any, also that which interrupts economy? That which, in suspending economic calculation, no longer gives rise to exchange? That which opens the circle so as to defy reciprocity or symmetry, the common measure, and so as to turn aside the return in view of the no-return? If there is gift, the *given* of the gift (*that which* one gives, *that which* is given, the gift as given thing or as act of donation) must not come back to the giving (let us not already say to the subject, to the donor). It must not circulate, it must not be exchanged, it must not in any case be exhausted, as a gift, by the process of exchange, by the movement of circulation of the circle in the form of return to the point of departure. If the figure of the circle is essential to economics, the gift must remain *uneconomic*. Not that it remains foreign to the circle, but it must *keep* a relation of foreignness to the circle, a relation without relation of familiar foreignness. It is perhaps in this sense that the gift is the impossible.

Not impossible but *the* impossible. The very figure of the impossible. It announces itself, gives itself to be thought as the impossible. It is proposed that we begin by this.

And we will do so. We will begin later. By the impossible.

The motif of the circle will obsess us throughout this cycle of lectures. Let us provisionally set aside the question of whether we are talking about a geometric figure, a metaphorical representation, or a great symbol, the symbol of the symbolic itself. We have learned from Hegel to treat this problem. Saying that the circle will obsess us is another way of saying it will encircle us. It will besiege us all the while that we will be regularly attempting to exit [*la sortie*]. But why exactly would one desire, along with the gift, if there is any, the exit? Why desire the gift and why desire to interrupt the circulation of the circle? Why wish to get out of it [*en sortir*]? Why wish to get through it [*s'en sortir*]?

The circle has already put us onto the trail of time and of that which, by way of the circle, circulates between the gift and time. One of the most powerful and ineluctable representations, at least in the history of metaphysics, is the representation of time as a circle. Time would always be a process or a movement in the form of the circle or the sphere. Of this privilege of circular movement in the representation of time, let us take only one index for the moment. It is a note by Heidegger, the last and the longest one in *Sein and Zeit*. Some time ago I attempted a reading of it in "*Ousia* and *Grammè*: Note on a Note from *Being and Time*."[3] Since this Note and this Note on a note will be part of our premises, it will help to recall at least the part concerning the absolute insistence of this figure of the circle in the metaphysical interpretation of time. Heidegger writes:

> The priority which Hegel has given to the 'now' which has been levelled off, makes it plain that in defining the concept of time he is under the sway of the manner in which time is *ordinarily* understood; and this means that he is likewise under the sway of the traditional conception of it. It can even be shown that his conception of time has been drawn *directly* from the 'physics' of Aristotle. [. . . .] Aristotle sees the essence of time in the *nun*, Hegel in the 'now' [*jetzt*]. Aristotle takes the *nun* as *oros*; Hegel takes the 'now' as 'boundary' [*Grenze*]. Aristotle understands the *nun* as *stigmè*; Hegel interprets the 'now' as a point. Aristotle describes the *nun* as *tode ti*; Hegel calls the 'now' the 'absolute this' [*das 'absolute Dieses'*]. Aristotle follows tradition in connecting *khronos* with *sphaira*, Hegel stresses the 'circular course' [*Kreislauf*] of time. [. . .] In suggesting a direct connection between Hegel's conception of time and Aristotle's analysis, we are not accusing Hegel of any 'dependance' on

3. In *Margins*.

Aristotle, but are calling attention to the *ontological import which this filiation has in principle* for the *Hegelian logic.*[4]

There would be more to say on the figure of the circle in Heidegger. His treatment is not simple. It also implies a certain affirmation of the circle, which is assumed. One should not necessarily flee or condemn circularity as one would a bad repetition, a vicious circle, a regressive or sterile process. One must, in a *certain way* of course, inhabit the circle, turn around in it, live there a feast of thinking, and the gift, the gift of thinking, would be no stranger there. That is what *Der Ursprung des Kunstwerks* (*The Origin of the Work of Art*) suggests. But this motif, which is not a stranger to the motif of the hermeneutic circle either, coexists with what we might call a delimitation of the circle: the latter is but a particular figure, the "particular case" of a structure of *nodal* coiling up or interlacing that Heidegger names the *Geflecht* in *Unterwegs zur Sprache* (*On the Way to Language*).

If one were to stop here with this first somewhat simplifying representation or with these hastily formulated premises, what could one already say? That wherever there is time, wherever time predominates or conditions experience in general, wherever *time as circle* (a "vulgar" concept, Heidegger would therefore say) is predominant, the gift is impossible. A gift could be possible, there could be a gift only at the instant an effraction in the circle will have taken place, at the instant all circulation will have been interrupted and *on the condition* of this instant. What is more, this instant of effraction (of the temporal circle) must no longer be part of time. That is why we said "on the condition of this instant." This condition concerns time but does not *belong* to it, does not pertain to it without being, for all that, more logical than chronological. There would be a gift only at the instant when the *paradoxical* instant (in the sense in which Kierkegaard says of the paradoxical instant of decision that it is madness) tears time apart. In this sense one would never have the time of a gift. In any case, time, the "present" of the gift, is no longer thinkable as a now, that is, as a present bound up in the temporal synthesis.

The relation of the gift to the "present," in all the senses of this

---

4. *Being and Time*, division II, chapter 6, n. xxx; as quoted in *Margins*, pp. 39–41/36–38.

term, also to the presence of the present, will form one of the essential knots in the interlace of this discourse, in its *Geflecht*, in the knot of that *Geflecht* of which Heidegger says precisely that the circle is perhaps only a figure or a particular case, an inscribed possibility. That a gift is called a present, that "to give" may also be said "to make a present," "to give a present" (in French as well as in English, for example), this will not be for us just a verbal clue, a linguistic chance or *alea*.

We said a moment ago: "Let us begin by the impossible." By the impossible, what ought one to have understood?

If we are going to speak of it, we will have to name something. Not to present the thing, here the impossible, but to try with its name, or with some name, to give an understanding of or to think this impossible thing, this impossible itself. To say we are going to "name" is perhaps already or still to say too much. For it is perhaps the name of name that is going to find itself put in question. If, for example, the gift were impossible, the name or noun "gift," what the linguist or the grammarian believes he recognizes to be a name, would not be a name. At least, it would not name what one thinks it names, to wit, the unity of a meaning that would be that of the gift. Unless the gift were the impossible but not the unnameable or the unthinkable, and unless in this gap between the impossible and the thinkable a dimension opens up where *there is* gift—and even where *there is* period, for example time, where *it gives* being and time (*es gibt das Sein* or *es gibt die Zeit*, to say it in a way that anticipates excessively what would be precisely a certain essential excess of the gift, indeed an excess of the gift over the essence itself).

Why and how *can I think that the gift is the impossible?* And why is it here a matter precisely of *thinking*, as if thinking, the word *thinking*, found its fit only in this disproportion of the impossible, even announcing itself—as thought irreducible to intuition, irreducible also to perception, judgment, experience, science, faith—only on the basis of *this* figure of the impossible, on the basis of the impossible *in the figure of the gift?*

Let us suppose that someone wants or desires to give to someone. In our logic and our language we say it thus: someone wants or desires, someone *intends-to-give* something to someone. Already the complexity of the formula appears formidable. It supposes a subject and a verb, a constituted subject, which can also be collective—for example, a group, a community, a nation, a clan, a tribe—in any case, a subject identical to itself and conscious of its identity, indeed seeking through the gesture of the gift to constitute its own unity and, precisely, to get its own identity recognized so that that identity comes back to it, so that it can reappropriate its identity: as its property.

Let us suppose, then, an intention-to-give: Some "one" wants or desires to give. Our common language or logic will cause us to hear the interlace of this already complex formula as incomplete. We would tend to complete it by saying "some 'one'" (A) intends-to-give B to C, some "one" intends to give or gives "something" to "someone other." This "something" may not be a thing in the common sense of the word but rather a symbolic object; and like the donor, the donee may be a collective subject; but in any case A gives B to C. These three elements, identical to themselves or on the way to an identification with themselves, look like what is presupposed by every gift event. For the gift to be possible, for there to be gift event, according to our common language and logic, it seems that this compound structure is indispensable. Notice that in order to say this, I must already suppose a certain precomprehension of what *gift* means. I suppose that I know and that you know what "to give," "gift," "donor," "donee" mean in our common language. As well as "to want," "to desire," "to intend." This is an unsigned but effective contract between us, indispensable to what is happening here, namely, that you accord, lend, or give some attention and some meaning to what I myself am doing by giving, for example, a lecture. This whole presupposition will remain indispensable at least for the *credit* that we accord each other, the faith or good faith that we lend each other, even if in a little while we were to argue and disagree about everything. It is by making this precomprehension (credit or faith) explicit that one can authorize oneself to state the following axiom: In order for there to be gift, gift event, some "one" has to give some "thing" to someone other, without which "giving" would be meaningless. In other words, if giving indeed means what, in speaking of it among ourselves, we think it means, then it is necessary, in a certain situation, that some "one" give some "thing" to some "one other," and so forth. This appears tautological, it goes without saying, and seems to imply the defined term in the definition, which is to say it defines nothing at all. Unless the discreet introduction of "one" and of "thing" and especially of "other" ("someone other") does not portend some disturbance in the tautology of a gift that cannot be satisfied with giving or with giving (to) *itself* [se *donner*] without giving something (other) to someone (other).

For this is the impossible that seems to give itself to be thought here: These conditions of possibility of the gift (that some "one" gives some "thing" to some "one other") designate simultaneously the conditions of the impossibility of the gift. And already we could translate this into other terms: these conditions of possibility define or produce the annulment, the annihilation, the destruction of the gift.

Once again, let us set out in fact from what is the simplest level and let us still entrust ourselves to this semantic precomprehension of the word "gift" in our language or in a few familiar languages. For there to be a gift, there must be no reciprocity, return, exchange, countergift, or debt. If the other *gives* me *back* or *owes* me or has to give me back what I give him or her, there will not have been a gift, whether this restitution is immediate or whether it is programmed by a complex calculation of a long-term deferral or differance. This is all too obvious if the other, the donee, gives me back *immediately* the same thing. It may, moreover, be a matter of a good thing or a bad thing. Here we are anticipating another dimension of the problem, namely, that if giving is spontaneously evaluated as *good* (it is *well* and *good* to give and what one gives, the present, the *cadeau*, the gift, is a good), it remains the case that this "good" can easily be reversed. We know that as good, it can also be bad, poisonous (*Gift, gift*), and this from the moment the gift puts the other in debt, with the result that giving amounts to hurting, to doing harm; here one need hardly mention the fact that in certain languages, for example in French, one may say as readily "to give a gift" as "to give a blow" [*donner un coup*], "to give life" [*donner la vie*] as "to give death" [*donner la mort*], thereby either dissociating and opposing them or identifying them. So we were saying that, quite obviously, if the donee gives back the same thing, for example an invitation to lunch (and the example of food or of what are called consumer goods will never be just one example among others), the gift is annulled. It is annulled each time there is restitution or countergift. Each time, according to the same circular ring that leads to "giving back" ["*rendre*"], there is payment and discharge of a debt. In this logic of the debt, the circulation of a good or of goods is not only the circulation of the "things" that we will have offered to each other, but even of the values or the symbols that are involved there [*qui s'y engagent*]⁵ and the intentions to give, whether they are conscious or unconscious. Even though all the anthropologies, indeed the metaphysics of the gift have, *quite rightly and justifiably*, treated *together*, as a system, the gift and the debt, the gift and the cycle of restitution, the gift and the loan, the gift and credit, the gift and the countergift, we are here *departing*, in a peremptory and distinct fashion, from this tradition. That is to say, from tradition itself. We will take our point of departure in the dissociation, in the overwhelming evidence of this other axiom: There is gift, if there is any, only in what interrupts the system as well as the symbol, in a partition without return and without division [*répartition*], without being-with-self of the gift-counter-gift.

For there to be a gift, *it is necessary* [*il faut*] that the donee not give back, amortize, reimburse, acquit himself, enter into a contract, and that he never have contracted a debt. (This "it is necessary" is already the mark of a duty, a debt owed, of the duty-not-to [*le devoir de-ne-pas*]: The donee owes it *to himself* even not to give back, he *ought* not *owe* [*il a le devoir de ne pas devoir*] and the donor ought not count on restitution.) Is is thus necessary, at the limit, that he not *recognize* the gift as gift. If he recognizes it *as* gift, if the gift *appears to him as such*, if the present is present to him *as present*, this simple recognition suffices to annul the gift. Why? Because it gives back, in the place, let us say, of the thing itself, a symbolic equivalent. Here one cannot even say that the symbolic re-constitutes the exchange and annuls the gift in the debt. It does not re-constitute an exchange, which, because it no longer takes place as exchange of things or goods, would be transfigured into a symbolic exchange. The symbolic opens and constitutes the order of exchange and of debt, the law or the order of circulation in which the gift gets annulled. It suffices therefore for the other to *perceive the gift*—not only to perceive it in the sense in which, as one says in French, "on *perçoit*," one receives, for example, merchandise, payment, or compensation—but to perceive its nature of gift, the

---

5. We will translate *engager* variously as to involve, to commit, and rarely as to engage. Here and there we will insert the French term as a reminder that *engager*, which also commonly means to set in motion (as in "to engage a mechanism"), elicits *gage*, that is, pledge, token exchanged in an *engagement*, a promise or agreement. It marks thereby the symbolics of debt that Derrida is concerned with throughout. (Trans.)

meaning or intention, the *intentional meaning* of the gift, in order for this simple *recognition* of the gift *as* gift, *as such*, to annul the gift as gift even before *recognition* becomes *gratitude*. The simple identification of the gift seems to destroy it. The simple identification of the passage of a gift as such, that is, of an identifiable thing among some identifiable "ones," would be nothing other than the process of the destruction of the gift. It is as if, between the event or the institution of the gift *as such* and its destruction, the difference were destined to be constantly annulled. *At the limit, the gift as gift* ought *not appear as gift: either to the donee or to the donor.* It cannot be gift as gift except by not being present as gift. Neither to the "one" nor to the "other." If the other perceives or receives it, if he or she keeps it as gift, the gift is annulled. But the one who gives it must not see it or know it either; otherwise he begins, at the threshold, as soon as he intends to give, to pay himself with a symbolic recognition, to praise himself, to approve of himself, to gratify himself, to congratulate himself, to give back to himself symbolically the value of what he thinks he has given or what he is preparing to give. The temporalization of time (memory, present, anticipation; retention, protention, imminence of the future; "ecstases," and so forth) always sets in motion the process of a destruction of the gift: through keeping, restitution, reproduction, the anticipatory expectation or apprehension that grasps or comprehends in advance.

In all these cases, the gift can certainly keep its phenomenality or, if one prefers, its appearance as gift. But its very appearance, the simple phenomenon of the gift annuls it as gift, transforming the apparition into a phantom and the operation into a simulacrum. It suffices that the other perceive and *keep,* not even the object of the gift, the object given, the thing, but the meaning or the quality, the gift property of the gift, its intentional meaning, for the gift to be annulled. We expressly say: It suffices that the gift *keep* its phenomenality. But *keeping* begins by *taking.* As soon as the other accepts, as soon as he or she takes, there is no more gift. For this destruction to occur, it suffices that the movement of acceptance (of prehension, of reception) last a little, however little that may be, more than an instant, an instant already caught up in the temporalizing synthesis, in the *syn* or the *cum* or the being-with-self of time. There is no more gift as soon as the other *receives*—and even if she refuses the gift that she has perceived or recognized as gift. As soon as she keeps for the gift the signification of gift, she loses it, there is no more *gift*. Consequently, if there is no gift, there is no gift, but if there is gift held or beheld *as* gift by the other, once again there is no gift; in any case the gift does not *exist* and does not *present* itself. If it presents itself, it no longer presents itself.

We can imagine a first objection. It concerns the at least implicit recourse that we have just had to the values of subject, self, consciousness, even intentional meaning and phenomenon, a little as if we were limiting ourselves to a phenomenology of the gift even as we declared the gift to be irreducible to its phenomenon or to its meaning and said precisely that it was destroyed by its own meaning and its own phenomenality. The objection would concern the way in which we are describing the intentionality of intention, reception, perception, keeping, recognition—in sum, everything by means of which one or the other, donee and donor, *take part* in the symbolic and thus annul the gift in the debt. One could object that this description is still given in terms of the self, of the subject that says I, *ego*, of intentional or intuitive perception-consciousness, or even of the conscious or unconscious ego (for Freud the ego or a part of the ego can be unconscious). One may be tempted to oppose this description with another that would substitute for the economy of perception-consciousness an economy of the unconscious: Across the forgetting, the non-keeping, and the non-consciousness called up by the gift, the debt and the symbolic would reconstitute themselves for the subject of the Unconscious or the unconscious subject. As donee or donor, the Other would keep, bind himself, obligate himself, indebt himself according to the law and the order of the symbolic, according to the figure of circulation,[6] even as the conditions of the gift — forgetfulness, non-appearance, non-phenomenality, non-perception, non-keeping—would have been fulfilled. We are indicating here only the principle of a problematic displacement that we would have to go into more carefully.

The necessity of such a displacement is of the greatest interest. It offers us new resources of analysis, it alerts us to the traps of the would-be *gift* without debt, it activates our critical or ethical vigilance.

---

6. On this subject, see Lacan's "Seminar on 'The Purloined Letter'" and the reading I proposed of it in "Le facteur de la vérité," especially around the circle of reappropriation of the gift in the debt (*The Post Card*, pp. 464 ff./436 ff.).

It permits us always to say: "Careful, you think there is gift, dissymmetry, generosity, expenditure, or loss, but the circle of debt, of exchange, or of symbolic equilibrium reconstitutes itself according to the laws of the unconscious; the 'generous' or 'grateful' consciousness is only the phenomenon of a calculation and the ruse of an economy. Calculation and ruse, economy in truth would be the truth of these phenomena."

But such a displacement does not affect the paradox with which we are struggling, namely, the impossibility or the double bind of the gift: For there to be gift, it is necessary that the gift not even appear, that it not be perceived or received as gift. And if we added "not even *taken* or *kept*," it was precisely so that the generality of these notions (of *taking* and especially of *keeping*) could cover a wider reception, sense, and acceptation than that of consciousness or of the perception-consciousness system. We had in mind also the keeping in the Unconscious, memory, the putting into reserve or temporalization as effect of repression. For there to be gift, not only must the donor or donee not perceive or receive the gift as such, have no consciousness of it, no memory, no recognition; he or she must also forget it right away [*à l'instant*] and moreover this forgetting must be so radical that it exceeds even the psychoanalytic categoriality of forgetting. This forgetting of the gift must even no longer be forgetting in the sense of repression. It must not give rise to any of the repressions (originary or secondary) that reconstitute debt and exchange by putting in reserve, by keeping or saving up what is forgotten, repressed, or censured. Repression does not destroy or annul anything; it keeps by displacing. Its operation is systemic or topological; it always consists of keeping by exchanging places. And, by keeping the meaning of the gift, repression annuls it in symbolic recognition. However unconscious this recognition may be, it is effective and can be verified in no better fashion than by its effects or by the symptoms it yields up [*qu'elle donne*] for decoding.

So we are speaking here of an absolute forgetting—a forgetting that also absolves, that unbinds absolutely and infinitely more, therefore, than excuse, forgiveness, or acquittal. As condition of a gift event, condition for the advent of a gift, absolute forgetting should no longer have any relation with either the psycho-philosophical category of forgetting or even with the psychoanalytic category that links forgetting to meaning or to the logic of the signifier, to the economy of repression, and to the symbolic order. The thought of this radical forgetting as thought of the gift should accord with a certain experience of the *trace* as *cinder* or *ashes* in the sense in which we have tried to approach it elsewhere.[7]

And yet we say "forgetting" and not nothing. Even though it must leave nothing behind it, even though it must efface everything, including the traces of repression, this forgetting, this *forgetting of the gift* cannot be a simple non-experience, a simple non-appearance, a self-effacement that is carried off with what it effaces. For there to be gift event (we say event and not act), something must come about or happen, in an instant, in an instant that no doubt does not belong to the economy of time, in a time without time, in such a way that the forgetting forgets, that it forgets *itself*, but also in such a way that this forgetting, without being something present, presentable, determinable, sensible or meaningful, is not nothing. What this forgetting and this forgetting of forgetting would therefore give us to think is something other than a philosophical, psychological, or psychoanalytic category. Far from giving us to think the possibility of the gift, on the contrary, it is on the basis of what takes shape in the name *gift* that one could *hope* thus to think forgetting. For there to be forgetting in this sense, there must be gift. The gift would also be the *condition* of forgetting. By condition, let us not understand merely "condition of possibility," system of premises or even of causes, but a set of traits defining a given situation in which something, or "that" ["*ça*"], is established (as in the expressions "the human condition," "the social condition," and so forth). We are not talking therefore about conditions in the sense of conditions posed (since forgetting and gift, if there is any, are in this sense unconditional),[8] but in the sense in

---

7. For example in *Feu la cendre* (Paris: Des femmes, 1987; *Cinders*, trans. Ned Lukacher [Lincoln: University of Nebraska Press, 1991) and the other texts intersecting with it at the point where, precisely, a certain "il y a là" [there is there] intersects with the giving of the gift (pp. 57, 60 and *passim*/00).

8. Of course, this unconditionality must be absolute and uncircumscribed. It must not be simply declared while in fact dependent in its turn on the condition of some context, on some proximity or family tie, be it general or specific (among human beings, for example, to the exclusion of, for example, "animals"). Can there be any gift *within the family*? But has the gift ever been thought *without the family*? As for the unconditionality evoked by Lewis Hyde in *The Gift: Imagination and the Erotic Life of Property* (New York: Vintage Books, 1983), it is explicitly limited to gifts among close

which forgetting would be in the *condition of the gift* and the gift in the *condition of forgetting;* one might say on the mode of being of forgetting, if "mode" and "mode of being" did not belong to an ontological grammar that is exceeded by what we are trying to talk about here, that is, gift and forgetting. But such is the condition of all the words that we will be using here, of all the words given in our language—and this linguistic problem, let us say rather this problem of language before linguistics, will naturally be our obsession here.

Forgetting and gift would therefore be each in the condition of the other. This already puts us on the path to be followed. Not a particular path leading here or there, but on *the* path, on the *Weg* or *Bewegen* (path, to move along a path, to cut a path), which, leading nowhere, marks the step that Heidegger does not distinguish from thought. The thought on whose path we are, the thought as path or as movement along a path is precisely what is related to that *forgetting* that Heidegger does not name as a psychological or psychoanalytic category but as the condition of Being and of the truth of Being. This truth of Being or of the meaning of Being was foreshadowed, for Heidegger, on the basis of a question of Being posed, beginning with the first part of *Sein und Zeit,* in the transcendental horizon of the question of time. The explicitation of time thus forms the horizon of the question of Being as question of presence. The first line of *Sein und Zeit* says of this question that it "has today fallen into oblivion [*in Vergessenheit*]. Even though in our time [*unsere Zeit*] we deem it progressive to give our approval to 'metaphysics' again. . . . "

Here we must be content with the most preliminary and minimal selection within the Heideggerian trajectory; we will limit ourselves to situating that which links the question of time to the question of

---

friends, relatives, and most often close relatives. Which is to say that it is not what it is or claims to be: unconditional. This is what the literature on organ donation brings out. One of these studies records that the son who donates a kidney to his mother does not want any gratitude from her because she had borne him in the first place. Another who donates to his brother insists that the latter should not feel either indebted or grateful: "those who prize their closeness to the recipient," notes Hyde, "are careful to make it clear that the gift is not conditional" (p. 69). Earlier, it had been pointed out that if, in fact, something comes back, after the gift, if a restitution takes place, the gift would nevertheless cease to be a gift from the moment this return would be its "explicit condition" (p. 9).

the gift, and then both of them to a singular thinking of forgetting. In fact, forgetting plays an essential role that aligns it with the very movement of history and of the truth of Being (*Sein*) which is nothing since it is not, since it is not being (*Seiendes*), that is, being-present or present-being. Metaphysics would have interpreted Being (*Sein*) as being-present/present-being only on the basis of, precisely, a pre-interpretation of time, which pre-interpretation grants an absolute privilege to the now-present, to the temporal ecstasis named present. That is why the transcendental question of time (and within it a new existential analysis of the temporality of *Dasein*) was the privileged horizon for a reelaboration of the question of Being. Now, as we know, this movement that consisted in interrogating the question of Being within the transcendental horizon of time was not interrupted (even though *Sein und Zeit* was halted after the first half and even though Heidegger attributed this interruption to certain difficulties linked to the language and the grammar of metaphysics), but rather led off toward a further turn or turning (*Kehre*). After this turning, it will not be a matter of subordinating the question of Being to the question of the *Ereignis*, a difficult word to translate (event or propriation that is inseparable from a movement of dis-propriation, *Enteignen*). This word *Ereignis*, which commonly signifies event, signals toward a thinking of appropriation or of de-propriation that cannot be unrelated to that of the gift. So from now on it will not be a matter of subordinating, through a purely logical inversion, the question of Being to that of *Ereignis*, but of conditioning them otherwise one by the other, one with the other. Heidegger sometimes says that Being (*das Seyn*, an archaic spelling that attempts to recall the word to a more thinking—*denkerisch*—mode) is *Ereignis*.[9] And it is in the course of this movement that Being (*Sein*)—which is not, which does not exist as being present/present being—is signaled on the basis of the gift.

9. See for example the *Beiträge zur Philosophie (Vom Ereignis), Gesamtausgabe* vol. 65, chap. 8, ed. Friedrich-Wilhelm von Herrmann (Frankfurt am Main, 1989). A French translation of ¶267 has recently been proposed by Jean Greisch in *Rue Descartes*, an issue titled "Des Grecs" (pp. 213 ff.). Beginning with the first pages of the *Vorblick*, a certain *Ereignis* is defined as the truth of Being [*die Wahrheit des Seyns*]. "L'être est l'*Ereignis* [*Das Seyn ist das Er-eignis*]" (¶267, p. 470); or again: "L'être est (este, s'essencie) comme l'*Ereignis* [*Das Seyn west als Ereignis*]" (¶10, p. 30).

This is played out around the German expression *es gibt,* which, moreover, in *Sein und Zeit* (1928) had made a first, discreet appearance that was already obeying the same necessity.[10] We translate the idiomatic locution *es gibt Sein* and *es gibt Zeit* by "il y a l'être" in French and in English "there is Being" (Being is not but there is Being), "il y a le temps," "there is time" (time is not but there is time). Heidegger tries to get us to hear in this [*nous donner à y entendre*] the "it gives," or as one might say in French, in a neutral but not negative fashion, "ça donne," an "it gives" that would not form an utterance in the propositional structure of Greco-Latin grammar, that is, bearing on present-being/being-present and in the subject-predicate relation (S/P). The enigma is concentrated both in the "it" or rather the "*es,*" the "ça" of "ça donne," which is not a thing, and in this giving that gives but without giving anything and without anyone giving anything— nothing but Being and time (which are nothing). In *Zeit und Sein* (1952), Heidegger's attention bears down on the giving (*Geben*) or the gift (*Gabe*) implicated in the *es gibt.* From the beginning of the meditation, Heidegger recalls, if one can put it this way, that in itself time is nothing temporal, since it is nothing, since it is not a thing (*kein Ding*). The temporality of time is not temporal, no more than proximity is proximate or treeness is woody. He also recalls that Being is not being (being-present/present-being), since it is not something (*kein Ding*), and that therefore one cannot say either "time is" or "Being is," but "*es gibt Sein*" and "*es gibt Zeit.*" It would thus be necessary to think a thing, something (*Sache* and not *Ding,* a *Sache* that is not a *being*) that would be Being and time but would not be either a being or a temporal thing: "*Sein—eine Sache, aber nichts Seiendes, Zeit—eine Sache, aber nichts Zeitliches,*" "Being—a thing in question, but not a being. Time—a thing in question, but nothing temporal." He then adds this, which we read in translation for better or worse:

> In order to get beyond the idiom and back to the matter [*Sache*], we must show how this "there is" ["*es gibt*"] can be experienced [*erfahren*] and seen [*erblicken*]. The appropriate way [*der geeignete Weg*] to get there is to explain [elucidate, localize: *erörten*] what is given [*gegeben*] in the "it gives" ["*Es*

gibt"], what "Being" means, which—It gives [*das—Es gibt*]; what "time" means, which—It gives [*das—Es gibt*]. Accordingly, we try to look ahead [*vorblicken*] to the It [*Es*] which—gives [*gibt*] Being [*Sein*] and time [*Zeit*]. Thus looking ahead, we become foresighted in still another sense. We try to bring the It [*Es*] and its giving [*Geben*] into view, and capitalize the "It."[11]

And after having thus written the "It gives Being" and "It gives time," "there is Being" and "there is time," Heidegger in effect asks the question of what it is in this gift or in this "there is" that relates time to Being, conditions them, we would now say, one to the other. And he writes:

First, we shall think [in the trace of: *nach*] Being in order to think It itself into its own element [*um es selbst in sein Eigenes zu denken*].

Then, we shall think [in the trace of: *nach*] time in order to think it itself into its own element.

In this way, the manner must become clear how there is, It gives [*Es gibt*] Being and how there is, It gives [*Es gibt*] time. In this giving [*Geben*; in this *"y avoir" qui donne* says the French translation; in this "there Being" that gives, one might say in English], it becomes apparent [*ersichtlich*] how that giving [*Geben*] is to be determined which, as a relation [*Verhältnis*], first holds [*hält*] the two toward each other and brings them into being [*und sie er-gibt*; by producing them or obtaining them as the result of a donation, in some sort: the *es* gives Being and gives time by giving them one to the other insofar as it holds (*hält*) them together in a relation (*Verhältnis*) one to the other].[12]

In the very position of this question, in the formulation of the project or the design of thinking, namely, the "in order to" (we think "in order to" [*um . . . zu*] think Being and time in their "own element" [*in sein Eigenes, in ihr Eigenes*]), the desire to accede to the proper is already, we could say, surreptitiously ordered by Heidegger according to the dimension of "giving." And reciprocally. What would it

11 Heidegger, *On Time and Being,* trans. Joan Stambaugh (New York: Harper and Row, 1972), p. 5.

12. Ibid.

mean to think the gift, Being, and time *properly* in that which is most proper to them or in that which is properly their own, that is, what they can give and give over to the movements of propriation, expropriation, de-propriation or appropriation? Can one ask these questions without anticipating a thought, even a desire of the proper? A desire to accede to the property of the proper? Is this a circle? Is there any other definition of desire? In that case, how to enter into such a circle or how to get out of it? Are the entrance and the exit the only two modalities of our inscription in the circle? Is this circle itself inscribed in the interlacing of a *Geflecht* of which it forms but one figure? These are so many threads to be pursued.

The only thread that we will retain here, for the moment, is that of *play.* Whether it is a matter of Being, of time, or of their deployment in presence (*Anwesen*), the *es gibt* plays (*spielt*), says Heidegger, in the movement of the *Entbergen,* in that which frees from the withdrawal [*retrait*], the withdrawal of the withdrawal, when what is hidden shows itself or what is sheltered appears. The *play* (*Zuspiel*) also marks, works on, manifests the unity of the three dimensions of time, which is to say a fourth dimension: The "giving" of the *es gibt Zeit* belongs to the play of this "quadridimensionality," to this *properness* of time that would thus be quadridimensional. "True time [authentic time: *die eigentliche Zeit*]," says Heidegger, "is four-dimensional [*vier-dimensional*]." This fourth dimension, as Heidegger makes clear, is not a figure, it is not a manner of speaking or of counting; it is said of the thing itself, on the basis of the thing itself (*aus der Sache*) and not only "so to speak." This thing itself of time implies the play of the four and the play of the gift.

Faced with this play of *fours,* of the four, as play of the gift, one thinks of the hand dealt by this game [*la donne de ce jeu*], of the locution "ça donne" (it gives), of the French imperative "donne" that, given by grammar to be an imperative, perhaps says something other than an order, a desire, or a demand. And then one thinks of *la doña,* of the woman who has been soliciting us since the epigraph, of all the questions of language that are crossing, in German and in French, in the locutions *es gibt* and *ça donne.* Thinking of all that and the rest, we will also evoke a very fine book by Lucette Finas[13] which interlaces all these motifs: the *alea,* the play of the four [*quatre*] and of cards [*cartes*],

13. *Donne* (Paris: Le Seuil, 1976).

the verb "give," the locution *ça donne* (for example, when it is said in French of a purulent body). All these motifs and a few others find themselves woven into a narration, into a narration of narration or into a passion of narration. We will have to recognize that the question of *récit* (narration) and of literature is at the heart of all those we are talking about now. Lucette Finas's novel knots all these threads into the absolute idiom, the effect of the absolute idiom, which is a proper name (*Donne* is a proper name in the novel), a proper name without which perhaps there would never be either a narration effect or a gift effect. Even though we do not meet Heidegger in person in this novel, it is hard to resist the impression that he is hiding behind a series of men's proper names whose initial, with its German assonance, is H.

This detour was meant first of all to remind us that the forgetting we're talking about, if it is constitutive of the gift, is no longer a category of the *psyche*. It cannot be unrelated to the forgetting of Being, in the sense in which Blanchot also says, more or less, that forgetting is another name of Being.

As the condition for a gift to be given, this forgetting must be radical not only on the part of the donee but first of all, if one can say here first of all, on the part of the donor. It is also on the part of the donor "subject" that the gift not only must not be repayed but must not be kept in memory, retained as symbol of a sacrifice, as symbolic in general. For the symbol immediately engages one in restitution. To tell the truth, the gift must not even appear or signify, consciously or unconsciously, *as* gift for the donors, whether individual or collective subjects. From the moment the gift would appear as gift, as such, as what it is, in its phenomenon, its sense and its essence, it would be engaged in a symbolic, sacrificial, or economic structure that would annul the gift in the ritual circle of the debt. The simple intention to give, insofar as it carries the intentional meaning of the gift, suffices to make a return payment to oneself. The simple consciousness of the gift right away sends itself back the gratifying image of goodness or generosity, of the giving-being who, knowing itself to be such, recognizes itself in a circular, specular fashion, in a sort of auto-recognition, self-approval, and narcissistic gratitude.

And this is produced as soon as there is a subject, as soon as donor and donee are constituted as identical, identifiable subjects, capable of identifying themselves by keeping and naming themselves. It is even a matter, in this circle, of the movement of subjectivation, of the constitutive retention of the subject that identifies with itself. The becoming-subject then reckons with itself, it enters into the realm of the calculable as subject. That is why, if there is gift, it cannot take place between two subjects exchanging objects, things, or symbols. The question of the gift should therefore seek its place before any relation to the subject, before any conscious or unconscious relation to self of the subject—and that is indeed what happens with Heidegger when he goes back before the determinations of Being as substantial being, subject, or object. One would even be tempted to say that a subject as such never gives or receives a gift. It is constituted, on the contrary, in view of dominating, through calculation and exchange, the mastery of this *hubris* or of this impossibility that is announced in the promise of the gift. There where there is subject and object, the gift would be excluded. A subject will never give an object to another subject. But the subject and the object are arrested effects of the gift, arrests of the gift. At the zero or infinite speed of the circle.

If the gift is annulled in the economic odyssey of the circle as soon as it appears *as* gift or as soon as it signifies *itself as* gift, there is no longer any "logic of the gift," and one may safely say that a consistent discourse on the gift becomes impossible: It misses its object and always speaks, finally, of something else. One could go so far as to say that a work as monumental as Marcel Mauss's *The Gift*[14] speaks of everything but the gift: It deals with economy, exchange, contract (*do ut des*), it speaks of raising the stakes, sacrifice, gift *and* countergift—in short, everything that in the thing itself impels the gift *and* the annulment of the gift. All the gift supplements (potlatch, transgressions and excesses, surplus values, the necessity to give or give back more, returns with interest—in short, the whole sacrificial bidding war) are destined to bring about once again the circle in which they are annulled. Moreover, this figure of the circle is evoked *literally* by Mauss (literally in French since I am for the moment setting aside an essential problem of translation to which we will return). On the

14. *Essai sur le don, forme archaïque de l'échange* in Marcel Mauss, *Sociologie et Anthropologie* (Paris: Presses Universitaires de France, 1950); *The Gift: The Form and Reason for Exchange in Archaic Societies*, trans. W. D. Halls (London: Routledge, 1990). Page references to the translation, which has occasionally been modified, will be included in parentheses in the text.

subject of the Kula, a kind of "grand potlatch" practiced in the Trobriand Islands and the "vehicle for busy intertribal trade [extending] over the whole of the Trobriand Islands," Mauss writes:

> Malinowski gives no translation of *kula*, which doubtless means "circle." Indeed it is as if all these tribes, these expeditions across the sea, these precious things and objects for use, these types of food and festivals, these services rendered of all kinds, ritual and sexual, these men and women,—were caught up in a *circle** following around this *circle* a *regular movement* in time and space.
> *Note: Malinowski favors the expression "*kula* ring." (Pp. 21–22; emphasis added)[15]

Let us take this first reference to Mauss as a pretext for indicating right away the two types of questions that will orient our reading.

1. The question of language or rather of languages. How is one to legitimate the translations thanks to which Mauss circulates and travels, identifying from one culture to another what he understands by gift, what he calls *gift*? He does this essentially on the basis of the Latin language and of Roman law. The latter plays a singular role throughout the essay, but Mauss also takes German law into account, which is the occasion for him to remark that a "detailed study of the very rich German vocabulary of the words derived from *geben* and *gaben* has not yet been made" (p. 60). This question of the idiom, as

---

15. This circle of the "Kula Ring" is evoked at length by L. Hyde (*The Gift*, pp. 11 ff.) at the beginning of a chapter that is itself titled "The Circle" and that opens with these words from Whitman: "The gift is to the giver, and comes back most to him—it cannot fail. . . ." In a later chapter, we will evoke once again the scene of the gift and the debt, not as it is studied scientifically, but rather as it is first of all assumed or denied by French sociologists. Let us note here, while citing the work of Americans who are "indebted" to Mauss, that they extend this chain of the debt in a necessary and paradoxical manner. Hyde notes that Mauss's essay was the "point of departure" for all the research on exchange of the last half-century. Citing as well Raymond Firth and Claude Lévi-Strauss, he recognizes a particular debt to Marshall Sahlins, notably to the chapter titled "The Spirit of the Gift" in Sahlins' *Stone Age Economics* (Chicago: University of Chicago Press, 1972), which holds Mauss's *The Gift* to be a "gift," "applies a rigorous *explication de texte*" to its sources, and situates "Mauss's ideas in the history of political philosophy." "It was through Sahlins' writings," says Hyde, "that I first began to see the possibility of my own work, and I am much indebted to him" (p. xv).

we shall see, is in itself a question of gift in a rather unusual sense that amounts to neither the gift of languages nor the gift of language.

2. The second type of question cannot be separated from the first, in its widest generality. It would amount to asking oneself in effect: What and whom is Mauss talking about in the end? What is the semantic horizon of anticipation that authorizes him to gather together or compare so many phenomena of diverse sorts, which belong to different cultures, which manifest themselves in heterogeneous languages, under the unique and supposedly identifiable category of gift, under the sign of "gift"? What remains problematic is not only the *unity* of this semantic horizon, that is, the presumed identity of a meaning that operates as general translator or equivalent, but the very existence of something like *the* gift, that is, the common referent of this sign that is itself uncertain. If what Mauss demonstrates, one way or the other, is indeed that every gift is caught in the round or the contract of usury, then not only the unity of the meaning "gift" remains doubtful but, on the hypothesis that giving would have a *meaning* and *one* meaning, it is still the possibility of an effective existence, of an effectuation or an event of the gift that seems excluded. Now, this problematic of the difference (in the sense that we evoked earlier) between "the gift exists" and "there is gift" is never, as we know, deployed or even approached by Mauss, no more than it seems to be, to my knowledge, by the anthropologists who come after him or refer to him. Questions of this type should be articulated with other questions that concern the metalinguistic or meta-ethnological conceptuality orienting this discourse, the category of totality ("total social fact"), the political, economic, and juridical ideology organizing the classification and the evaluation, for example the one that permits Mauss, at the end (it is especially at the end that these evaluations are openly declared), to say that "segmented" societies—Indo-European societies, Roman society before the Twelve Tables, Germanic societies up to the writing of the *Edda*, Irish society up to the writing of its "chief literature"—were ones in which individuals were "less sad, less serious, less miserly, and less personal than we are. Externally at least, they were or are more generous, more giving than we are" (p. 81).

Everything thus seems to lead us back toward the paradox or the aporia of a nuclear proposition in the form of the "if . . . then": If the gift appears or signifies itself, if it exists or if it is presently *as gift*, as what it is, then it is not, it annuls itself. Let us go to the limit: The truth of the gift (its being or its appearing such, its *as such* insofar as it guides the intentional signification or the meaning-to-say) suffices to annul the gift. The truth of the gift is equivalent to the non-gift or to the non-truth of the gift. This proposition obviously defies common sense. That is why it is caught in the impossible of a very singular double bind, the bond without bond of a bind and a non-bind. On the one hand, Mauss reminds us that there is no gift without bond, without bind, without obligation or ligature; but on the other hand, there is no gift that does not have to untie itself from obligation, from debt, contract, exchange, and thus from the bind.

But, after all, what would be a gift that fulfills the condition of the gift, namely, that it not appear as gift, that it not be, exist, signify, want-to-say as gift? A gift without wanting, without wanting-to-say, an insignificant gift, a gift without intention to give? Why would we still call that a gift? That, which is to say what?

In other words, what are we thinking when we require simultaneously of the gift that it appear and that it not appear in its essence, in what it has to be, in what it is to be, in what it will have had to be (in its *to ti en einai* or in its *quiddltus*)? That it obligate and not obligate? That it be and not be that for which it is given? What does "to give" mean to say? And what does language give one to think with this word? And what does "to give" mean to say *in the case* of language, of thinking, and of meaning-to-say?

It so happens (but this "it so happens" does not name the fortuitous) that the structure of this impossible *gift* is also that of Being—that gives itself to be thought on the condition of being nothing (no present-being, no being-present)—and of time which, even in what is called its "vulgar" determination, from Aristotle to Heidegger, is always defined in the paradoxia or rather the aporia of what is without being, of what is never present or what is only scarcely and dimly. Once again let us refer to all the texts, notably those of Aristotle, that are cited in *"Ousia* and *grammè,"* beginning with the Fourth Book of the *Physics*, which says, in the exoteric phase of its discourse, *dia tôn exoterikôn logôn*, that time "is not at all or only scarcely and dimly is [*olôs ouk estin ē molis kai amudrôs*]." Such is the aporetic effect—the "what does not pass" or "what does not happen"—of time defined on the basis of the *nun*, of the now, as *peras*, limit, and as *stigmē*, the point of the instant. "Some of it has been and is not [*gegone kai ouk esti*], some of it is to be and is not yet [*mellei kai oupo estin*]. From these both infinite time [*apeiros*] and time in its incessant return [*aei lambanomenos*] are composed. But it would seem to be impossible that what is composed of things that are not should participate in being [*ousia*]."[16]

We will not analyze here the context and the situation of this proposition called exoteric. Let us take it simply as a marker in the history of an aporetics that will become law and tradition: From the moment time is apprehended on the basis of the *present* now as general form and only modifiable or modalizable in such a way that the past and the future are still presents-past and presents-to-come, this predetermination entails the aporetics of a time that is not, of a time that is what it is *without being (it)* [sans l'être], that is not what it is and that is what it is not, which is to be it *without being (it)* [*qui est de l'être* sans l'être].

If it shares this aporetic paralysis with the gift, if neither the gift nor time exist as such, then the gift that *there* can *be* [*qu'il peut* y avoir] cannot in any case *give time*, since it is nothing. If there is something that can in no case be given, it is time, since it is nothing and since in any case it does not properly belong to anyone; if certain persons or certain social classes have more time than others—and this is finally the most serious stake of political economy—it is certainly not *time itself* that they possess. But inversely, if giving implies in all rigor that one gives nothing that is and that appears as such—determined thing, object, symbol—if the gift is the gift of the giving itself and nothing else, then how to give time? This idiomatic locution, "to give time," seems to mean in common usage "leave time for something, leave time to do something, to fill time with this or that." As usual, it intends less time itself and properly speaking than the temporal or what there is in time. "To give time" in this sense commonly means to give something other than time but something other that is measured by time as by its element. Beyond this historical hardening or sedimentation, perhaps the idiomatic locution "to give time" gives

16. Aristotle, *Physics* 4.10.217b–18a, in *A New Aristotle Reader*, ed. J. L. Ackrill (Princeton: Princeton University Press, 1987), p. 122.

one at least to think—to think the singular or double condition both of the gift and of time.

What there is to give, uniquely, would be called time.

What there is *to give,* uniquely, would be called time.

What there is to give, uniquely, *would be called time.*

For finally, if the gift is another name of the impossible, we still think it, we name it, we desire it. We intend it. And this *even if* or *because* or *to the extent that* we *never* encounter it, we never know it, we never verify it, we never experience it in its present existence or in its phenomenon. The gift *itself*—we dare not say the gift *in it-self*—will never be confused with the presence of its phenomenon. Perhaps there is nomination, language, thought, desire, or intention only there where there is this movement still for thinking, desiring, naming that which gives itself neither to be known, experienced, nor lived—in the sense in which presence, existence, determination regulate the economy of knowing, experiencing, and living. In this sense one can think, desire, and say only the impossible, according to the measureless measure [*mesure* sans *mesure*] of the impossible.[17] If one wants to recapture the proper element of thinking, naming, desiring, it is perhaps according to the measureless measure of this limit that it is possible, possible as relation *without* relation to the impossible. One can desire, name, think in the proper sense of these words, if there is one, *only* to the *immeasuring* extent [*dans la mesure* démesurante] that one desires, names, thinks *still* or *already,* that one still lets announce itself what nevertheless cannot *present itself* as such to experience, to knowing: in short, here *a gift that cannot make itself (a) present* [un don qui ne peut pas se faire présent]. This gap between, on the one hand, thought, language, and desire and, on the other hand, knowledge, philosophy, science, and the order of presence is also a gap between gift and economy. This gap is not present anywhere; it resembles an empty word or a transcendental illusion. But it also gives to this struc-

---

17. On the singular modality of this "impossible," permit me to refer to *Psyché* ("Psyche: Inventions of the Other" in *Reading de Man Reading,* ed. Wlad Godzich and Lindsay Waters [Minneapolis: University of Minnesota Press, 1989]), pp. 26–59/35–60; to *Mémoires,* pp. 54 ff./35 ff., and to *L'Autre Cap* (Paris: Minuit, 1991), pp. 46 ff. On the strange grammar of this "sans," cf. "Pas" in *Parages,* pp. 85 ff.; on that of the "sans l'être," cf. *Dissemination,* p. 241/213.

ture or to this logic a form analogous to Kant's transcendental dialectic, as relation between thinking and knowing, the noumenal and the phenomenal. Perhaps this analogy will help us and perhaps it has an essential relation to the problem of "giving-time."

We are going to give ourselves over to and engage in the effort of thinking or rethinking a sort of transcendental illusion of the gift. For in order to think the gift, a *theory of the gift* is powerless by its very essence. One must engage oneself in this thinking, commit oneself to it, give it tokens of faith [*gages*], and with one's person, risk entering into the destructive circle. One must promise and swear. The effort of thinking or rethinking a sort of transcendental illusion of the gift should not be a simple reproduction of Kant's critical machinery (according to the opposition between thinking and knowing, and so forth). But neither is it a matter of rejecting that machinery as old-fashioned. In any case, we are implicated in it, in particular because of that which communicates, in this dialectic, with the problem of time on one side, that of the moral law and of practical reason on the other side. But the effort to think the groundless ground of this quasi-"transcendental illusion" should not be either—if it is going to be matter of *thinking*—a sort of adoring and faithful abdication, a simple movement of faith in the face of that which exceeds the limits of experience, knowledge, science, economy—and even philosophy. On the contrary, it is a matter—desire beyond desire—of responding faithfully but also as rigorously as possible both to the injunction or the order of the *gift* ("give" ["*donne*"]) as well as to the injunction or the order of meaning (presence, science, knowledge): *Know* still what giving *wants to say, know how to give,* know what you want and want to say when you give, know what you intend to give, know how the gift annuls itself, commit yourself [*engage-toi*] even if commitment is the destruction of the gift by the gift, give economy its chance.

For finally, the overrunning of the circle by the gift, if there is any, does not lead to a simple, ineffable exteriority that would be transcendent and without relation. It is this exteriority that sets the circle going, it is this exteriority that puts the economy in motion. It is this exteriority that *engages* in the circle and makes it turn. If one must *render an account* (to science, to reason, to philosophy, to the economy of meaning) of the circle effects in which a gift gets annulled, this account-rendering requires that one take into account that which, while not simply belonging to the circle, engages in it and sets off its motion. What is the gift as the first mover of the circle? And how does it contract itself into a circular contract? And from what place? Since when? From whom?

That is the contract, between us, for this cycle of lectures. (Recall that Mauss's essay *The Gift* has its premises in his work and that of Davy on the contract and on sworn faith.)[18]

Even if the gift were never anything but a simulacrum, one must still *render an account* of the possibility of this simulacrum and of the desire that impels toward this simulacrum. And one must also render an account of the desire to render an account. This cannot be done against or without the *principle of reason* (*principium reddendae rationis*), even if the latter finds there its limit as well as its resource. Otherwise, why would I commit myself—making it an obligation for myself—to speak and to render an account? Whence comes the law that obligates one to give even as one renders an account of the gift? In other words, to *answer* [répondre] still for a gift that calls one beyond all responsibility? And that forbids one to forgive whoever *does not know how to give?*

"I will never forgive him the ineptitude of his calculation," concludes the narrator of "La fausse monnaie" (Counterfeit Money), the brief story by Baudelaire that we will read together. Was he reproaching his friend in effect for not having *known how to give?* That is one of the questions waiting for us. Here is "Counterfeit Money":

> As we were leaving the tobacconist's, my friend carefully separated his change; in the left pocket of his waistcoat he slipped small gold coins; in the right, small silver coins; in his left trouser pocket, a handful of pennies and, finally, in the right he put a silver two-franc piece that he had scrutinized with particular care.
>
> "What a singularly minute distribution!" I said to myself.
>
> We encountered a poor man who held out his cap with a trembling hand.—I know nothing more disquieting than the

18. See Georges Davy, *La Foi jurée, Etude sociologique du problème du contrat et de la formation du lien contractuel* (*L'Année Sociologique*, 1922), and Mauss, "Une forme ancienne de contrat chez les Thrace," *Revue des Etudes grecques*, no. 24 (1921):388–97.

mute eloquence of those supplicating eyes that contain at once, for the sensitive man who knows how to read them, so much humility and so much reproach. He finds there something close to the depth of complicated feeling one sees in the tear-filled eyes of a dog being beaten.

My friend's offering was considerably larger than mine, and I said to him: "You are right; next to the pleasure of feeling surprise, there is none greater than to cause a surprise." "It was the counterfeit coin," he calmly replied as though to justify himself for his prodigality.

But into my miserable brain, always concerned with looking for noon at two o'clock (what an exhausting faculty is nature's gift to me!), there suddenly came the idea that such conduct on my friend's part was excusable only by the desire to create an event in this poor devil's life, perhaps even to learn the varied consequences, disastrous or otherwise, that a counterfeit coin in the hands of a beggar might engender. Might it not multiply into real coins? Could it not also lead him to prison? A tavern keeper, a baker, for example, was perhaps going to have him arrested as a counterfeiter or for passing counterfeit money. The counterfeit coin could just as well, perhaps, be the germ of several days' wealth for a poor little speculator. And so my fancy went its course, lending wings to my friend's mind and drawing all possible deductions from all possible hypotheses.

But the latter suddenly shattered my reverie by repeating my own words: "Yes, you are right; there is no sweeter pleasure than to surprise a man by giving him more than he hopes for."

I looked him squarely in the eyes and I was appalled to see that his eyes shone with unquestionable candor. I then saw clearly that his aim had been to do a good deed while at the same time making a good deal; to earn forty cents and the heart of God; to win paradise economically; in short, to pick up gratis the certificate of a charitable man. I could have almost forgiven him the desire for the criminal enjoyment of which a moment before I assumed him capable; I would have found something bizarre, singular in his amusing himself by compromising the poor; but I will never forgive him the ineptitude of his calculation. To be mean is never excusable, but there is some merit in knowing that one is; the most irreparable of vices is to do evil out of stupidity.[19]

The following three chapters will maintain a constant relation to the letter of this text, sometimes by referring to it directly. Readers who wish consult it at any moment may do so by unfolding the page at the end of this book.

19. Charles Baudelaire, *Oeuvres complètes*, vol. 1, ed. Claude Pichois (Paris: Bibliothèque de la Pléiade, 1975), p. 323; *Paris Spleen*, trans. Louise Varèse (New York: New Directions, 1970), pp. 58–59; translation modified. The French text of "La fausse monnaie" is printed below, p. 175.

2

The Madness of Economic Reason: A Gift without Present

At the same time we are thinking the impossible, and it is at the same time.

What does "at the same time" mean to say? Where could one ever place oneself in order to say "at the same time"? And to say what is meant, for example in some language or another, by "at the same time"?

It is as if we were looking for complications, for *midi à quatorze heures* as we say in French, literally, for noon at two o'clock, and as if we wanted to show that we were given to, and even gifted at, tracking the impossible. That is what the narrator of "Counterfeit Money" says when speaking of the "exhausting faculty" that "nature" has given him as a "gift." To look for noon at two o'clock is to torment one's mind trying to find that which, by definition, cannot be found where one is looking for it and especially not at the moment one is looking for it. At no *given moment*, at no *desired moment* [moment voulu] can one reasonably hope to find, outside any relativity, noon at two o'clock. This contradiction is the logical and chronological form of the *impossible* simultaneity of two times, of two events separated in time and which therefore cannot be given *at the same time*. To look for the impossible is that form of madness in which we seem to have enclosed ourselves up to now. It is true that looking for "noon" is not just any madness and it is not looking for just any moment; perhaps it is to dream, at whatever time and always too late (at two o'clock it's already too late), of an origin without shadow, without dialectical negativity, in the solar course on the basis of which we calculate time;

it is to dream while strolling along, like the two friends in "Counterfeit Money"; it is to sleepwalk in the vicinity of the impossible.

Perhaps what was said or told the last time sounded a little mad. How is one to speak reasonably, in a sensible fashion, that is, accessible to common sense, of a gift that could not be what it was except on the condition of not being what it was? On the condition of not being or appearing to be the gift of anything, of anything that is or that is present, come from someone and given to someone? On the condition of "being" a gift without given and without giving, without presentable thing and act? A gift that would neither give *itself*, nor give itself *as such*, and that could not take place except on the condition of not taking place—and of remaining impossible, without dialectical sublation of the contradiction? To desire, to desire to think the impossible, to desire, to desire to give the impossible—this is obviously madness. The discourse that orders itself on this madness cannot not let itself be contaminated by it. This discourse on madness appears to go mad in its turn, *alogos* and *atopos*. *Alogos* as well because it claims to render an account (the demand to *render account* that we mentioned at the conclusion), to render account and reason (*reddere rationem*) of that very thing, the gift, that demands an unheard-of-accounting since it must not conclude in either a balancing of income and expenses, in an economic circle, or in the regulated rationality of a calculation, a metrics, a symmetry, or any kind of relation, which is to say in a *logos*, to stay with this injunction of the Greek term, which means at once reason, discourse, relation, and account. It is *logos* and *nomos* that, as we saw, are sent into crisis by the madness of the gift—but perhaps as well *topos*. *Atopos*, as we know, means that which is not in its place (noon at two o'clock) and thus it means the extraordinary, the unusual, the strange, the extravagant, the absurd, the mad. Only an *atopic* and *utopic* madness, *perhaps* (a certain *perhaps* or *maybe* will be both the modality and the modality to be modified or our meditation), could thus give rise to the gift that can give only on the condition of not taking place, taking up residence or domicile: *the gift may be, if there is any.*

This madness, let us recall, would also be that of a forgetting, of a given and desired forgetting, not as a negative experience therefore, like an amnesia and a loss of memory, but as the affirmative condition of the gift. How, without madness, can one desire the forgetting of that which will have been, like the gift, a gift without ambivalence, a gift that would not be a *pharmakon* or a poisoned present (*Gift/gift*)[1] but a good, a good that would not be an object (a good given as a thing) but the good of the gift, of giving or donation itself? How does one desire forgetting? How does one desire not to keep? How does one desire mourning (assuming that to mourn, to work at mourning does not amount to keeping—and here we touch on what remains no doubt the unavoidable problem of mourning, of the relation between gift and grief, between what should be non-work, the non-work of the gift, and the work of mourning)? How does one desire forgetting or the non-keeping of the gift if, implicitly, the gift is evaluated as good, indeed as the very origin of what is good, of the good, and of value?

Linked to the double bind (double ligature, double stricture,[2] double obligation to link and unlink absolutely, thus to absolve and to forgive by giving), this madness is all the more maddened and maddening that it besieges reason at its two borders, so to speak, from the inside and the outside. It is at once reason and unreason because it also manifests that madness of the rational *logos* itself, that madness of the economic circle the calculation of which is constantly

---

1. In a note to "Plato's Pharmacy" (*Dissemination*, pp. 150–51/131–32), the subject of which is therefore being continued here, I had already cited this note of Mauss's:

> *Mélanges Ch. Andler*, Strasbourg, 1924. We are asked why we do not examine the etymology of *gift*, translation of the Latin *dosis*, itself a transcription of the Greek *dosis*, dose, dose of poison. This etymology supposes that High and Low German dialects had retained a scientific word for a commonly used thing, which is contrary to the usual semantic rule. Moreover, one would still have to explain the choice of the word *gift* for this translation and the inverse linguistic taboo that has weighed on the sense of 'gift' for this word in certain Germanic languages. Finally, the Latin and especially Greek use of *dosis* to mean poison shows that with the Ancients as well there was association of ideas and moral rules of the kind we are describing.
>
> We compare the uncertainty of the meaning of *gift* with that of the Latin *venenum* and the Greek *philtron* and *pharmakon*; one should also add (cf. Bréal, *Mélanges de la société linguistique*, Vol. 3, p 140) *venia, venus, venenum*, from *vanati* (Sanskrit, to give pleasure) and *gewinnen, win*.

Cf. as well Gloria Goodwin Raheja, *The Poison in the Gift: Ritual, Prestation, and the Dominant Caste in a North Indian Village* (Chicago: University of Chicago Press, 1988). There, one may follow an interesting discussion of Mauss on the subject of the gift and the (non-reciprocal) reception of the *dan* (pp. 249ff.).

2. Cf. on this subject *Glas* and *The Post Card*.

reconstituted, logically, rationally, annulling the excess that itself, as we underscored at the conclusion of the preceding chapter, entails the circle, makes it turn without end, gives it its movement, a movement that the circle and the ring can never comprehend or annul. Whence the difficulty in knowing whom and what one is talking about. Is madness the economic circulation annulling the gift in equivalence? Or is it the excess, the expenditure, or the destruction?

To make another indicative and preliminary appeal to *The Gift*, we will lift an exemplary fragment from it in which madness is named. Evoking it in passing and in the form of an adverb ("madly"), Mauss seems to be quite unaware of what he is naming and whether one can still call one thing by the name of gift and another thing by the name of exchange.

Mauss is describing the potlatch.[3] He speaks of it blithely as "gifts exchanged." But he never asks the question as to whether gifts can remain gifts once they are exchanged. A long *nota bene* has just specified that "there are potlatches everywhere. . . . As in Melanesia it is a constant give-and-take." This latter expression, also in English in the original, is translated "donner et recevoir." So, translating "take" by "recevoir," Mauss continues: "The potlatch *itself*, so typical a phenomenon, and at the same time so characteristic of these tribes, *is none other than* the system of gifts exchanged" (p. 35). (We underscore "itself," this word that marks the assurance and the certainty that one has touched the essential property of an identifiable thing corresponding to a proper name: potlatch; we also underscore the locution "is none other than": It confirms once again the identificatory tranquility of this assurance.)

Mauss does not worry enough about this incompatibility between gift and exchange or about the fact that an exchanged gift is only a tit for tat, that is, an annulment of the gift. By underscoring this, we do not mean to say that *there is no* exchanged gift. One cannot deny the *phenomenon*, nor that which presents this precisely phenomenal aspect of exchanged gifts. But the apparent, visible contradiction of these two values—gift and exchange—must be problematized. What must be interrogated, it seems, is precisely this being-together, the at-the-same-time, the synthesis, the symmetry, the syntax, or the system, the *syn* that joins together two processes that are by rights as

3. In Chapter 2, section 3, "The American Northwest: Honor and Credit," pp. 33ff.

incompatible as that of the gift and that of exchange. Can one speak without any second thoughts of something that would be "none other," in "*itself*," "than the system of gifts exchanged"?

The *syn* of this system, as we shall see in a moment, has an essential relation to *time*, to a certain delay, to a certain *deferral/differing* [différer] in time. The "it is none other than" takes on all its relief when, right after this, Mauss marks a difference: "the only differences are . . . ," he is going to note. This difference is precisely that of the *excessive.* An essential exaggeration marks this process. Exaggeration cannot be here a feature among others, still less a secondary feature. The problem of the gift has to do with its nature that is *excessive in advance, a priori exaggerated.* A donating experience that would not be delivered over, *a priori,* to some immoderation, in other words, a moderate, measured gift would not be a gift. To give and thus do something other than calculate its return in exchange, the most modest gift must pass beyond measure. Mauss continues:

> The potlatch . . . is none other than the system of gifts exchanged. The only differences are in the violence, exaggeration, and antagonisms it arouses, on the one hand and, on the other, by a certain lack of juridical concepts, and in a simpler, more brutal structure than in Melanesia, especially with the two northern nations, the Tlingit and the Haida . . ." (Ibid.)

And before describing this exaggeration of the Indians in a passage where precisely "madness" will be named and where, at least twice, the question of the lexicon will appear inevitable, Mauss stays a moment longer with the Melanesians or the Polynesians so as to describe both the circle, the regular circulation of what he insists on calling *gifts,* and the role played by *time* in this circulation. The decisive concepts here are those of "credit" and "term" (in the sense of the term of a loan or a debt) in the potlatch:

> Gifts *circulate* [emphasis added; how can gifts circulate?], as we have seen, in Melanesia and Polynesia, with the certainty that they will be reciprocated. Their "guarantee" [*sûreté*: also security deposit] is in the virtue of the thing given [we will come back to this] which is itself that "guarantee." But in every possible form of society, it is in the nature of a gift to impose an

obligatory *time limit or term* [emphasis added]. By definition, even a meal shared in common, a distribution of *kava,* or a talisman that one takes away, cannot be reciprocated immediately. "Time" [an expression that Mauss puts in quotation marks, no doubt aware of the obscure character of this notion and the fact that, beneath the word time, it is no doubt a matter, in the homogeneous element of chronology, of a more complex and qualitatively more heterogeneous structure of delay, of interval, of maturation, or of differance] is needed to perform any counter-service. The notion of a *time limit or term* [emphasis added again] is thus logically implied when it is a question of paying or returning visits [*rendre des visites:* an interesting expression in the French idiom: a visit is always repaid or returned even when it is the first], contracting marriages and alliances, establishing peace, attending games or regulated contests, celebrating alternative festivals, rendering ritual and honorific services [*rendre les services:* an equally interesting expression: This language of restitution is necessary even for services that one "gives" for the first time], "showing recip rocal respect" [a Tlingit expression]—all the things that are exchanged at the same time as other things that become increasingly numerous and valuable, as these societies become richer. (P. 36)

The term "term" marks a mark: It is the limit of a due date, the cadence of a falling due [*échéance*]. It thus implies time, the interval that separates reception from restitution. In Mauss's view, the *term* forms the original and essential feature of the *gift*. The interval of this delay to deadline allows Mauss to pass unnoticed over that contradiction between gift and exchange on which I have insisted so much and which leads to madness in the case both where the gift must remain foreign to circular exchange as well as where it is pulled into that exchange, unless it is the gift itself that does the pulling. The differance marked by the term "term" is comparable here to a guardrail, *un garde-fou,* against the madness of the gift. Mauss is not at all bothered about speaking of exchanged gifts; he even thinks there is gift only in exchange. However the *syn*-, the *syn*thesis, the *sys*tem, or the *syn*tax that joins together gift and exchange is temporal—or more precisely temporizing—differance, the delay of the term or the term of delay that dislocates any "at the same time." The identity between gift and exchange would not be immediate and analytical. It would have in effect the form of an *a priori* synthesis: a synthesis because it requires temporization and *a priori*—in other words necessary—because it is required at the outset by *the thing itself*, namely by the very object of the gift, by the force or the virtue that would be inherent to it. Here is, it seems, the most interesting idea, the great guiding thread of *The Gift:* For those who participate in the experience of gift and countergift, the requirement of restitution "at term," at the delayed "due date," the requirement of the circulatory differance *is inscribed in the thing itself* that is given or exchanged. Before it is a contract, an intentional gesture of individual or collective subjects, the movement of gift/countergift is a *force* (a "virtue of the thing given," says Mauss), a property immanent to the thing or in any case apprehended as such by the donors and donees. Moved by a mysterious force, the thing itself demands gift *and* restitution, it requires therefore "time," "term," "delay," "interval" of temporization, the becoming-temporization of temporalization, the animation of a neutral and homogeneous time by the desire of the gift and the restitution. Differance, which (is) nothing, is (in) the thing itself. It is (given) in the thing itself. It (is) the thing itself. It, differance, the thing (itself). It, without anything other. Itself, nothing.

The transformation of temporalization into temporization would be the movement of this desire for the gift/countergift. It would be inscribed in, *upon* [à même] the given-exchanged thing. This demand of the thing, this demand for term and temporization, would be the very structure of the thing. The thing would demand limit and time, at once the mark or the margin—that is, the measure that sets a boundary—and temporality. And the thing would be a thing, that is, it would have its "virtue" or its essence of thing, only in this demand. The demand dawns in what is called the gift-counter-gift.

What is a thing that one can talk about it in this fashion? Later we will have to encounter this question in or beyond its Heideggerian modality, but it seems to be posed in a certain way at the very opening of *The Gift*, right after the definition of a program and the quotation of a poetic text in epigraph. (Why must one begin with a poem when one speaks of the gift? And why does the gift always appear to be the *gift of the poem*, the *don du poème* as Mallarmé says?) Here are the first words in italics: *"What rule of legality and self-interest, in societies of a* backward or archaic type, compels the present that has been received to be obligatorily reciprocated? What force is there in the given thing that causes its recipient to pay it back?" (p. 3).

One can translate as follows: The gift is not a gift, the gift only gives to the extent it *gives time*. The difference between a gift and every other operation of pure and simple exchange is that the gift gives time. *There where there is gift, there is time.* What it gives, the gift, is time, but this gift of time is also a demand of time. The thing must not be restituted *immediately and right away*. There must be time, it must last, there must be waiting—without forgetting [*l'attente—sans oubli*]. It demands time, the thing, but it demands a delimited time, neither an instant nor an infinite time, but a time determined by a term, in other words, a rhythm, a cadence. The thing is not *in* time; it is or it has time, or rather it demands to have, to give, or to take time—and time as rhythm, a rhythm that does not befall a homogeneous time but that structures it originarily.

The gift gives, demands, and takes time. The thing gives, demands, or takes time. That is one of the reasons this thing of the gift will be linked to the—internal—necessity of a certain narrative [*récit*] or of a certain poetics of narrative. That is why we will take account of "Counterfeit Money" and of the impossible account [*compte-rendu*] that is Baudelaire's tale. The thing as given thing, the given of the gift arrives, if it arrives, only in narrative. And in a poematic simulacrum of narrative. The opening of *The Gift* inscribes, then, in epigraph an "old poem from the Scandinavian *Edda*" of which one stanza (45) is made to stand out:

> It is better not to beg [ask for something]
> Than to sacrifice too much [to the gods]:
> A present given always expects one in return.
> It is better not to bring any offering
> Than to spend too much on it. (P. 2)

Mauss maneuvers laboriously with this notion of time or term. He is seeking in it the distinctive trait of the gift, that which distinguishes the latter from credit, debt, or payment as these are determined by modern Western law or economy. In criticizing the vocabulary of certain authors, Mauss tries to restitute, so to speak, the value of gift, of "present made" and of "present repaid" where others wanted to describe the same operation of exchange with interest as a purely economic, commercial, or fiduciary operation, without needing in the least to have recourse to the category of the gift. For it might seem tempting to get rid of the mysterious and elusive character of this value of gift. And since we are saying with such insistence that it is impossible, why not denounce it as an illusion, even a sophism or paralogism, as well as a pseudo-problem that reason would require us, in good logic, to evacuate? Does it not suffice in fact to describe scientifically the objective exchange of values with usurious supplement, in short, the logic of credit, of interest rates, and of repayment due dates? By reintroducing the word and the category of gift where other authors attempt or are tempted to get by without it, Mauss would like to bring off several operations (and this is one of the admirable things about his essay: it seeks to match the stubbornness of this impossible non-thing that would be the gift with a certain stubbornness of its own): (1) to succeed in maintaining an originary specificity of the process of gift in relation to cold economic rationality, to capitalism, and mercantilism—and in that way to recognize in the gift that which sets the circle of economic exchange going; (2) to succeed in describing the symbolicity that runs throughout cold economic reason, to render an account of religious, cultural, ideological, discursive, esthetic, literary, poetic phenomena that are inseparable from the process of the gift and that organize it from within this *total social fact* which Mauss makes the very object of sociology (here it would be necessary to evoke his critique of a certain economism in Marx and the whole context of the *Cahiers de Sociologie,* and so forth); (3) to succeed in understanding the at least relative homogeneity of all human cultures, whatever may be the type or the level of economic and juridical functioning; (4) to succeed in making credit, time, "term"—or the supplementary differance (the "return-more-later")—into a demand, an *interest of the thing itself,* thus an interest that cannot be derived from anything other than the thing, an interest of the given thing, of the thing that calls for the gift, of the given "it" or *ça* (*ça* is not in Mauss's vocabulary): not the *ça* of *ça donne* (*es gibt, il y a,* there is) but of the *ça donné,* of the given it, although the thing's requirement that it be given-returned allows one to dispense with the distinction between the *it* of *it gives* and the *it* of the *given.* The given *it* will have required that *it* gives. The *it* is giving-given, giving-giving.[4]

---

4. That is, *donnant donnant.* This is also a colloquial expression in French that might be translated: fair's fair, i.e., you give me this and I'll give you that. (Trans.)

Finally, with the sole difference of a distancing in time and of the interest of usury, the *it* is at once, "at the same time," given-given and giving-giving.

To substantiate these remarks, let us consider a certain lexical maneuver by Mauss. We will give or take two examples of it.

First example. This example can interest us as well for the relation between the *date* and the *gift*, a relation that Mauss does not thematize.[5] On the question of the credit demanded by the thing in the potlatch among tribes of northwestern Canada, a note quotes Boas:

> "In all his undertakings, the Indian trusts to the aid of his friends. He promises to pay them for this assistance at a later date. If the aid provided consists of valuable things, which are measured by the Indians in blankets, just as we measure them in money, he promises to pay back the value of the loan with interest. The Indian has no system of writing and consequently, to guarantee the transaction, the promise is made in public. To contract debts on the one hand, and to pay those debts on the other, constitutes the potlatch. This economic system is developed to such an extent that the capital possessed by all the individuals associated with the tribe far exceeds the quantity of available valuables that exists; in other words, the conditions are entirely analogous to those prevailing in our own society: if we desired to pay off all our debts, we would find that there was not nearly enough money, in fact, to settle them. The result of an attempt by all creditors to seek reimbursement of their loans [that is, together and immediately] is a disastrous panic that the community takes a long time to recover from." (P. 11, n. 131)

Let us notice first of all, in passing, this allusion to writing. To repeat the, in our view, very problematic expression of Boas, "the Indian has no system of writing." We thus see a certain relation shaping up between writing or its substitute (but what is a substitute for writing if not a writing?) and the process of the gift. The latter is perhaps not determined only as the content or the theme of a piece of writing—accounting, archive, memoirs, narrative, or poem—but already, in itself, as the marking of a trace. The gift would always be

5. I take the liberty of referring here to *Schibboleth, pour Paul Celan* (Paris: Galilée, 1986), in particular pp. 72–77, 93–108.

the gift of a writing, a memory, a poem, or a narrative, in any case, the legacy of a text; and writing would not be the formal auxiliary, the external archive of the gift, as Boas suggests here, but "something" that is tied to the very act of the gift, *act* in the sense both of the archive and the performative operation.

Boas concludes that, in the potlatch, the Indian wants *both* to pay his debts in public and to invest the fruits of his labor for the future, to prepare an inheritance for his children. Now, what does Mauss do after having quoted this long passage? He raises no essential objection, he judges the description to be exact, but he proposes a correction to the vocabulary. Here it is: "By correcting the terms 'debt,' 'payment,' 'reimbursement,' 'loan' and replacing them with such terms as 'presents made' and 'presents repaid,' terms that Boas moreover ends up by using himself, we have a fairly exact idea of how the notion of credit functions in the potlatch."

This correction inverts, therefore, the direction of the definitional circle. It appears tautological, but what is at stake in this correction is important for Mauss. For him, it is a matter of thinking the economic rationality of credit on the basis of the gift and not the reverse. The gift would be originary. It would be the true producer of value, being in itself the value of values. As Valéry says of spirit, the gift would be at once a value and the—priceless—origin of all value.[6] For Mauss's discourse is oriented by an ethics and a politics that tend to valorize the generosity of the giving-being. They oppose a liberal socialism to the inhuman coldness of economism, of those two economisms that would be capitalist mercantilism *and* Marxist communism.

Second example. Right after this, another apparently lexical maneuver objects to a sort of evolutionism. In failing to understand debt in its relation to the originary gift, in failing to understand "term" and deferred interest as gift effects, evolutionism ends up believing credit to be a late invention of very evolved societies.

Current economic and juridical history is largely mistaken in this matter. Imbued with modern ideas, it forms *a priori* ideas of development,* and follows a so-called necessary logic. All in all, it remains within old traditions. There is nothing more

6. Paul Valéry, *Oeuvres complètes* (Paris: Bibliothèque de la Pléiade, 1960), vol. 2, pp. 1077–85. Cf. on this subject, *L'Autre cap*, pp. 94ff.

dangerous than this "unconscious sociology," as Simiand has
termed it. For example, Cuq still states: "In primitive societies,
only the barter regime is conceived of; in those more advanced,
sales for cash are the practice. Sale on credit is characteristic of
a higher phase in civilization. It first appears in an oblique form
as a combination of cash sale and loans." In fact, the point of
departure lies elsewhere. It is provided in a category of rights
neglected by jurists and economists as uninteresting. This is
the gift, a complex phenomenon, particularly in its most ancient form, that of *the total prestation which we are not studying in
this essay. Now, the gift necessarily entails the notion of credit* [em-
phasis added]. The evolution in economic law has not been
from barter to sale, and from cash sale to credit sale. It is on
the foundation of a system of gifts given and returned over
time [*à terme*] that have been established both barter, through
simplification, by drawing together moments of time earlier
dissociated, and purchase and sale, both credit and cash sale,
as well as loans. For we have no evidence that any of the legal
systems that have evolved beyond the phase we are describing
(in particular, Babylonian law) remained ignorant of the credit
process that is known in every archaic society that still survives
today. This is another simple, realistic way of resolving the
problem of the two "moments of time" brought together in the
contract, which Davy has already studied. (P. 36)
*Note: We have failed to notice that the notion of "term" was
not only as ancient, but also as simple, or, if you wish, as complex, as the notion of cash. (P. 111, n. 133)

These propositions belong to a subchapter titled "Honor and
Credit," that is, two motifs that would be proper to this American
potlatch. The subject of credit has just been addressed. It is on the
subject of honor that madness irrupts into the scene that, in truth, it
secretly organizes. We have made ourselves take this detour in order
to arrive at this madness. The madness that insinuates itself even into
Mauss's text is a certain excess of the gift. It goes so far perhaps as to
burn up the very meaning of the gift; at the very least it threatens
the presumed semantic unity that authorizes one to continue speaking of gift. Whereas, in the preceding paragraphs, he has shown himself to be so scrupulous, so demanding with regard to the *name* gift

and the necessity of calling a gift a gift, Mauss will begin to proliferate signs—to give signs, as one says—of a lexical uncertainty, as if his language were about to go a little mad one page after it had insisted so strenuously on keeping the meaning of gift for the gift. His language goes mad at the point where, in the potlatch, the process of the gift *gets carried away with itself* [s'emporte lui-même] and where, as Mauss comes to say, "it is not even a question of giving and returning, but of destroying, so as not to want even to appear to desire repayment. . . . " The trembling of this uncertainty affects the word "gift" but also the word "exchange" with which Mauss regularly associates it. Here is the passage of madness:

> No less important in these transactions of the Indians is the role played by honor. Nowhere is the individual prestige of a chief and that of his clan so closely linked to what is spent and to the meticulous repayment with interest of gifts that have been accepted, so as to transform those who have obligated you into the obligated ones. Consumption and destruction are here really without limits. In certain kinds of potlatch, one must expend all that one has, keeping nothing back. It is a competition to see who is the richest and also *the most madly extravagant* [le plus follement *dépensier*; emphasis added]. Everything is based upon the principles of antagonism and of rivalry. The political status of individuals in the brotherhoods and clans, and ranks of all kinds are gained in a "war of property," just as they are in real war, or through chance, inheritance, alliance, and marriage. Yet everything is conceived of as if it were a "struggle of wealth."* Marriages for one's children and places in the brotherhoods are only won during the potlatch exchanged and returned. They are lost at the potlatch as they are lost in war, by gambling or in running and wrestling. In a certain number of cases, *it is not even a question of giving and returning, but of destroying, so as not to want even to appear to desire repayment* [emphasis added]. Whole boxes of olachen (candlefish) oil or whale oil are burnt, as are houses and thousands of blankets. The most valuable copper objects are broken and thrown into the water, in order to crush and to "flatten" one's rival. In this way one not only promotes oneself, but also one's family, up the social scale. It is therefore a system of law and

ecnomics in which considerable wealth is constantly being expended and transferred. *One may, if one so desires, call these
transfers by the name of exchange or even trade and sale; but* [empha-
sis added] such trade is noble, replete with etiquette and generosity. At least, when it is carried on in another spirit, with a
view to immediate gain, it is the object of very marked scorn.
(P. 37)
*Note: See especially the myth of Haiyas . . . who has lost face
while gambling and dies. His sisters and his nephews go into
mourning, give a "revenge" potlatch, and he comes to life
again. On this subject it would be necessary to study gambling,
which even in French society, is not considered to be a contract, but a situation in which honor is committed and where
goods are handed over that, after all, one could refuse to hand
over. Gambling is a form of potlatch and the gift system. Its
spread even as far as the American Northwest is remarkable.
(P. 112, n. 138 and 139)

This madness has a somewhat monstrous face, but its face or its
defacement is regular up to a certain point. One can recognize in it a
few interlaced traits. Linked to the redoubled double bind, between
the bind and the non-bind or the letting loose [*débandade*], this madness is surely double since it threatens *a priori* the closed circle of
exchangist rationality as well as frantic expenditure, without return,
of a gift that forgets itself: madness of keeping or of hypermnesic
capitalization *and* madness of the forgetful expenditure. But because
it wreaks havoc on the two sides of the circle, this madness manages
to eat away at language itself. It ruins the semantic reference that
would allow one reasonably to say, to state, to describe this madness,
in short, it ruins everything that claims to know what gift and non-
gift *mean to say*. There is always a moment when this madness begins
to burn up the word or the meaning "gift" itself and to disseminate
without return its ashes as well as its terms or germs. We could interrogate this essential passage between the gift and this dissemination—what I in the past defined as that which does not return to the
father, or that which does not *return* in general.[7] Let us, then, try to
find the unifying principle of all the idiomatic locutions in which one

7. Cf. *Dissemination*, passim, especially "Outwork."

finds the noun "gift," the verb "to give," the adjective "given." Such a semantic *center* [foyer] around which an organized economy or polysemia would gather seems indeed to be lacking. If this lack were to be confirmed, one would have to give up a concept of language regulated by deep semantic anchoring points that would authorize, for example, questions of the type: What is the guiding sense or *etymon* of the gift on the basis of which all semantic diversities, all idioms, and all usages are diffracted? What is the consensus on the basis of which an implicit linguistic contract would permit us to understand one another, to pre-understand one another, right here, to extend credit to each other when we speak of gift, giving, or given? What would happen if the lack of a guiding sense or of a regulated polysemia were to force us to renounce this style of question in favor of a certain concept of dissemination? This concept, which would not be the only one possible, would lead us to consider only usage, play, and the contextual functionings of idioms, if indeed it were still possible to speak of idioms in this sense, without postulating a semantic regulation, a system of prescriptions inscribed in language or in the continuum of a linguistic tradition. This alternative, let us note in passing, would in both cases concern a sort of given of the language: what is given by the language or the language as given, as a given language [*une sorte de donné ou de donnée de la langue*], in other words, two ways of determining the gift of the language said to be maternal or natural.

This hypothesis of a dissemination without return would prevent the locution from circling back to its meaning. It thus also concerns—whence this paradoxical fold—the without-return of the gift. One must say that we are constantly encouraged in this direction by the experience of language each time that the words "gift," "to give," "given," "donation," "donee," or "donor" occur there. Not only because of great frontiers, great lines of demarcation that seem to set up a secure barrier between different meanings or different functionings. For example, one might wonder if the same semantic order governs the logic of the gift whether it is under the regime of *to have* or *to be*. In general, it is thought that one can give only what one has, what one possesses as one's own, and give it to the other who, in his or her turn, can thus have it, come into possession. The very paradox of "giving what one does not have," which we have already talked about, has the value of paradox only because of what links, in common sense, giving with having. One might wonder if the same semantic order governs locutions that, on the contrary, imply the transfer of what one *is* to the other who takes—or becomes—what is thereby given to him or her. Think of the expression "to give one-self," of the metonymies or synecdoches concerning partial "objects," the fragments or signs of what one is and which one can give as something one has, abandons, or lets be taken. All the figures of this tropic are difficult to contain within the limits of a rhetoric the margins or "terms" of which can no longer, in principle and in all rigor, be fixed.

Likewise, one might wonder if the same order governs locutions which imply that one gives something (a determined object, either material or symbolic, to make provisional use of this distinction) and those in which the given of the donation is not an object, a material thing, but a symbol, a person, or a discourse. In other words, does not the direct "object" of the act of "giving," does not the given of the giving alter radically the meaning of the act each time? What do the following have in common: on the one hand, to give a ring, a bracelet, to give something to drink and to eat and, on the other hand, to give an impression, to give a feeling, to give a show or a play? The latter are all expressions that appeal irreducibly to the idiom and in principle therefore they have only a limited translatability. What is common to and what is the connection between "to give the time" and "to give a price" (in the sense of the auction bid: "I will give you so much for it"), between "donner une facilité" [to facilitate, as in a facilitated payment plan] and "give an order," between "give information," "give a course, a class, and a seminar," "give a lesson" (which is something completely different) and "give chase,"[8] "give signs," and so forth? Each time a structural difference of the given presents itself: It can be an apparently natural or material thing (water), a symbolic thing (a ring), a person (to give one's daughter or son in marriage, to give a child, to give a king to one's country),[9] a

8. Derrida's example here is "donner le change," which is a hunting expression that means to decoy or to put off the scent. (Trans.)

9. Or to give a slave: When this lecture was read in Chicago, W. J. T. Mitchell elaborated the question of the slave in a very interesting manner and linked it to that of narrative (in an unpublished text to which I hope to return one day). In a word, what happens when "the Given is a person," the slave who "has nothing to give"? Slavery is that which gives back or gives ("What gives?" in American slang) but also deprives of "narrative."

discourse (still another order of the gift: to give a lecture, to give an order; once again the nature of the discourse alters each time the structure of the gift). Each time, then, the structural difference of the giv*en* seems, and we do say *seems*, to transmit to the operation of the giv*ing* an irremediable heterogeneity.

In this very short list of examples, we have all the same tried to put things in order. We distinguished, for the convenience of the presentation, between the orders of *given* (to be *vs.* to have; sensible, natural thing, if such exists in the pure state, *vs.* symbol, person, discourse, and so forth—all of which are problematic categories since all of them determine being-given and since, thereby, the gift may perhaps efface their boundaries). We have indeed tried to establish an order, a principled taxonomy, a classification (given as either to be or to have, either thing or person, either natural, sensible thing or signifying, symbolic thing, either thing or word, and so forth), but if you consult the *Littré* or what is called an analogic dictionary, you would be at great pains to find a unifying or classifying principle for all the idiomatic locutions. We could take as guide *four types of questions:*

1. In the style of analytic philosophy or of ordinary language analysis, one could ask oneself: What are the conditions (conventional, contextual, intentional, and so forth) for the functioning of, for example, an expression or a speech act that consists in, let us say it in French, *donner sa parole*, giving one's word (to promise or to swear) or *donner un ordre*, giving an order (jussive act) and what is going on with giving in each of these cases? Such an analysis can go back before speech acts, in the phenomenological style of an intentional analysis, toward the intentional act of giving in general. On what conditions does it take place? What is a "donating consciousness"? and so on. This latter expression, moreover, is immediately and massively complicated by reason of a figure of donation that is constantly used by phenomenologists, beginning with Husserl, to designate the ultimate recourse, phenomenology's principle of principles, namely the originary *donating* intuition (*gebende Anschauung*),[10]

---

10. Following here the problematic outline I tried to put in place during the 1977–78 seminar, I will not for the moment enter into the long developments, the patient reading and discussion that would be required concerning the important work since published by Jean-Luc Marion (*Réduction et donation, Recherches sur Husserl, Heidegger et la phénoménologie* [Paris: Presses Universitaires de France, 1989]). In order to indicate a few preliminary points of reference in the space of this future exchange and in order

the one that delivers up the thing or the sense themselves, in person or in flesh and blood, as people still say, in their immediate presence.

2. One may wonder whether this multiplicity of meanings that transmits the multiplicity of *givens* and refracts it in the multiplicity of the *to give* has a sort of general equivalent which would permit

---

to situate the stakes of the semantics of donation in phenomenology, I will quote the conclusion of the first chapter, where Marion discusses in particular certain aspects of my reading of Husserl's *Logical Investigations* in *Speech and Phenomena:*

Categorial intuition allows one only to take the measure—which is from now on measureless —of donation. It marks the open abyss of donation without covering it over—at least in Heidegger's view, if not in Husserl's. For here, the most sober of the two in the face of the fascination with superabundant and unconditional presence is no doubt not the one you expected. Husserl, in fact, completely dazzled by limitless donation, does not seem to realize the strangeness of such a beyond-measure [*démesure*], and does nothing more than *manage* its excess, without interrogating it. Unless the bedazzlement betrays—by covering it over—a fright in face of the broadening of presence by donation.

This is no doubt where the question arises that Husserl could not answer, perhaps because he never understood it as an authentic question: What then is given? Not only "What is it that is given?" but more essentially: "What does giving mean, what is then being played out by the fact that everything is given, how is one to think the fact that everything that is only is insofar as it is given?" It seems legitimate to suppose that Husserl, as if he were submerged by the imperative—at once threatening and jubilatory—to *manage* the superabundance of givens in presence, at no point (at least in the *Logical Investigations*) inquires into the status, the scope, and even the identity of this donation. This silence amounts to admitting (following Jacques Derrida's thesis) that Husserl, leaving donation uninterrogated even though he had accomplished its broadening, does not free it from the prison of presence; rather he maintains it in metaphysical detention. Heidegger, on the contrary . . ." (p. 62; cf. as well especially pp. 68 ff., 87 ff., and naturally all the pages called up by the whole course of the book [unless it is the book that is called up by them] on the basis of a thinking of the *call* as thinking of the gift: ("After the transcendental reduction and the existential reduction, the reduction of and to the call intervenes. What is given is given only to whoever gives himself over to the call and only in the pure form of a confirmation of the appeal, repeated because received. . . . The call thus appears as the originary schema of the two former reductions, precisely because it alone permits one to go back to . . . in that it demands that one give oneself over to the call as such—to answer the call, in the double sense of abandoning oneself to it and of going toward it. . . . It would already suffice to specify that which, before or without *Dasein*, receives or challenges the call, in short hears it. Neither the constituting *I* nor *Dasein*

translation, metaphorization, metonymization, exchange within an ultimately homogeneous semantic circle. This general equivalent would be a transcendental signified or signifier. Playing the role of a transcendental given, it would orient the multiplicity and furnish the transcendental category of which all the other categories of given (to

---

which is—if precisely it can still be—the one that gives itself over to the call that gives?" [Pp. 296–97])

What I have attempted to articulate on the subject of the call, as well as of the "come," the "yes," especially their irreducible iterability, of the "destinerrance" of a sending determined by the response, and of the "gift" in general would lead me no doubt to subscribe to the "logic" and the necessity of this analysis.

To limit ourselves here to the most basic schema, let us say that the question, if not the discussion, would remain open at the point of the determination of the call or of the demand, there where the circle seems to turn between the call of Being (*Anspruch des Seins*), the call of the father (*Anspruch des Vaters*), the primacy of which Heidegger contests, and a "call which is brother to the one Heidegger dismisses," namely, the one that "Levinas will not fail to take up." Nor, I will add, does Marion, who seems to me also to make "*the* call as such," "the pure form of the call," conform to the call of the father, to the call that returns to the father and that, in truth, would speak the truth of the father, even the name of the father, and finally of the father inasmuch as he gives the name.

Marion indeed writes: "In fact, the speech that demands 'Listen!' does not so much pronounce *a* call among other possible ones to the advantage of some authority or other as it performs *the* call as such—the call to answer the call itself, in the sole intention of holding oneself to it by exposing oneself to it. The call even intervenes as such, without or before any other 'message' except to *overtake* with surprise [surprendre] whoever hears it, to *take* up [prendre] even whoever does not expect it. The model of the call is in practice before the simple claim of Being and more fully." And then this in a note: "In fact the claim is no longer exerted here in the name of Being (but of the Father), neither at destination nor from a being. Thus the pure form of the call arises" (p. 295; I have italicized the words "prendre" and "surprendre" in order to situate, in advance, some stakes that will appear later on, notably in the reading of "Counterfeit Money"). Having *declared* that it excludes any determinable content, why does Marion determine "the pure form of the call" (and therefore of the gift) as call "in the name of the Father"? As unique call, despite "the gap between the two calls (the one Christian, the other Jewish)" that it is "important to maintain"? Is it possible to hear a "pure form of the call" (and first of all must one presume such a purity? And if one does, on what basis?) that would still not be from Being, nor from the father, nor in the fraternal difference of the "there," if one can put it that way, between the Jew and the Christian, nor therefore in the language of the "Hear, O Israel: The Lord our God is one Lord" (*Deuteronomy* 6:4) in which, Marion tells us, they "both have their source" (p. 295)? Cf. also Marion, "Réponses à quelques questions," *Revue de Métaphysique et de Morale*, no. 1 (1991), in particular p. 69.

be/to have; thing/person; sensible, natural/symbolic; and so forth) would be particular determinations, metaphorico-metonymic substitutes. We know that the adjective "transcendental" modifies first of all the category that surpasses every genus (*transcendit omne genus*), thereby making possible every other categorial determination. This great transcendentalist tradition can inscribe the transcendental given in the present in general (the present appearing of that which appears in the light, or else created being, the originary given of a gift which comes down to and comes back to [*revient à*] Nature, Being, God, the Father—or the Mother) as well as in the phallus in general (transcendental signifier sealing, according to Lacan, a "symbolic order" that guards the gift against its dissemination, which is perhaps to say, against itself). For this tradition, which is the most powerful and the most irrefutable, there must be a general equivalent of the given if one is to understand what happens with the gift in general and how gifts and exchanges in general (total or partial) are ordered—and, finally, what the Thing given is. For in the end, it must always be the Thing, the same thing that gives itself, even if it does so by dividing itself or by partitioning itself into partial objects. But the Thing is not a partial object, which is why Lacan, for example, insists on the fact that the phallus, the signifier of all signifiers, condition of every gift and every exchange, cannot be a partial object.[11] Difficult problematic of the partial object and the whole chain of supposed gifts (*cadeaux*, feces, penis, child, weapons of war). It is this problematic that we are talking about here, directly or indirectly.

3. How is one to explain these breaks, within certain idioms (French for example), between the syntax of giving (verb) and the syntax of the gift (noun)? From the meaning of "to give" to the meaning of "gift," is the idiom logically consistent? For example, I would say in French that a window "*donne* sur la rue," it gives onto the street (understanding by that, I suppose, that it gives visual access, just as a stairway gives onto, gives access to, and so forth). But it would never occur to me (and why?) that what we have here is a gift. In any case, I would not say literally the gift of the window or of the staircase. What is the significance of these breaks? Why does "giving someone up to the police" not amount to offering a gift, a generous gift, of someone to the police (although the latter may indeed receive

11. Cf. "Le Facteur de la vérité," in *The Post Card*, pp. 500 ff./pp. 470 ff.

it as such), whereas parents who give one of their children in marriage or to the fatherland could more easily speak of a gift, since they could think that they are depriving themselves of what they give? Let us not accumulate these examples; they would be numerous but also different from one language to another. Let us merely draw from them a *conclusion* (which is that the essential link that passes from the thinking of the gift to language, or in any case to the trace, will never be able to avoid idioms) and a *doubt* (is it not impossible to isolate a concept of the essence of the gift that transcends idiomatic difference?).

4. The transcendental question or rather the question *on* the transcendental gets complicated, it even goes a little mad if, among all the *givens,* all the "things" given that we have so far enumerated, one attempts to draw a line dividing two major structures of the gift, such at least as these are to be located in the idiom. There would be, *on the one hand,* the gift that gives something determinate (a given, a present in whatever form it may be, personal or im-personal thing, "natural" or symbolic thing, thing or sign, nondiscursive or discursive sign, and so forth) and, *on the other hand,* the gift that gives not a given but the *condition* of a present given in general, that gives therefore the element of the given in general. It is thus, for example, that "to give time" is not to give a given present but the condition of presence of any present in general; "donner le jour" (literally to give the day, but used in the sense of the English expression "to give birth") gives nothing (not even the life that it is supposed to give "metaphorically," let us say for convenience) but the *condition* of any given in general. To give time, the day, or life is to give nothing, nothing determinate, even if it is to give the giving of any possible giving, even if it gives the condition of giving. What distinguishes in principle this division from the transcendental division it resembles? One perceives there no longer the sharp line that separates the transcendental from the conditioned, the conditioning from the conditioned, but rather the fold of undecidability that allows all the values to be inverted: The gift of life amounts to the gift of death, the gift of day to the gift of night, and so on. And we will say nothing further—it would take us into another dimension—about the strange crossings of idioms such as those that translate "se donner la mort" by "to take one's life." This inversion follows from the great law of the *Gift-gift.*[12] It was the locu-

---

12. See above, note 1, p. 36.

tion "donner le jour" that elsewhere led us to explore this logic, which is a logic of madness but also of narration, the condition of possibility and impossibility of narration, in the margins of a text by Blanchot titled *La folie du jour, The Madness of the Day.*[13]

All these questions concern a certain madness of the gift, which is first of all the madness of the dissemination of the meaning "gift." To look for a unity of this meaning would be, to quote the narrator of "Counterfeit Money," to "look for noon at two o'clock." Mauss is not unaware of this madness. His essay *The Gift* begins more and more to look like an essay not on the gift but on the word "gift." It would basically be an attempt to see if one can speak of the gift, an assaying of the "gift" (in quotation marks because it is mentioned rather than used), an assaying, in a word, of the word "gift" to see if and how it can be used. At the end of this essay, of these assays, a few pages before the final word, he writes the following, which leaves one wondering or perplexed since it comes from someone who has taken an incessant pleasure in giving self-satisfied terminology lessons to the authors he has been citing:

> However, we can go even farther than we have gone up to
> now. We can dissolve, mix up, color, and redefine the principal
> notions that we have used. The terms that we have used—
> present, gift, *cadeau*—are not themselves entirely exact. It's just
> that we can find no others. These concepts of law and econom-
> ics that we like to oppose: freedom and obligation; liberality,
> generosity, and luxury, as against savings, interest, and util-
> ity—it would be good to put them into the melting pot once
> more. (P. 73)

In place of this impossible concept and of this missing term, Mauss then proposes only brief indications and an example, an "example," an example of, precisely, a "hybrid," which defies the oppositions permitting one to construct concepts. Is this significant? Here is how Mauss in fact continues:

> We can only give the merest indications on this subject. Let us
> choose, for example,* the Trobriand Islands. There they still
> have a complex notion that inspires all the economic acts we
> have described. Yet this notion is neither that of the free,

---

13. Cf. *Parages*, pp. 240 ff. and pp. 280 ff.

purely gratuitous prestation, nor that of production and exchange purely interested in what is useful. It is a sort of hybrid
that has flourished there.
*Note: We could just as well have chosen the Arab *sadaqa:*
alms, price of the betrothed, justice, tax.

The madness of this essay: It ends where it should have begun,
and the result is that, just as in Blanchot's *Madness of the Day*, one no
longer knows according to what impossible figure an interminable
end is included in an interminable beginning.[14] It is a narrative, but
an interdicted narrative in this sense. As if Mauss were saying to us:
Forget everything that has been said in all the preceding pages; we
will have to begin all over again.

This madness still hesitates between the "I am talking madness"
and the "don't go off thinking that I am talking madness even when I
speak of madness." And it is inscribed in the command to forget that
is uttered with every gift. But the command to forget, the command
given to forget is a strange command, whose very structure remains
as maddened as it is maddening. One sees it appear in "Aumône"
(Alms) by Mallarmé:

Ne t'imagine pas que je dis des folies
La terre s'ouvre vieille à qui crève la faim
Je hais une autre aumône et veux que tu m'oublies.
Et surtout ne va pas, frère, acheter du pain.

Do not suppose that I am talking madness
The earth opens up old to one dying of hunger
I hate another alms and want you to forget me.
And most of all, brother, do not go buy bread

We will not interpret this poem, not even this last line. It gives the
command, it requires, it asks that the gift not be converted into its
equivalent merchandise, into some useful goods (in the first two versions, it was "Je hais l'aumône utile," "I hate the useful alms") and
especially into edible food, into an incorporable thing. Let us merely
underscore the structure of an impossible command: "I want you to
forget me." Like every negative command, like every interdiction that
folds back in a contradictory manner toward the subject who utters it
(for example, "do not listen to me," "do not read me"), it engenders

14. Ibid., pp. 232 ff. and pp. 266 ff.

that schism in the response or the responsibility in which some have sought to recognize the schizopathogenic power of the double bind.

Here the addressee must keep the command not to keep, without forgetting the request to forget: Grieve for me, therefore keep me enough to lose me as you must.

We will encounter later, in all its dimensions (religious, anthropological, cultural, socioeconomic), the question of alms—and of whether alms is a gift. For the moment, let us not forget the fold of a supplementary question: Is that which is given, whether or not it is alms, the content, which is to say the "real" thing one offers or of which one speaks? Is it not rather the act of address to the other, for example the work as textual or poetic performance? Along with all the internal perversion or madness we are talking about, is not the gift first of all the essay titled *The Gift*, precisely to the extent to which it would be incapable of speaking adequately of the gift that is its theme? Or the poem titled "Aumône"? Or very close to it, that song of mourning which is "Don du poème" (The Gift of the Poem)? "Aumône" also names "tabac," "opium," the "pharmacie," and the act of "supputer" (calculation), all of which are motifs that will stay with us. This poem went through at least four versions and several earlier titles: "Haine du pauvre" (Hatred of the Poor Man), "A un mendiant" (To a Beggar), and "A un pauvre" (To a Poor Man).[15]

Aumône

Prends ce sac, Mendiant! tu ne le cajolas
Sénile nourrisson d'une tétine avare
Afin de pièce à pièce égoutter ton glas.

Take this bag, Beggar! you cajoled it
Senile nurseling of a miser teat
Only to drain from it coin by coin your *glas*.

A un mendiant

Pauvre, voici cent sous . . . Longtemps tu cajolas,
—Ce vice te manquait,—le songe d'être avare?
Ne les enfouis pas pour qu'on te sonne un glas.

15. On this poem and on the "glas" that comes to resonate there, cf. *Glas*, pp. 171 ff./150 ff.

Poor man, here is twenty cents . . . Long you cajoled,
—You lacked this vice—the dream of being miserly?
Don't bury them to have a *glas* sounded for you.

A un pauvre

Prends le sac, Mendiant. Longtemps tu cajolas
—Ce vice te manquait—le songe d'être avare?
N'enfouis pas ton or pour qu'il te sonne un glas.

Take the bag, Beggar. Long you cajoled
—You lacked this vice—the dream of being miserly?
Don't bury your gold so it will sound a *glas* for you.[16]

The sadistic aggressivity with regard to the donee, the perversity which threatens a beggar suspected of speculating, all this already belongs to a certain tradition. We will attempt to recognize that tradition and we cite Mallarmé here only in order to sketch in this descent. It is for example the tradition of Baudelaire's "Counterfeit Money" and "Assommons les pauvres," (Beat Up the Poor). This tradition will have left traces in *The Madness of the Day* where one may read, for instance: "At forty, somewhat poor, I was becoming destitute. . . . What is irritating about poverty is that it is visible, and anyone who sees it thinks: You see, I'm being accused; who is attacking me? But I did not in the least wish to carry justice around on my clothes."[17] Is not the gift precisely the madness of the day?[18] Like "Aumône," Mallarmé's "Don du poème" went through several versions. One of them was titled precisely "Le jour" (The Day), and the other "Le poème nocturne" (The Nocturnal Poem) and the "Dédicace du poème nocturne" (Dedication of the Nocturnal Poem). Like the narrative of "Counterfeit Money" that we will take up soon, like its

16. Stéphane Mallarmé, *Oeuvres complètes*, ed. Henri Mondor et G. Jean-Aubry (Paris: Bibliothèque de la Pléiade, 1961), pp. 39, 1434–36.
17. "A quarante, un peu pauvre, je devenais misérable . . . la misère a ceci d'ennuyeux qu'on la voit et ceux qui la voient pensent: Voilà qu'on m'accuse; qui m'attaque là? Or je ne souhaitais pas du tout porter la justice sur mes vêtements" (Paris: Fata Morgana, 1973), pp. 23–24; *The Madness of the Day*, trans. Lydia Davis (Barrytown, N.Y.: Station Hill Press, 1981), p. 13.
18. Cf. *Parages*, pp. 234 ff. and 278 ff.

dedication, which gives itself by giving nothing other than the gift in question with no possible oversight [*surplomb*] of that performance, this "Gift of the Poem" would be given as the gift itself, enacted; it begins "Je t'apporte l'enfant d'une nuit d'Idumée!" [I bring you the child of an Idumean night!]. Idumea, the land of the Edom, would be the pre-Adamic kingdom: Before Esau was replaced by Jacob, who received his blind father's blessing, the kings of Idumea were supposed to reproduce themselves without sex and without woman. They were not hermaphrodites but men without sex and without women. The poem is compared to a work that would have been born from the poet alone, without couple or without woman. "Horrible naissance" (Horrible birth), says "Don du poème," a birth in which the child, that is, the poem, finds itself thus *given, confided*, offered—to the reader to whom it is dedicated, to its addressee or its donee, to be sure, but by the same token to the nurse who *in her turn, in exchange, will give* it the breast (" . . . *accueille une horrible naissance: / Et ta voix rappelant viole et clavecin, / Avec le doigt fané presseras-tu le sein / Par qui coule en blancheur sibylline la femme / Pour les lèvres que l'air du vierge azur affame?*" [. . . receive a horrible birth: / And your voice recalling viola and harpsichord, / With faded finger will you press the breast / From which flows the woman in sibylline whiteness / For the lips famished by the virgin azure air?]) [19]

From the hand of the donor to that of the beggar, we have just seen the passage of gifts in the form of cash money. We can no longer avoid the question of what money is: true money or counterfeit money, which can only be what it is, false or counterfeit, to the extent to which no one knows it is false, that is, to the extent to which it circulates, appears, functions *as good and true money*. The enigma of this simulacrum should begin to orient us toward the triple and indissociable question of the *gift*, of *forgiveness*, and of the *excuse*. And to the question of whether a gift can or *ought* to *secure itself* against counterfeit money.

At the end of a long note on the notion of money (pp. 93–94), Mauss deems it necessary to excuse himself. He does so in the grammar of the magisterial "we": "We excuse ourselves for having been obliged to take sides on these very vast questions, but they touch too closely upon our subject and it was necessary to be clear." He does

19. *Oeuvres complètes*, pp. 40, 1438–39.

not ask to be excused; he *excuses himself*. In the code of French etiquette, it is not the most refined formula of politeness. What is he
excusing himself for? Well, for having been obligated to take sides.
When one is obligated, in principle, one does not have to excuse oneself; one has every excuse as when one does something "beyond one's
control." In this formulation, which must not be pushed too far, he
excuses himself for having been obligated. This may seem strange.
But since he has a good excuse, he does not have to ask forgiveness.
Without waiting for the reader's reply, he takes the liberty of excusing
himself. What is the fault he was obligated to commit and for which
he has such a good excuse? Having "taken sides" ["*pris parti*"] and
having taken sides on "very vast questions." He would thus have the
right to excuse himself because these questions "touch too closely"
upon the subject and it was necessary to be rather "clear." In this
unique sentence, which is all of a piece, one cannot tell what the real
fault is. In "taking sides" or in taking sides on "very vast questions"?
One first has the feeling that, in his view, a sociologist, a theoretician,
a scholar guided by a principle of objectivity and neutrality should
not take sides, should not be *involved* or *committed* [engagé]. He
should not give any *token* [gage] in the debate or in the problem. In
this scene, he should not occupy a position (*take* a position, as one
says) in order to try to win, to win his case, as if the normative ideal
for whoever would speak scientifically—for instance of the *gift*—
were to neither give nor take, nor to make of one's scientific discourse
a *piece* of the analyzed structure, a piece in the play [*pièce*] or in
the scene, an act in the play or a scene in the play (the word *pièce*
in French, which means piece, play, but also coin as in "pièce de
monnaie," could give the title to any possible discourse on the gift,
indeed of any possible gift, if one did not immediately have to say the
same thing of the word "title").[20]

Unless Mauss is excusing himself not for having broken with a sort
of metalinguistic neutrality or uninvolved distant reserve but for having taken sides where he should not have done so: on "very vast
questions." He would have gone too quickly and too superficially
over questions that deserve a wider treatment, an analysis that would

20. We have attempted to analyze this word "pièce" and put it in play in a reading
of *Droit de regards* by M.-F. Plissart (Paris: Minuit, 1985), pp. XVII, XX ("Right of In-
spection," trans. David Wills, in *Art & Text*, no. 32, Autumn 1989 pp. 60, 62).

be fitting to their—very vast—scale. Mauss would be excusing himself for having concluded too quickly, for having given insufficient *guarantees* of his statements, for having insufficiently demonstrated his justificatory reasons. Which implies that by good ethical standards—and here the good ethical standards of scientific discourse—one must not take sides unless one is able to do so neither in the dark, nor at random, nor by making allowance for chance, that is, for what cannot be thoroughly anticipated or controlled. One should only take sides rationally, one should not get involved beyond what analysis can *justify* and beyond what can accredit or legitimate the taking of sides; one should accredit, guarantee, and legitimate the discourse in which the taking of sides, the *parti pris* or bias is stated. Otherwise, one pays with words or *on se paie de mots*, as we say in French, [one gets paid in words, i.e., one talks a lot of hot air], by which one understands that words in this case are simulacra, money without value—devalued or counterfeit—that is, without gold reserves or without the correspondent accrediting value. By excusing himself for having been obliged to take sides on very vast questions, Mauss excuses himself for not having given to his taking of sides, that is, to the discourse that explains his taking of sides, a kind of fiduciary guarantee. He has not been able to accredit sufficiently the signs he has given of his taking of sides. He excuses himself, therefore, for seeming to take the risk of giving us a kind of counterfeit money without corresponding gold reserves.

He does not say, of course, that in taking sides he is unjustified or that the money he gives us is counterfeit, that he is paying us with words (which implies without proven value [*titre*]). No, he says that perhaps it looks as if—but this is only an appearance—he is giving us counterfeit money, or more exactly and what is even worse (since giving someone money that the other knows to be counterfeit is not a deception), money that we cannot know to be sufficiently credited, true or counterfeit, guaranteed or not, since the relation is not established, visible, or verifiable between the terms of his taking sides and the extent of these "very vast questions." He may be deceiving us, he may have the appearance of being able to deceive us by deceiving himself, paying us with words while talking a lot of hot air. This is in sum what he excuses himself for in this long note on money ("A *Note* of principle concerning the use of the notion of money").

For Mauss is not opposed to all taking of sides. Even if it does not look that way, we can verify that *The Gift*, from beginning to end, is one long taking of sides, a continuous involvement [*engagement*]. And it cannot be otherwise. A discourse on the gift, a treatise on the gift *must* and can only be *part* or *party* [partie prenante *ou* parti pris] in the field it describes, analyzes, defines. That is why, that is the way in which, *that is the very thing he must, he owes, he ought to* [il doit]: He is first of all and from the first *indebted*. The theoretical and supposedly constative dimension of an essay on the gift is *a priori* a piece, only a part, a part and a party, a *moment* of a performative, prescriptive, and normative operation that gives or takes, indebts itself, gives and takes, refuses to give or accepts to give—or does both at the same time according to a necessity that we will come back to. But in every case, this discursive gesture is from the outset an example of that about which it claims to be speaking. It is part of the whole, it belongs [*appartient*] to the whole process, it is part of it even as it claims to designate only an object of that process or a part of a set that would be dominated by its discourse. Thus the mass of prescriptive (ethical, moral, juridical, political) "il faut" (it is necessary, one must, one should, one ought to and so forth) that are unleashed in the last chapter titled "Conclusion" and especially in its first subchapter ("Moral Conclusions"). These "il faut" accumulate according to a regular law. Not that the "il faut" are lacking before this moral conclusion. But here they are assumed in a declared fashion and are regulated by a law that may appear strange but that alone can account for the little sentence I began by quoting. No doubt, as with every "il faut," this law of the "il faut" is that one must—*il faut*—go beyond constatation and prescribe. One must—*il faut*—opt *for* the gift, for generosity, for noble expenditure, for a practice and a morality of the gift ("il faut donner," one must give). One cannot be content to speak of the gift and to describe the gift without giving and without saying *one must* give, without giving by saying one must give, without giving to think that one must give but a thinking that would not consist merely in thinking but in doing what is called giving, a thinking that would call upon one to give in the proper sense, that is, to do more than call upon one to give in the proper sense of the word, but to give beyond the call, beyond the mere word.

But—because with the gift there is always a "but"—the contrary is also necessary: It is necessary [*il faut*] to limit the excess of the gift and of generosity, to limit them by economy, profitability, work, exchange. And first of all by reason or by the principle of reason: It is *also* necessary to render an account, it is also necessary to give consciously and conscientiously. It is necessary *to answer for* [répondre] the gift, the given, and the call to giving. It is necessary to answer to it and answer for it. One must be *responsible* for what one gives and what one receives.

Whence a series of "il faut" worked over, as you will hear, by this contradiction, sometimes going so far as to take the most ingenuous and naïvely hypocritical form, which is also the most inconsistent and incoherent, betraying thereby Mauss's predicament when he tries to define the right rule, the right economy: *between* economy and non-economy, in the "not too much," "neither too much this nor too much that," "a good but moderate blend of reality and the ideal." In this long litany of "il faut," we will also underscore, among other things, the words "to state," "revolution," and "return."

> But it is not enough *to state* the fact. *One must* [il faut] deduce practice from it, and a moral precept. It is not sufficient to say that law is in the process of ridding itself of a few abstractions such as the distinction between real law and personal law; or that it is intent on adding other rights to the cold-hearted law of sale and payment for services. One *must* [Il faut] *also say* that this is a salutary *revolution*.
>
> First of all, we *return*, as *return we must* [il faut], to customs of "noble expenditure." *It is essential* [Il faut] that, as in Anglo-Saxon countries and so many other contemporary societies, both primitive and highly civilized ones, that the rich *return*, freely or by obligation, to considering themselves as the financial guardians, as it were, of their fellow citizens. Among ancient civilizations, from which ours has sprung, some had a (debtors') jubilee, others liturgies (of duty) such as choregies and trierarchies, and *syussitia* (meals in common), and the obligatory expenditure by the aedile and the consular dignitaries. *We should* [On devra] go back to laws of this kind. Then *there must be* [il faut] more care for the individual, his life, his health, his education (which is, moreover, a profitable investment), his family, and their future. *There must be* [Il faut] more good faith, more sensitivity, more generosity in contracts dealing with hiring of services, the renting of houses, the sale of

vital foodstuffs. And *it will indeed be necessary* [il faudra bien] to find a way to limit the rewards of speculation and interest.

However, the individual *must* work [il faut *que l'individu travaille*]. *He must* [il faut] be made to rely upon himself rather than upon others. On the other hand, *he must* [il faut] defend his interests, both personally and as a member of a group. Overgenerosity and communism would be as harmful to himself and to society as the egoism of our contemporaries and the individualism of our laws. In the *Mahabharata* a malevolent genie of the woods explains to a Brahmin who gave away too much, and too injudiciously: "That is why you are thin and pale." The life of the monk and the life of a Shylock *must be* [doivent] equally shunned. This new morality will surely consist of a *good but moderate blend of reality and the ideal.* (Pp. 68–69)

A few remarks, since perhaps not everything goes without saying upon first encountering these declarations:

1. First of all, it would be wrong to consider these "Moral Conclusions" (in a final chapter that is itself titled "Conclusion") as a moral epilogue external to the work, as a taking sides that could be harmlessly dissociated from the work that goes before. These axiomatics were at work in *all* the preceding analyses. They provided the conceptual material, the instruments of analysis, the theoretical organization of the discourse.

2. It would be rather thoughtless to laugh at the often indecent mediocrity of the mediating desire, at this median, measured, measuring morality, this rule of the compromise and of the "good but moderate blend of reality and the ideal." The moderation of this *mediocritas* signals perhaps the most difficult task. Better—or worse—it announces perhaps a sort of paradoxical *hubris,* the *hubris* of the right measure (who ever dares to fix the right measure?) and even that vocation of the impossible to which all responsibility and every effective decision has to answer. What is recommended is not just any compromise; it is the good one, the right one. Now, from his reflection and his inquiry into the gift, Mauss has learned that the *pure* gift or the gift that is *too good,* the excess of generosity of the gift—in which the pure and good gift would consist—turns into the bad; it is even the worst. The best becomes the worst. It is because he has understood this turnabout to be the law of the gift that the anthro-

pologist tends toward this wisdom, this policy, this morality of the *mediocritas* and of the happy medium. And as we have just suggested, but it should be said in Mauss's favor perhaps, this "happy medium" is, moreover, as impossible, as untenable, and as inaccessible as the two extremes, just as the role of Sancho Panza is as unlivable as that of Don Quixote.

3. Mauss repeatedly says that one must *return to*—. Return to what? This "returning" is not a regression but a revolution. Analogous to the natural revolution of the Earth around the Sun, of the absolute sun at its high noon (and this is why we began by making the question of the gift turn around a Sun-King), it would bring about a return to man's nature, to that "eternal morality" ("This morality is eternal," Mauss will write further on), to that "bedrock" which has remained closest to the surface in those societies said to be "the least advanced that we can imagine"—those societies that have been the object of *The Gift*, its particular but also obviously *exemplary* object in Mauss's eyes. They offer the example of a natural—and thus universal—structure of this *socius* set in motion by the gift. That description ought to hold true beyond those societies. To be sure, Mauss does not *directly extend* his analysis to "evolved" societies, but by way of the axis of a certain historicity and a certain exemplarity, with the ethico political movement of the "one must return . . . ," he assures a revolutionary circulation to his discourse. We must return to the *example* given us by those "least advanced societies" that are closer to "bedrock." We must return to the example they give us concerning the gift. "Thus we can and we ought to return to the archaic and to the elemental," says Mauss.

> We will rediscover motives for living and acting that are still prevalent in many societies and classes: the joy of public giving; the delight in generous expenditure on the arts; the pleasure in hospitality and in private and public festival. Social security, the solicitude of the mutuality, of the cooperative, of the professional group, of all those legal entities upon which English law bestows the name of "Friendly Societies"—all are of greater value than the mere personal security that the lord guaranteed to his tenant, better than the mean life afforded by the daily wage set by management, and even better than capitalist saving—which is only based on a changing form of credit. (Ibid.)

We will find a surer guide back to this archaic originarity, which we have left behind or allowed to become perverted, in a non-Marxist socialism, a liberal anti-capitalism or anti-mercantilism. That is the morality or the politics that organizes the structure, even the theoretical *telos*, of this essay. As for the formal characteristic of this profound identity between the theoretical and the ethical, we could invoke a Platonic or Aristotelian tradition. However, as for its content, one glimpses rather a Rousseauist schema. This is not only the model that will soon be reclaimed by the very one who introduces, not without formulating a few admiring criticisms, Mauss's essay, namely Lévi-Strauss; it is already Mauss's model, even if he does not refer to it as explicitly as Lévi-Strauss does.

This question of the natural or exemplary universality of the "bedrock" and the (inductive or reflexive) extension of Mauss's analyses is formulated or resolved in his very language. A question of *restitution:* The anthropologist proposes to *give back* and to *come back* in a circular manner to the good example, to return to the good inheritance that archaic societies have given or rather bequeathed us. The inheritance that is thus passed down is nothing other, finally, than nature. It is nature that gives, and one must show oneself worthy of this gift. One must take and learn [*prendre et apprendre*] the gift of nature. From giving nature, one must learn to give, in a manner that is both generous and ordered; and by giving as nature says one must give, one will give it back its due, one will show oneself to be worthy, one will mark the right equivalence. This equivalence (whose naturalist law we will find staged once again in "Counterfeit Money") is nothing other that that of the giving-returning or of the giving-taking. It is the logic of exchange or the symbolics of *restitution*—or one could also say of the *re-institution*—of nature, beyond the oppositon nature/culture, *phusis/nomos*, or *phusis/thesis*, and so forth.

Archaic society, the archaic, or the originary in general can be replaced by *anything whatsoever* (by X or by Chi), by nature, the mother, father, creator, supreme being, prime mover, *logos*, masculine or feminine possessor of the *phallus:* One will always find again the same schema, one will find (oneself) back there all the time—in a circular manner. And it is by setting out from the question of the "giving-taking" or the "giving-returning" that one accedes to all the instances we have just enumerated or piled up. Now, this equivalence of giving-taking is precisely stated in the form of a "beautiful Maori proverb" that, once again as epiloguing epigraph, comes to close the "Moral Conclusions":

"Ko Maru kai atu
Ko Maru kai mai
Ka ngohe ngohe"

"Give as much as you take, all shall be very well." (P. 69)

In a note to the translation, Mauss clarifies as follows: "Rev. Taylor, *Te Ika a Maui, Old New Zealand* (p. 130, proverb 42), translates very briefly as 'give as well as take and all will be right,' but the literal translation is probably as follows: 'As much as Maru gives, so much Maru takes, and this is good, good' (Maru is the god of war and justice)."

The equivalence of the taken and the given is *posed*, it is a thesis and a theme. It happens to be posed as the moral, ethical, and political rule: the rule of what there is but also of *what is necessary* [*de ce qu'il faut*], of what *there must be* [*de ce qu'il* doit y avoir]. The law of what happens implies an imperative: "give as much as you take." The original text has a descriptive form and not, precisely, an imperative one; yet the statement is followed by a positive evaluation that transforms natural necessity into a good thing: "As much as Maru [god of war and justice] gives, so much Maru takes, *and this is good*." The logic of the utterance remains complex. By posing the equivalence between what the god gives and what he takes, by posing this equivalence as "good," one affirms the excess of the gift; one lets the gift overflow. The equivalence given by Maru or that he gives by his example is good and this *goodness* of the given equivalence is in *excess* over the equivalence itself. It will thus be necessary to restore, reconstitute, give back, *restitute* the equilibrium by following the *example*, by reflecting it in imitation. We are not through with this "logic," and what is more one is never through with it.

The schema of exemplarity is all the more significant in this precise place in that it poses the equivalence of the giving and taking, of the given and the taken, but on the basis of their opposition or at least their distinction. To say that *one must* reach equivalence and that equivalence is good is to recall that it is not simply given and that giving is not taking. There is at the outset neither real equivalence nor semantic equivalence: To give does not mean to take—on the contrary!

But like the *il faut*, the *on doit* [one must, one ought, one owes]—which, along with debt and duty, supposes an inequality—regulates itself according to an "it is thus," *there is* [il y a] equivalence; this is a natural law of nature, a necessity. One must therefore think this equivalence of equivalence and non-equivalence. Any discourse on this problematic must then presuppose a clarity, if possible and even before taking sides, concerning the values of "giving" and "taking," concerning their possible opposition or their equivalence, whether real or semantic. Now, Mauss makes a brief allusion to the fact that, in certain languages, notably in Papuan and Melanesian, there is "one single term to designate buying and selling, lending and borrowing," in the words of Holmes who has studied these tribes and according to whom operations that are "opposites are expressed by the same word" (p. 32). This concerns only the opposition of selling and buying (and not in general that of giving and taking). Mauss notes that the uncertainty of this verbal opposition "selling/buying" is not specific to the societies of the Pacific; it is present in Chinese where only a tonal difference distinguishes the two monosyllables that designate the purchase as well as the sale; and in our ordinary language, the word "sale" [*"vente"*] covers the sale as well as the purchase. This seems rather careless on Mauss's part: Although the word *vente* can cover a chain of operations of which purchase is one link, there is no ambiguity in ordinary language regarding the opposition between selling and buying, but that little matters here. What matters more is this possibility of an effacement, inside and outside of language, of the opposition in general, and singularly of the opposition between giving and taking. There would be, there should be an equivalence between what one gives and what one takes, between the given and the taken, but also between the meaning of giving and the meaning of taking. This is the logical lever of two, almost contemporary texts that each have a very different relation to the essay *The Gift*. I mean first *The Introduction to the Work of Marcel Mauss*, by Lévi-Strauss. It opens the 1950 volume of *Sociologie et Anthropologie* in which Mauss's essay was reprinted. One should remember that Mauss died during the printing of this volume.[21] The other text is that

21. This fact is recalled in the Postscriptum (at once extraordinary and flatly conventional) that Georges Gurvitch, who was then director of the collection and professor at the Sorbonne, adds on 12 April 1950 to the Foreword dated 20 September 1949. The several lines of this Postscriptum deserve to be quoted. In their fashion, perhaps in-

of Benveniste, "Gift and Exchange in Indo-European Vocabulary."[22] This pair of texts will lead us back to the excuses presented by Mauss and then to the forgiveness refused by one of the two friends in Baudelaire's "Counterfeit Money."

The same unrest will never quiet down, that of the gift as well as that of forgiveness. *Ought* they not—but beyond duty and debt[23]—

---

advertently, they say something about the *Gift-gift*, the poisoned gift of which legacies are made, particularly those exemplary legacies that are intellectual legacies: gifts, in sum, whose poison almost never fails to call forth the counter-poison which is presented in the guise of the counter-gift (restitution, tribute, celebration, commentary, critical reading, "personal interpretation"). And when a third party says of an "interpretation," which an inheritor offers to the one from whom he inherits, that it is a "very personal interpretation," one may suspect that there is more here than a disagreement or reservation: some venom is surely being distilled, like a counter-poison in its turn, in the body of this tribute to a tribute, to this already venomous tribute that was the interpretation in question. Not that death *really* results, or always, but here is that which sometimes—impressive *imprimatur*, murderous perfidy of academic politeness, mask over mortuary mask—literally follows death: "Postscriptum—During the printing of this volume, Marcel Mauss died. The reader will find in M. Claude Lévi-Strauss's introduction an impressive image of the inexhaustible wealth of the intellectual legacy bequeathed by this great scholar, as well as a very personal interpretation of his work. Georges Gurvitch, Paris, 12 April 1950."

22. *L'Année sociologique*, vol. 2, 1950; reprinted in *Problèmes de linguistique générale* (Paris: Gallimard, 1966); *Problems in General Linguistics*, trans. Mary Elizabeth Meek (Coral Gables, Fla.: University of Miami Press, 1971).

23. Another form of the same aporia, this *ought-to without owing, duty without duty* [devoir sans devoir] prescribes that the gift not only *owes* nothing, remains foreign to the circle of the debt, but must not *answer* to its own essence, must not even be what it has to be, namely, a gift. On the immense question (at once etymological, semantic, philosophical, and so forth) of what does or does not link duty to debt, we will refer not only to the well-known texts of Nietzsche, Heidegger, and so forth, but, closer to home, to the analyses of Emile Benveniste (*Le vocabulaire des institutions européennes* [Paris: Minuit, 1969], vol. 1, chap. 16, "Prêt, emprunt et dette," and chap. 17, "Gratuité et reconnaissance," pp. 181 ff.) Cf. as well Charles Malamoud's admirable "Présentation" of the very rich contributions, including his own ("Dette et devoir dans le vocabulaire sanscrit et dans la pensée brahmanique"), collected in *Lien de vie, noeud mortel, Les représentations de la dette en Chine, au Japon et dans le monde indien* (Paris: EHESS, 1988). The question of the "false money of a true sacrifice" is evoked there in relation to "Les Monnaies de la Trésorerie et la notion de Destin fondamental," by Hou Chin-lang (p. 14). Cf. aussi Charles Malamoud, "La théologie de la dette dans le brâhmanisme," in *Purusartha* 4: "La Dette" (Paris: EHESS, 1980).

These questions have also been approached in *The Post Card*, notably at the beginning of "To Speculate—on 'Freud'" (pp. 278 ff./260 ff.). On the indissociable question

deprive themselves of any security against the counterfeit, of any mistrust regarding counterfeit money, so as to preserve the chance of being what they *ought to be*, but ought to be beyond duty and debt? A gift that would claim to control money and preserve itself from any simulacrum, will that still be a gift or already a calculation clinging or recalling one—naïvely, sometimes with authority—to the reassuring distinction between the natural and the artificial, the authentic and the inauthentic, the originary and the derived or borrowed?

---

of the fetish, in Marx or Freud, on its link to the "rest of time" to be given, cf. *Glas*, pp. 231 ff./206 ff.

3

"Counterfeit Money" I:
Poetics of Tobacco
(Baudelaire, Painter of Modern Life)

> . . . one has to be on one's guard to recognize the counterfeit money
> given by a friend . . .*

*". . . il faut bien être sur ses gardes pour reconnaître la fausse monnaie que
donne un ami," Honoré de Balzac, *Splendeurs et misères des courtisanes,* in a
chapter titled "Ce que c'est que les filles" (What Prostitutes Are), from Part I
"Comment aiment les filles" (How Prostitutes Love).¹ One should recall at
least the immediate context of this warning that also speaks about the "literary critic of today":

> Women who led the life that Esther had then so violently repu
> diated reach an absolute indifference concerning men's external ap-
> pearance. They are not unlike the literary critic of today who, in
> several ways, can be compared to them and who attains to a profound
> lack of concern with the formulas of art: He has read so many works,
> he sees so many of them pass by, he has suffered through so many
> climaxes, he has seen so many plays, he has written so many articles
> without saying what he thinks, while betraying so often the cause of
> art in favor of his friendships and his enmities, that he reaches a state
> of disgust with everything and yet he continues to judge. It would
> take a miracle for this writer to produce a work, just as pure and noble
> love demands another miracle before it can flower in the heart of a

1. Paris: Garnier, 1964, p. 41.

courtesan. The tone and the manners of this priest, who appeared to have stepped out of a painting by Zurbaran, seemed so hostile to the poor girl, for whom appearance counted little, that she thought she was less the object of some solicitude than the necessary subject of some plot. Without being able to distinguish between smooth-talking self-interest and the balm of charity, for one has to be on one's guard to recognize the counterfeit money given by a friend, she felt as if she were being held in the claws of a monstrous and ferocious bird that swept down on her after having soared overhead for a long time; in her fright, she said these words in a voice filled with alarm: "I thought priests were supposed to console us, and you are killing me!"

Beyond this immediate context, one should also read the scene in which the figures of forgiveness, of time expended ("If it were only his money he spent! But he will expend his time, his force . . ."), of the "cured blind man" who "can lose his sight again if struck by a light that is too bright," of "tears," and of the "Give it to me!" that Esther says to the priest when asking him in fact for a letter, a paper that is held in his belt: "She grabbed the man, covered his hand with kisses; she made use of all the kittenish devices of her caresses, but in a saintly outpouring of gratitude; she lavished the dearest names on him, said to him, through her sweetened phrases, a thousand times over: 'Give it to me!' in as many different tones . . .

Conclusion: "Finally it is Art that irrupted into Morality."

The priest, ashamed at having given into this show of affection, pushed Esther away sharply and she sat down, ashamed as well, for he said to her: "You are still a courtesan." And he coldly put the letter back in his belt. Like a child that has only one wish in mind, Esther did not take her eyes off the place on the belt where the paper was.

In his *Introduction to the Work of Marcel Mauss*,[2] Lévi-Strauss insinuates a discreet and respectful critique. Even if one supposes that it does not take away with one hand what it gives with the other, this critique may still poison the vibrant generosity of the tribute.[3] And what Lévi-Strauss puts in question [*met en cause*] with this highly ambivalent

2. Trans. Felicity Baker (London: Routledge & Kegan Paul, 1987); the quoted passages from this translation will occasionally be modified. We will extend here in another direction the reading proposed of this Introduction in *Writing and Difference*, pp. 409ff./278ff.

3. For example:

The revolutionary character of *The Gift* is that it sets us on that path. The facts it puts forward are not new discoveries. Two years before [. . . .] So what is the source of the extraordinary power of those disordered pages of the essay, which look a little as if they are still in the draft stage, with their very odd juxtaposition of impressionistic notations and (usually compressed into a critical apparatus that dwarfs the text) inspired erudition, which gathers American, Indian, Celtic, Greek or Oceanian references seemingly haphazardly, and yet always penetratingly? Few have managed to read *The Gift* without feeling the whole gamut of the emotions that Malebranche described so well when recalling his first reading of Descartes: the pounding heart, the throbbing head, the mind flooded with the imperious, though not yet definable, certainty of being present at a decisive *event* in the evolution of science.

What happened in that essay, for the *first time* in the history of ethnological thinking, was that an effort was made to transcend empirical observation and to reach deeper realities. For the *first time*, the social ceases to belong to the domain of pure quality—anecdote, curiosity, material for *moralizing* description or for scholarly comparison—and becomes a system, among whose parts connections, equivalences and interdependent aspects can be discovered. (*Introduction*, pp. 37–38)

In this tribute, the ambivalence of which signals the most radical criticisms and which has its equal only in the ambivalence we noted earlier (pp. 68–69, n. 24) in Gurvitch's Postscriptum, we have emphasized the words *event*, *first time*, and *moralizing* so as to recall two central focuses of our reflection. The first, a classical question, concerns the event as "first time," not only in the sudden appearance, said to be historical, of a philosophical discourse or scientific configuration (for example in the case of Mauss, as Lévi-Strauss suggests), but also that which in principle links such an event to the possibility of a gift, that is, of an invention or of an intervention that interrupts the continuous chain, the program, or the economy. The second focus, around "moralizing," because the first question always gets complicated, precisely in Mauss and contrary to what Lévi-Strauss suggests, by a moralization that it is impossible to separate—we will come back to this—from the "scientific" concern. We would not be tempted to see in this only a residue of non-scientificity left over after some "epistemological break," but precisely, and this is what interests us here in the most consistent fashion, another co-

gesture of filiation is nothing less than the cause or more exactly *the thing* [chose] *itself*. His critique tends to eliminate with a wave of the hand the difficulties regarding the *question of the thing*. For a logic of the thing, insofar as it would include the substantial power, the intrinsic virtue of the gift and the call for the countergift, Lévi-Strauss substitutes a logic of relation and exchange which causes all difficulties to vanish and even the very value of gift.

What is the lever of this critique? Precisely the fact that in a given linguistic idiom "antithetical operations are expressed by the same word." Lévi-Strauss recalls that Mauss "does not fail to note" this fact, but "he does not make as much of it as he should" (p. 49). If he had done so, he would not have needed the notion of *hau*, that virtue of the thing which carries out the synthesis between two antithetical operations. "Hau" is unnecessary to produce the synthesis because, according to Lévi-Strauss, the antithesis does not exist. This antithesis would be a kind of phantasm or illusion of ethnographers who often reflect or reproduce in their theory the theories of indigenous

---

implication between the possibilities of the event, of discourse (scientific or not), of invention, and of the gift. Moreover, if the moralizing tone is in general easy enough to identify in numerous discourses and in determined contexts, if it sometimes denotes everything but morality itself, it remains difficult to say where the limit is drawn, a rigorous and sharp limit, between *moral duty* and the moralizing discourse on the subject of moral duty, as well as between, for example, a scientific task, the *ethos* of science, and morality in general. Is morality absent from this evocation of "duty" by means of which Lévi-Strauss justifies his criticism of Mauss, in a paragraph where the figure of *leading* and *leader* [conduite *et* conducteur] reinscribes the refounding moment of French sociology in the landscape of the Promised Land and the legacy of Moses? Who will have been the Great Lawgiver, the Leader of this new science? And what is the relation between gift, law, promise, revelation, and fragments? Why is it that the event, like the gift—if there is any—cannot give evidence of itself but only promise itself? Let us read:

> Why did Mauss halt at the edge of those immense possibilities, like Moses conducting his people all the way to the promised land whose splendor he would never behold? I am impelled [*nous sommes conduits*] to seek the reason, not from any wish to criticize, but out of a *duty* not to let the most fruitful aspect of his thinking be lost or vitiated. Mauss might have been expected to produce the twentieth-century social sciences' *Novum Organum*; he held all the guidelines [*fils conducteurs*] for it, but it has only come to be revealed in fragmented form. There must be some crucial move, somewhere, that Mauss missed out. (Ibid., p. 45; emphasis added).

peoples who sometimes behave like sociologists. And against this illusion of theory (of spontaneous, subjective, illusory theory in the sense in which Freud could speak of the "sexual theory" of children), against this theoretical projection, whether it be Western or indigenous ("indigenous or Western, theory is only ever a theory" [p. 48]), Lévi-Strauss proposes what he calls an "objective" critique that will permit one "to reach the underlying reality." He defines this underlying reality as an unconscious, more exactly as a set of "unconscious mental structures" (p. 49). These unconscious structures can be reached, he tells us, through institutions and "better yet, through language." And it is in the name of the recourse to the unconscious, of the "objectivist" recourse ("objective" critique) to the unconscious that he is going to make a search of language, of the treasury of language and linguistic features so as to find the objectivity that interests him and that he thinks is going to protect him from illusory theories. "*Hau*," writes Lévi-Strauss,

> is a product of indigenous reflection; but reality is more conspicuous in certain linguistic features which Mauss does not fail to note, although he does not make as much of it as he should. "Papuan and Melanesian," he notes, "have one single term to designate buying and selling, lending and borrowing. Operations that are opposites are expressed by the same word." That is ample proof that the operations in question are far from "opposite"; that they are just two modes of a selfsame reality. We do not need *hau* to make the synthesis, because the antithesis does not exist. The synthesis is a subjective illusion of ethnographers, and sometimes also of indigenous people who, when reasoning about themselves—as they quite often do—behave like ethnographers, or more precisely, like sociologists; that is, as colleagues with whom one may freely confer.
>
> When I endeavor to reconstruct Mauss's thinking in this way, without recourse to magical or affective notions (whose use by Mauss seems to me to be merely residual), some may reproach me for drawing him too far in a rationalist direction. My reply to such a reproach is that Mauss took upon himself, from the very start of his career, in the *Outline of A General Theory of Magic,* this same effort to understand social life as a system of relations, which is the lifeblood of *The Gift.*
> (Pp. 49–50)

By eliminating or moving into a secondary role what he calls "affective" notions, whose intervention would remain "residual" (and everything that is at stake seems to consist here in this residue, that is, in a remainder that no one knows what to do with), Lévi-Strauss has no trouble privileging the logic of exchange and relation in order to eliminate the question of the thing. And let us recall here the principle guiding us in this reflection on the gift: To reduce the latter to exchange is quite simply to annul the very possibility of the gift. This annulment is perhaps inevitable or fatal. No doubt its possibility must always remain open. Still one has to deal with this annulment, still one has to render an account of the law of its possibility or its process, of what happens or can not happen in the form of the gift, to the gift and by way of the gift; still one must not treat the question of the thing, of the gift of the thing, and of the thing-gift as a false problem one need merely expose to the fresh air of reason for it to be snuffed out like a candle or, inversely, for it to dissolve in the transparent light of an *Aufklärung* of relational logic.

Since we are interested in *legacies* and before quoting several more statements by Lévi-Strauss that I will qualify here as *exchangist, linguisticist,* and *structuralist,* let us underscore once more the historic importance of the role that such statements played in the formation of the paradigm or, if you prefer, of the *epistemē* or the *themata* of French structuralism in the 60s (all these categories remaining for me the names of problems rather than secure concepts). In the conventional code of the history of ideas or the history of intellectuals, one would say that the "influence" then being exerted on Lacan and Foucault, Barthes or Althusser, is easy to decipher here:

> The only way to avoid the dilemma would have been to perceive that the primary, fundamental phenomenon is exchange itself, which gets split up into discrete operations in social life. . . . Here as elsewhere—but here above all—it was necessary to apply a precept Mauss himself had already formulated in the essay on magic: "The unity of the whole is even more real than each of the parts." But instead, in *The Gift*, Mauss strives to reconstruct a whole out of parts; and as that is manifestly not possible, he has to add to the mixture a supplemental quantity which gives him the illusion of squaring his account. This quantity is *hau.* (P. 47)

In the logic of this discussion, Lévi-Strauss thematizes the concept of "floating signifier," of "supplementary symbolic content," the appeal made by linguists to the "zero phoneme" which would come along to resolve all the contradictions produced when one has recourse to primitive notions of *hau, wakan, orenda* or *mana* as mysterious forces inherent in the thing. We have elsewhere insisted on this value of supplementarity,[4] and it is indeed a question of resorting to a "supplemental symbolic content" (p. 64), to the "distribution of a supplementary ration" (p. 63), to the addition of a "supplemental quantity" (p. 47) so as *to give* (the word is Lévi-Strauss's) himself "the illusion of squaring his account." The account that has gotten unbalanced (but why? by what? and why must it be "squared"?) is that of a "complementarity"—without "supplementarity"—and of a complementarity that would condition "the exercise of symbolic thinking." ("That distribution of a *supplemental* ration—if I can express myself thus—is absolutely necessary to ensure that, *in total*, the available signifier and the mapped-out signified may remain in the relationship of *complementarity* which is the very condition of the exercise of symbolic thinking" [p. 63; emphasis added].) The logic of this statement, it seems, can hardly be criticized. Like the supplemental *ratio* that comes "in total" to complete or complement the totality of the whole, it belongs to reason itself, to the rationality of the principle of reason. Without criticizing it for a moment, one must note that if it intervenes in the constitution of the symbolic, it is as the substitution of exchange for gift. *In total*, there is no gift as concerns reason, not even as concerns a practical reason. There is no reason for there ever to be the least gift. The gift, if there is any, must pass beyond the whole. Before all or after all. Not that it is *opposed* to reason or to anything whatsoever—not at all, through and through [*du tout, du tout au tout*][5]—but perhaps it passes them by so that something may come to pass, including something like reason, including everything [*tout*].

4. "Structure, Sign and Play in the Discourse of the Human Sciences," *Writing and Difference*, pp. 422ff./288ff. In an analogous sense, Remo Guidieri has discussed the rationalist relativism of Lévi-Strauss and his reading of Mauss. He writes: "Lévi-Strauss settled the score of the positive substantivists all too quickly," *La route des morts* (Paris: Le Seuil, 1980), p. 392.

5. Alternatively, this last phrase could be translated: Not that it is *opposed* to reason or to anything whatsoever—of the whole, or the whole to the whole . . . (Trans.).

The apparently, elliptically rationalist gesture that attributed to Mauss the idea that "all social phenomena can be assimilated to language" (ibid.) did quite a lot, let us emphasize once more, for the hegemonic institution of French structuralism as a linguisticism in the 60s: "all social phenomena can be assimilated to language" is what Mauss would say according to Lévi-Strauss; "the unconscious is structured like a language" is what Lacan will say.

In responding also, very differently it is true, to this problem of equivalence between *giving* and *taking* in *The Gift*, the article that Benveniste published at about the same time, "Gift and Exchange in Indo-European Vocabulary,"[6] calls Mauss's essay a "now classic" study. Can what Mauss describes in archaic societies be verified in the ancient societies of the Indo-European world? That is the question. It is difficult to have access to these ancient societies by reason of the state of "usable documents" and uncertain and imprecise accounts in the "evidence." With a gesture that up to a certain point resembles that of Lévi-Strauss in its attention to "unconscious mental structure," Benveniste then proposes to seek the unconscious in language. Might there not be in the vocabulary of the Indo-European languages facts that are "all the more valuable for not having run the risk of being distorted by conscious interpretations" (p. 271)? Out of the very interesting material he then assembles, Benveniste begins with that verb from the root *dô*—which means "to give" in "most Indo-European languages." But at the heart of this certainty concerning an assured constant an uneasiness arises when it is established that the Hittite verb *dâ* signifies not to give but to take. Since it is difficult to believe that the Hittite *dâ* is a different verb, one is prompted to wonder whether the "original meaning" of *dô* was not "to take"; this original meaning would have been maintained in Hittite or even in certain composites such as the Indo-Iranian *a-da*, which means to receive. But that still leaves the question of how "to give" could have

6. "Don et échange dans le vocabulaire indo-européen," in *Problèmes de linguistique générale*. Benveniste himself refers to this article (which includes "a more detailed analysis," he writes, "of the vocabulary of the 'gift'") in Chapter 5 of *Vocabulaire des institutions indo-européennes*, (p. 70), titled "Gift and Exchange." It is nevertheless the case that the great richness of this chapter, as well as of the two succeeding ones ("Donner, prendre, recevoir" and "L'hospitalité") is not altogether taken up in the article we are considering here.

come from "to take." To tell the truth, notes Benveniste, "the problem seems insoluble if we seek to derive 'take' from 'give' or 'give' from 'take.' But the problem is wrongly put" (p. 272).

Benveniste then proposes to resort to syntax rather than to semantics. *Dô* would "properly" mean, he says, neither give nor take "but either one or the other depending on the construction." Analogy: in English, "to take something *from* someone" means to take something that belongs to someone, *prendre quelque chose à quelqu'un*, whereas "to take something *to* someone" means to deliver, to give something to someone. Thus *dô* in itself would mean only "to take hold" (not to take but, more originally, to take hold) and sometimes one takes hold in order to offer, sometimes in order to keep, each language having made "one of the acceptations prevail at the expense of the other." But in the very logic to which Benveniste resorts, does this variation or this syntactic decidability resolve all the problems, even supposing that one could distinguish clearly syntax and semantics in this fashion and that all the same problems did not return in "to take hold" and in syntactic operators of the type "to," "from," "of," and "for"? This syntactic decidability can function only against a background of "semantic ambivalence," which leaves the problem intact. Benveniste seems to recognize this:

> It seems, then, that the most characteristic verb for "to give" was marked by a curious semantic ambivalence, the same sort of ambivalence affecting more technical expressions like "buy" and "sell" in Germanic (Germ. *kaufen : verkaufen*) or "borrow" and "lend" in Greek (*daneizô : daneizomai*). "To give" and "to take" thus proclaim themselves here, in a very ancient phase of Indo-European, as notions organically linked by their polarity and which were susceptible of the same expression. (Ibid.)

How is one to treat here this linguistic phenomenon? What is language? For one must ask oneself not only what use can be made, what type of necessity can be drawn from this philological analysis, to what type of history and objectivity it belongs, what epistemological problems it poses and so forth—all of which are serious questions that Benveniste does not address in this article. Perhaps first of all, however, one must ask oneself, in a manner that is in some way absolutely preliminary: What is the relation between a language and *giving-taking* in general? The definition of language, of a language, as

well as of the text in general, cannot be formed without a certain relation to the gift, to giving-taking and so forth, having been involved
[*engagé*] there in advance. In our relation to language, for example to
those languages called natural or material, to idioms, we are in advance involved in a relation that *obliges* us to think the gift, and, to
repeat Benveniste's own terms, "the very name of 'gift' in the form
which is the most constant throughout most of the Indo-European
languages" (p. 273). That it is a matter there of only certain languages
and only "most of the Indo-European languages," that *dô* is "not the
only example of this" (p. 272), that *nemô* (from which comes *nomos*,
the law), precisely like *partager* in French, signifies both to give and
to have a share (ibid.)—all of this emphasizes still further the urgency
of that obligation. Even before speaking of some gift or division [*partage*] of languages, it is not insignificant that one speaks of language
as a given, as a system that is necessarily there before us, that we
receive from out of a fundamental passivity. (The idiom—or the dialect [*Mundart*]—says Heidegger speaking of J. P. Hebel, is not only
the maternal tongue but also, indeed in the first place, the mother of
the tongue.)[7] Language gives one to think but it also steals, spirits
away from us, whispers to us [*elle nous souffle*], and withdraws the
responsibility that it seems to inaugurate; it carries off the property of
our own thoughts even before we have appropriated them. We will
simply recall this necessary and well-known schema, its principle and
its scope, which no doubt extends far beyond language in the strict
sense of the spoken idiom, to all textuality in general.

Reduced to its barest formality, the structural principle of this complication, which is supplementary and originary, originarily supplementary, is that all semantic ambivalence and the syntactico-semantic
problem of giving-taking are not situated only within language, the
words of language or the elements of a textual system. Language is
also an example of it as is any textual determination. In short, one

---

7. "Die Mundart ist nicht nur die Sprache der Mutter, sondern zugleich und zuvor
die Mutter der Sprache," "Sprache und Heimat," in *Dauer im Wandel, Festschrift zum 70
Geburtstag von C. J. Burckhardt* (Munich, 1961). Cf. as well *Hebel, Der Hausfreund* (Pful-
lingen: Neske, 1957). There Heidegger interrogated dialect (*Mundart*) as the "secret
source" of every developed language, the origin from which we are given everything
that is sheltered by the spirit of the language (*der Sprachgeist*). "What does the spirit of
an authentic language conceal?" ("Was birgt der Geist einer echten Sprache?") (p. 7).

must not only ask oneself, in something close to rapturous wonder, how it is possible that to give and/or to take are said this way or that way *in* a language, but one must also remember first of all that language is as well a phenomenon of gift-countergift, of giving-taking— and of exchange. All the difficulties of nomination or writing in the broad sense are also difficulties of *self*-naming, of *self*-writing [se *nommer, s'écrire*]. Everything said in language and everything written about giving-taking in general *a priori would fold back* on language and writing as giving-taking. Giving *would come back, come down* to taking and taking to giving, but this would also come back to fold itself over not only on language or writing but toward the text in general, beyond its linguistic or logocentric closure, beyond its narrow or common meaning. What then does the "come" of this "come-back" mean? That is one of the questions toward which we are heading. It will not simplify things; it will efface or invaginate all the borders, all the limits and will redouble endlessly not only the semantic ambivalence of which Benveniste speaks but also the ambivalence of the gift as good *and* bad, as gift and poison (*Gift-gift*).

After *dô-*, Benveniste recalls other examples. "to take," in German: *niman* (Gothic), *nehmen*, is seen to relate to the Greek *nemein* with which we began. Each of the Greek nouns that we translate by gift or present, of which there are at least five (*dôs, dosis, dôron, dôrea, dôtinē*), function in a very singular fashion. Along the way, Benveniste quotes a passage from the *Topics* (125a, 18) in which Aristotle speaks of the *dôrea* as a *dosis anapodotos*, a gift that, for once, would not require restitution. The importance of this allusive citation is in truth beyond measure. It announces the link between the economy of the proper, appropriation, expropriation, exappropriation, and the coming or coming-back of the event as restitution or beyond restitution, in the *Ereignis* or in the *Enteignis*.[8]

But let us stay a while with the extreme difficulty of this equivalence or this ambivalence of the giving-taking. If giving is not simply the contrary or something other than taking, if the gift is not totally foreign to taking, if it is not even contrary to it, then we have no take on the gift. *The Gift* is not complicated only because it is also an essay on

8. Linked to that of the gift, of the *es gibt*, of the event and of exappropriation, this problematic of symbolic restitution is developed, in particular around Heidegger, throughout *The Truth in Painting*, notably pp. 320ff./281ff.

the "word" rather than the "thing" "gift," thus implying, as we have already suggested, invisible quotation marks in the title, which designate that the word "gift" is always cited, mentioned, but nowhere used. The complication does not depend only on a word concerning which it is unclear under what conditions, finally, one could ever rightfully use it. *The Gift* complicates itself, *gets taken up* [se prend] in its own internal complication: giving itself to be an essay on the gift, it is also in truth an essay on taking. Even though it is given *to be* or *as* an essay on the gift, it can be taken as an essay on taking. Or yet again: even though it takes itself for an essay on the gift, it gives itself in fact, in truth, as an essay on taking. We don't know if we should take it for what it takes itself to be or as it gives itself, or for what it gives itself since what it gives one to think or to read is that giving must be equivalent to taking. Which does not mean "to take oneself for" and "to give oneself for" come down—or come back—to the same thing.

In other words, what we do not yet know is whether we should take its title for legal tender [*argent comptant*].

For, as we have remarked, all this comes down to, comes back to the *title*, to the question of the title as question of credit and to the title as question of counterfeit money.

This very long temporizing detour, as will perhaps be recalled, was supposed to explain a little phrase of Mauss's: He excuses himself for having been obliged to take sides on very vast questions. And so as to excuse his taking sides in conditions which are such that he cannot give himself the means to justify himself totally, he adds: "but they touch very closely upon our subject and it was necessary to be clear." He therefore assumes to his own account the taking of sides and the involvement [*l'engagement*]. But the haste with which sides have been taken must be justified, compensated, guaranteed. The involvement must be rationalized or shored up by an account or a *logos*. One must explain it with good reasons ("it was necessary to make things clear" and "they were too closely related to our subject," they were too closely related so one had to take sides and not remain indifferent; but in taking sides, one had to be reasonable). It is the system of calculated and not excessive generosity, of the profitable gift, of the good blend between reality and the ideal set forth in the "Moral Conclusions"; it is this "economic paradise," this gesture which consists of winning "paradise economically" that the narrator of "Counterfeit

Money"—we are approaching it slowly—says he cannot forgive his friend.

It happens, moreover (and in saying "it happens" one always simplifies things a little, but we will come back to the meaning of these apparently aleatory encounters when we follow the strolls taken by "Counterfeit Money"), that Mauss's sentence is the last of a long note, one of the longest of the essay, and a note that bears a title, which, for a note, is altogether unusual. The title of this note is "A *Note* of principle concerning the use of the notion of money." The Note bearing this title extends over three pages (100–102) and responds to the objections of those who would like to retain the strict sense for the notion of money and the word "money," and, at the same time, link the meaning of "economic value" to the emergence of money in the strict sense, that is, to the moment when "precious things, themselves intrinsic forms of wealth and signs of riches," we quote Mauss, "were really made into currency [*monnayées*], that is, tested [*titrées*], depersonalized, detached from all relationships with any legal entity, whether collective or individual, other than the state that mints them. But the question posed in this way," continues Mauss, "concerns only the arbitrary limit that must be placed on the use of the world. In my view, one only defines in this way a second type of money— our own."

This note tries to justify the extension of the notion of money and value. Bearing, then, as a *title* "A *Note* of principle concerning the use of the notion of money," it deals with the very *title* of money and with the question of whether money must be, as one says in French, *titrée*, titrated[9]—and titrated by the State—in order to earn its title as money. Everything turns around this value of title and the title of value. In sum, it is a matter of knowing when one is right to (entitled to, justified in) naming *money, true money* in opposition not to *counterfeit money* but to *non-money*. Mauss calls money what his objectors say is not true money and he claims that it is in truth true money, that it is truly authentic money, having the right to the title of true money even if it is not titrated or titled. Nevertheless, his adversaries would not say that this non-true money is counterfeit money.

9. I.e., tested "to ascertain the amount of constituent in a mixture," from the French "*titre,* title, qualification, fineness of alloyed gold or silver" (*OED*). In French, a *titre* is also a stock, bond, or security. (Trans.)

So what then is counterfeit money? When is there counterfeit money? When does one give counterfeit money? And what is given, under this title, *counterfeit money*? Counterfeit money must be *taken* for true money and for that it must *give itself* for correctly titled money.

This was a long introduction, with many detours, to a *chef d'oeuvre* by Baudelaire. About this very short "récit," bearing the title "Counterfeit Money," we will say very little at first. We have played for a lot of time with it since the beginning of these lectures and we are going to read it once again. We will take it at its word and I would say almost word for word. *First of all* [D'abord], we will simply skim its *borders*, what is given as the frame and the system of edges, margins, limits, those of a narrative that resembles in many of its features Poe's "Purloined Letter."[10] Among all these border or framing features, there is, before the first word, the title. The title is "La fausse monnaie," "Counterfeit Money," and its structure is quite complex. As title, it does not form a sentence, it does not say to what it refers, and its referential trait, as well as its referent, remains relatively undetermined. The referential structure of a title is always very tricky. Here it is understood conventionally that the title does not belong to the narrative, it does not constitute an element of the narration that will follow. It is not one of the sentences that the narrator will utter. The whole narrative is situated in the voice of a narrator who says *I*. This *I* takes *part* in *what* he recounts. Playing a role in it, he inscribes, involves, links, or indebts himself there through a tie of friendship (he always says "my friend") to the other character, namely, the one who is going to give counterfeit money *for* true. But the narrator is not Baudelaire, of course, and it goes without saying, according to

---

10. On the title, as well as in general on the threshold and the borders of the text, we once again refer to earlier works, notably to *The Truth in Painting, The Post Card* (in particular "Le facteur de la vérité"), *Parages*, "Préjugés—devant la loi," in *La faculté de juger* (Paris: Minuit, 1985; "Before the Law," trans. Avital Ronell in *Kafka and the Contemporary Critical Performance: Centenary Readings*, ed. Alan Udoff [Bloomington, Ind.: Indiana University Press, 1987]). As for the very limited but significant analogy between "Counterfeit Money" and "The Purloined Letter," precisely as concerns the gift, we will come back to it more than once. But let us note right away a coincidence that one would like to think is "fitting" for Poe, if one can ever say that about a coincidence: the complete text of "The Purloined Letter" was published for the first time in a journal whose title was simply *The Gift*.

the convention, that the title does not belong to the narrative discourse. The narrator is not the author of the title. The author is Baudelaire; the author supposed to be real is the author of the book. Which
does not mean for all that that the title, which does not belong to the
narrative fiction or to the narrative moment of the fiction, is foreign
to any and all fiction. It is as fictive, as freely chosen or *invented*
by the author (publishers ordinarily consider that real authors can
choose their title and that these are part of the book or the story even
if the title is not an element, a piece homogeneous with the rest of the
book). One may also say about the title of the book what we have said
about the title of this brief narrative even though it only entitles a
small piece of it.

So what can "Counterfeit Money," the title "Counterfeit Money"
mean? What does it give itself for, that is, what does it make itself out
to be? How can or should we take it? Its place and its structure as a
title leave a great indetermination and a great possibility for simulacra
that open the field precisely to *counterfeit money*. The title can mean—
and this is generally how it is understood—naïvely: Here is a story
about counterfeit money, under this title you are going to be told a
story in which it is a question of counterfeit money. At that moment,
for this common, immediate reading that is facilitated by so many
established and solid conventions, the title "Counterfeit Money" is
already divided, betrayed, displaced. It has two referents: (1) what is
called counterfeit money and (2) this text *here*, this story of counterfeit
money. It has two referents that both title it—or titrate it as one ti-
trates money and guarantees it: one is counterfeit money itself, the
other is the narrative that has counterfeit money as its referent or
narrated content, this story about counterfeit money. This first division then engenders many other dehiscences, virtually to infinity. For
if this title is double, if it refers at the same time to the thing and to
the narrative, to the text of the narrative, what is the consequence?
First of all, recall that the thing—as counterfeit money—is not a thing
like any other; it is a sign and an incorrectly titled sign, a sign without
value, if not without meaning. Next, the narrative is a fiction and a
fiction of fiction, a fiction on the subject of fiction, the very fiction of
fiction. It is a fiction by Baudelaire, entitled and written by Baudelaire, but it is a fiction that puts a narrative not in Baudelaire's hand
but in the mouth of a fictive narrator who is not Baudelaire and whose
discourse is not in principle assumed by the author. The latter, the

always presumed author, is not presumed to assume the remarks of the narrator, is not presumed to take them on his own account or, as one says in French, for *argent comptant,* at face value. No more than we are.

The fictive narrative is put forward (as non-fictive, *supposedly* [soi-disant] non-fictive) by a fictive narrator, that is, one who claims not to be fictive, in the fiction signed by Baudelaire. This narrative recounts the story of a fiction, of a fictive money, of a money that does not have a title, its legitimate and authentic title. This "storied," recounted, narrated content recounts, then, the whole text which is larger than it is even as the story seems to be only a bordered, framed piece of this larger whole. The smaller is metonymically larger than the larger. At that moment, the title "Counterfeit Money" becomes the title *of the* fictive text. It no longer says only: Here is a story of counterfeit money, but the story *as* literature is itself—perhaps—counterfeit money, a fiction about which one might say, at the limit and by looking for noon at two o'clock, everything that the narrator (who has the natural "gift," given him by nature, of the "exhausting faculty" of "looking for noon at two o'clock") could have said of the counterfeit money of his friend, of the intentions he attributes to his friend, of the calculation and all the exchanges that are thus provoked by the event that his friend has himself provoked with his counterfeit money.

Everything that will be said, *in* the story, *of* counterfeit money (and in the story of counterfeit money) can be said of the story, of the fictive text bearing this title. This text is also the coin, a piece of counterfeit money provoking an event and lending itself to this whole scene of deception, gift, forgiveness, or non-forgiveness. It is as if the title were the very text whose narrative would finally be but the gloss or a long note on the counterfeit money of the title, at the bottom of the page.

If this title is so bifid and abyssal as to say all that (the content of the narrative, the narrative itself as fiction, as counterfeit money, the *I* of the narrator as false signature, and so forth), one must still add a supplement of "counterfeit money." And what is that? The title says, in effect: "since I say so many things at once, since I appear to title this even as I title that at the same time, since I feign reference and since, insofar as it is fictive, my reference is not an authentic, legitimate reference, well then I, as title (but it does not say it . . .) am counterfeit money." It (I) entitles itself and "autonames" itself but without saying so, without saying *I* (otherwise it would not do it: in order to do it, it must not say so; and in order not to do it, it would have to say it). Counterfeit money is the title of the title, the (titleless) title of the title. The title is the title of the text. But does it give its title by saying: *I* am counterfeit money? No, since counterfeit money is only counterfeit on the condition of not giving its title.

The title of "Counterfeit Money" is, may be, counterfeit money. Counterfeit money is never, *as such,* counterfeit money. As soon as it is what it is, recognized *as such,* it ceases to act as and to be worth counterfeit money. It only is by being able to be, *perhaps,* what it is. This irreducible modality taken into account, and inasmuch as the title may belong to it, it obligates you. It obligates you first of all to wonder what money is: true money, false money, the falsely true and the truly false—and non-money which is neither true nor false, and so forth.

The other border about which I will say a few words is what is called the *dedication.* By giving it to be remarked, the dedication situates, then, the *dative* or *donor* movement that displaces the text. There is nothing in a text that is not dedicated, nothing that is not destined, and the destination of this dative is not reducible to the explicit dedication. The name of the dedicatee—or donee—supplies no more proof of the effective dedication than the patronymic name of the signatory (juridically identifiable by civil law) exhausts the effective signature, if there is one. Later, we will follow the dative movements *within* the narrative "Counterfeit Money." For the moment, let us *situate* the at least apparent dedication of the book *Le Spleen de Paris* (*Paris Spleen*) of which "Counterfeit Money," in its very unity, in its irreducible identity, is but an excised morsel, a piece, a segment, the cashing in of a whole [*monnayage d'un tout*]. Now, as for that whole, it is difficult to say whether this dedication on the border is or is not a part of it. Inserted in the book, inscribed between the name of the author and both the title, on the one hand, and the first narrative, on the other, the dedication letter seems not to belong to the system of the fiction of which "Counterfeit Money" is but one piece. But can one be so sure? In other words, how is one to take the dedication? Is it still fiction? Does Baudelaire sign it as he does the book, according to the same modality? Is it counterfeit money? By what title must one receive it? A decisive question whose knot is all the more difficult to *cut* [trancher] in that this dedication utters at the same time that question, the question of the title, the question of the whole and the part, the question even of the "slice" [*la "tranche"*] and of "cutting" [*"trancher"*]. It does so by waving the figure of the Serpent—the book being offered is a serpent—of a serpent in pieces, of a long elusive, segmented animal the "whole" of which [*"tout entier"*] Baudelaire says he wants to dedicate to his friend. What is one doing when one dedicates a serpent—a whole serpent or in segments? One could call up more than one corpus, beginning with other texts by Baudelaire, to provide an immense polylogic response to that question and to make it sing. Let us leave up in the air this question of a serpent that is to be made to sing, that is, blackmailed [*faire chanter*]. Here is the dedication in its two versions, the final one and the draft. For it is only in the draft that the question of the title is posed by name. But the final version puts in place a logic of what we could call a *jealousy of the gift*[11] that gives one to read, in its modernity, the very intrigue of "Counterfeit Money."

And this at the very moment when Baudelaire declares, at the same time as his "jealousy," that he speaks "to tell the truth."

To Arsène Houssaye

My dear friend, I send you a little work of which no one can say, without injustice, that it has neither head nor tail, since, on the contrary, everything in it is both head and tail, alternately and reciprocally. I beg you to consider the admirable convenience this offers all of us, you, me and the reader. We can cut wherever we like—me my reverie, you the manuscript, the reader his reading. For I do not keep the reader's restive will hanging in suspense on the threads of an interminable and superfluous plot. Take away a vertebra and the two parts of this tortuous fantasy will come together again painlessly. Chop it into numerous fragments and you will see that each one can exist on its own. In the hope that there is enough life in some of these segments to please and amuse you, I dare to dedicate the whole serpent to you.

---

11. As for the thinking of jealousy, the relation between gift and jealousy, a "déja-louser" beyond jealousy—and the excess of zeal, I refer to the remarkable text by Peggy Kamuf, "Reading Between the Blinds," Introduction to *A Derrida Reader: Between the Blinds* (New York: Columbia University Press, 1991).

I have a little confession to make to you. It is while paging through, for the twentieth time at least, the famous *Gaspard de la nuit* by Aloysius Bertrand (does not a book known to you, me and a few of our friends have every right to be called *famous*?) that the idea came to me of attempting something analogous, and of applying to the description of modern life, or rather of *a* modern and more abstract life, the same method he used in depicting the old days, so strangely picturesque.

Who among us, in his moments of ambition, has not dreamed of the miracle of a poetic prose, musical without rhythm or rhyme, supple enough and rugged enough to adapt itself to the lyrical impulses of the soul, to the undulations of reverie, the sudden movements of consciousness?

It is above all from frequenting huge cities, from the intersection of their innumerable relations that this obsessive ideal is born. You yourself, my dear friend, have you not tried to translate in a song the *Glacier's* strident cry and to express in lyric prose all the dismal suggestions that this cry sends up through the fog of the street to the highest garrets?

To tell the truth, however, I fear that my jealousy has not brought me good fortune. As soon as I began the work, I realized that not only did I remain far from my mysterious and brilliant model, but what is more I was doing something (if it can be called something) that is singularly different, an accident which anyone else but me would glory in, no doubt, but which can only deeply humiliate a mind convinced that the greatest honor for a poet is to succeed in doing exactly what he has set out to do.

Yours most affectionately,

C.B.[12]

[The draft]:

to Houssaye:

The title.
The dedication.

12. *Oeuvres complètes*, pp. 275–76; *Paris Spleen*, pp. ix–x; translation modified.

Without head nor tail. All head and tail.

Convenient for me. Convenient for you. Convenient for the Reader. We can all cut where we like, me my reverie, you the manuscript, the reader his reading. And I do not keep the restive will hanging on the interminable thread of a superfluous intrigue.

I have sought titles. The 66. Although however this work resembling the screw and the Kaleidoscope could be pushed as far as the Cabalistic 666 and even 6666. . . .

That is better than a 6,000-page intrigue; I should therefore be applauded for my moderation.

Who among us has not dreamed of a particular and poetic prose with which to translate the lyrical movements of the mind, the undulations of reverie and the sudden movements of consciousness?

My point of departure was Aloysius Bertrand. What he did for the old and picturesque days I wanted to do for modern and abstract life. And then, from the beginning, that I was doing something other than what I wanted to imitate. That which another would glory in, but which, for my part, humiliates me who thinks that the poet must always do exactly what he wants to do.

Note on the word famous.
Finally, little segments.
the whole serpent.[13]

In the *name* [titre] *of counterfeit money*, we set out from a sentence of Mauss's ("We excuse ourselves for having been obliged to take sides on these very vast questions, but they touch very closely upon our subject and it was necessary to be clear"). Then we wondered about the import of "taking sides" in a theoretical elaboration and in the whole problematic of the gift. Can one think the gift, speak or write about it without committing oneself to give, without giving at least tokens [gages] or signs? The problem remains intact, the problem of knowing whether one *gives* tokens and whether one gives when one gives tokens or signs or simulacra. As in the justification of his

---

13. *Oeuvres complètes*, pp. 366–67.

"taking sides," Mauss seemed to reproduce the calculation for which the narrator in Baudelaire's "Counterfeit Money" has so much trouble forgiving his friend—the calculation that consists in wanting to "win paradise economically"; it is as if the narrative to which Baudelaire gave the title "Counterfeit Money" comprehended in advance all the movements, all the possibilities—both theoretical and practical—of an essay on the gift in general, of any essay on the gift and of any attempt at a gift, the narrative comprehending the essay that comprehends it in turn like a note on the piece or the piece of a note.

To approach, to cross the borders [aborder], if one can put it that way, of Baudelaire's "Counterfeit Money" is all the more difficult: from the first approach, as we have begun to see and beginning with the title, the border seems to slip away, to divide or to multiply, to delinearize itself. The delinearization affects, to be sure, the rectilinear or circular continuity of a line but it also compromises the identity and indivisibility of the linear trait, its very consistency as a trait contracted with itself, its unity as trait. Now, what is a border or an approach [abord] once the indivisibility of the trait is no longer secure?

The gift, if there is any, will always be *without* border. What does "without" mean here? A gift that does not run over its borders, a gift that would let itself be contained in a determination and limited by the indivisibility of an identifiable *trait* would not be a gift. As soon as it delimits itself, a gift is prey to calculation and measure. The gift, if there is any, should overrun the border, to be sure, toward the measureless and the excessive; but it should also suspend its relation to the border and even its transgressive relation to the separable line or trait of a border. The "without" is not only the "besides" or the "beyond." A consequence, in passing, of this "logic" of a "without" that would be neither negative nor transgressive: Wherever there is castration and problematic of castration (as the dedication about the serpent, the whole, and the part might suggest), there is rationality of the border and there is no gift or even a possible problematic of the gift.

But who says there must be gift and problematic of the gift? Certainly not reason or a principle of reason in general. It is the question of reason that is asked of us here, have no doubt about it, of practical as well as theoretical or speculative reason. Let us leave the full import of that question in reserve and merely recall that, if one must always argue by giving one's reasons, there can never be a reason for giving (if there were, once again the gift would no longer be a gift but a calculation or an exchange), and this leaves open a completely other question: What happens when one gives reason to the other, *quand on donne raison à l'autre*, when, in other words, one concedes that the other is right (an act that also overruns the borders of the order of theoretical reason in the direction of the values of wrong and forgiveness)? What is it, finally, to *avoir raison* [to have reason, i.e., to be right]? And, in the French idiom, to *avoir raison de l'autre* [to have reason of the other, i.e., to win out over the other]?

All these themes or motifs are at work, more or less visibly, in the text signed by Baudelaire, "Counterfeit Money," the borders of which we have seen open out or collapse on themselves. First of all, on the side of the title ("Counterfeit Money"), which overruns its borders in an indefinitely supplementary and abyssal fashion as soon as it gives itself to be read. We will not get involved here in a general theory of the textual structure, typology, and topology of titles. Having attempted to do that elsewhere,[14] we gather up a few of the effects of that theory for this particular title. By reason of its referential structure and its *topos*, its situation as a title suspended in and above the text it entitles, neither in it nor outside it, the title "Counterfeit Money" divides itself, it divides its trait by a *double reference*: (1) It refers to what is commonly called counterfeit money (naïve and direct *thematic* reference *to what is in question in the narrative*); (2) it refers to the narrative itself, insofar as the title "Counterfeit Money" is the title of the narrative, the proper name of the narrative that has as narrated content or theme a story about counterfeit money. Already double or disunited, the title entitles twice at the same time, thereby posing, through the whole range of its indecision, a bifid question that, by playing between spoken signs and written signs (one of the presumed essential possibilities of counterfeit money), could be entitled:

"What is a title as/like counterfeit money?"[15]

The first division *engenders* a series of others that it bears in *embryo*.

---

14. Cf. above, n. 8.

15. This bifid title plays in French on the two grammatical senses of "comme" to mean either "as" or "like." The translation has not tried to render the other play with parentheses that in Derrida's text brings out this double possibility: *"Qu'est-ce qu'un titre comme (la) fausse monnaie?"* mais aussi bien, prenant acte de ce qu'une parenthèse efface ou suspend: *"Qu'est-ce un titre comme fausse monnaie?"* (Trans.)

Let us retain these generative or genealogical figures. A kind of scissiparity carries with it that which it engenders as so many genes, one encased in the other virtually to infinity. As double, the title names at once the "thing" (counterfeit money as thing) and the narrative of the story, and even the narrative act (the narration) of the narrative of the story. Now, the "thing" in question, the thematized thing, the object of narration defined as counterfeit money, is not a thing like any other, precisely, in the strictly determined sense of thing; it is "something" like a sign, and even a false sign, or rather a true sign with a false value, a sign whose signified seems (but that is the whole story) finally not to correspond or be equivalent to anything, a fictive sign without *secure* signification, a simulacrum, the double of a sign or a signifier. Next, the second referent of the title, in other words, the narrative, is a narrative that presents itself as [*se donne pour*] fictive. On the part of the author, in any case, and under the name of literature, but not on the part of the narrator. It is then a fiction the subject of which is a fictive money, a fiction of fiction; and if the recounted fiction also *says* the narrative fiction itself (if it gives one to think this fiction by means of emblematic or metonymic, but also reflexive or specular figuration), there is no end to the speculation.

In the civil code concerning ownership of literary works, the fiction is attributed to its signatory, Baudelaire, and is entitled by him. Now, by reason and by virtue of the same right—what is called the *droit d'auteur* in French, that is, the right of the author—this fiction places the narrative not in the mouth, in the hand, or within the responsibility of the author but, of course, of the narrator. The latter is himself fictive, a fiction of the author; as for the discourse of the narrator, his narrative, his deliberations, the conclusions of his deliberations (concerning in particular whether he can forgive his friend who has given counterfeit money to a beggar), we must always suppose that Baudelaire does not by rights take them on: he does not take them at face value. No more than we do, let us repeat. The (fictive) narrative is by right produced by the fictive narrator; but like the narrator, the narrative is fictive only between Baudelaire and us, if one may put it thus, since the fictive narrator produces his narrative *as* a true narrative and therein consists the fiction—or the simulacrum produced by the author. This is what it seems to share with the phenomenon of counterfeit money (to pass off a fiction as "true"). But since the convention permits us to know—Baudelaire and us the readers—that this fiction is a fiction, there is no phenomenon here of "counterfeit money," that is, of an abuse of trust that passes off the false for the true. It remains the case, however, that the possibility of counterfeit money, of the *effect* of counterfeit money, shares the same general condition: to pass off a fiction as "true." To be sure, dishonesty or the criminal misdeed has no place in literature, "within" the literary phenomenon delimited at its borders by conventions. Baudelaire is not lying, he is not deceiving. *Outside* of literature, but *in life such as it is represented,* imagined, recounted in a fiction like "Counterfeit Money," the moral fault or the criminal misdeed implies lying, the intention to deceive—and thus knowledge—only on the part of the emitting agent or the counterfeiter, to the exclusion of the receiver or the "dupes" (the beggar, for example, or the narrator before his friend's confession and, outside the narrative, in a heterogeneous space, the reader at least preceding the same confession; but the reader is not "deceived" or "duped" in the same sense as the narrator: in truth, his non-knowledge is not on the order of being-deceived; it is the experience of a *secret* without depth, a *secret without secret* to which we will return in conclusion).

Let us now consider this narrative. Truly fictive, but produced *as true narrative* by the fictive narrator in the fiction signed and forged by Baudelaire, here it goes and tells us the story of another fiction, of a fictive money. This money, as we would say in French, *n'a pas de titre,* has no title, does not have its legitimate and authentic title; it has only a false title [*faux titre*], or rather a "false" title [*title "faux"*], since in French a "faux-titre" means still something else.[16] This story (this narrated content) tells, then, at the same blow, but by way of a figure and obliquely, as a story of counterfeit money, of fiction or of simulacrum, *both* the (narrating) narration *and* the (narrated) narration. The story makes up a part of itself, it is part, a part of itself, it incorporates or interiorizes the very thing of which it is a part, the text entitled "Counterfeit Money." Framed, embedded, bordered, debordered, overrun, the smaller becomes, metonymically, larger than the larger—that borders and frames it. Such a frame fixes the space and time given, that is, instituted by a convention, a convention which is, by convention, irremovable. But this structure is rather a movement that also overruns and de-borders the coded language of

16. In typography, a "faux-titre" is a half title or bastard title. (Trans.)

rhetoric, here of metonymy as identifiable figure. For the very identity of figures supposes stable relations between the part and the whole. This relative stabilization always appears possible, to be sure, and it allows for rhetoric and the discourse on rhetoric. But as no natural stability is ever given, as there is only *stabilization in process*, that is, essentially precarious, one must presuppose "older" structures, let us not say originary structures, but more complicated and more unstable ones. We propose here to call them structures, and even to study them as such in literary processes, because they are not necessarily chaotic. Their relative "anteriority" or their greater complexity does not signify pure disorder.

Therefore, the title "Counterfeit Money" *can* become, it has the potential to signify twice in one blow, so to speak, and to divide itself in two referential directions: On the one hand, here is a story about counterfeit money, but also, on the other hand, the story is, *perhaps*, counterfeit money (*perhaps*: the *perhaps* remains essential here because, in order for there to be counterfeit money, the counterfeit money must not give itself *with certainty* to be counterfeit money; and this *perhaps* is also the intentional dimension, that is, the *credit*, the act of faith that structures all money, all experience or all consciousness of money, be it true or false). The story is perhaps counterfeit money, a fiction about which one can say in its turn, at the limit and by looking for noon at two o'clock, *all* that the narrator could have said about it, *gifted* as he is by nature, who has made him a *gift*—a gift without which none of this story would be possible—of the exhausting faculty of looking for noon at two o'clock. On the subject of itself, of its "own" text, the story says *all* that the narrator would have said of his friend's counterfeit money, of the intentions that he *lends* (that is his word, as we will see) to his friend, of the calculation that he attributes to him, in other words, that he credits to him, and of all the exchanges that are thus provoked with the counterfeit money. It is a little as if the narrator were speaking of the "author's intentions," namely Baudelaire's, as if Baudelaire were the narrator's friend, as if he presented "himself," in effect, without showing himself, disguised in the traits of the friend of the narrator whom he makes speak, as if he let the narrator (in the place of the reader or the critic) analyze the possible motifs and effects of the counterfeit money that is the text, the possible effects of "Counterfeit Money."

"It was the counterfeit coin," he calmly replied as though to justify himself for his prodigality.

But into my miserable brain, always concerned with looking for noon at two o'clock (what an exhausting faculty is nature's gift to me!), there suddenly came the idea that such conduct on my friend's part was excusable only by the desire to create an event in this poor devil's life, perhaps even to learn the varied consequences, disastrous or otherwise, that a counterfeit coin in the hands of a beggar might engender. Might it not multiply into real coins? Could it not also lead him to prison? A tavern keeper, a baker, for example, was perhaps going to have him arrested as a counterfeiter or for passing counterfeit money. The counterfeit coin could just as well, perhaps, be the germ of several days' wealth for a poor little spectator. And so my fancy went its course, lending wings to my friend's mind and drawing all possible deductions from all possible hypotheses.

But first of all, ought one to extend credit to such a friend? Ought one, as the narrator still seems to do, take him at his word when he says "It was the counterfeit coin"? What if he were an even greater counterfeiter than the narrator thinks? What if, with the simulacrum of a confession, he were passing off true money as false? We will let this question follow the path of the two friends leaving the "tobacconist's." Later we will come upon it again.

This text, then, is also the piece, *perhaps* a piece of counterfeit money, that is, a machine for provoking events: First of all, the event of the text that is there, like a narrative offering itself or holding itself open to reading (this event has taken place and continues to take place, it gives time and takes its time, it apparently gives itself time), but also and consequently, from there, in the order of the opened possibility and of the aleatory, an event pregnant with other events that have in common, however, a certain propitiousness for this staging of a trap or a deception [*leurre*]. And the trap is the affair of nothing less than reason, of the reason one *has* or the reason one *gives* [*de la raison qu'on a ou de la raison qu'on* donne]. What does "avoir raison" mean [to "have reason," i.e., to be right]? What does "donner reason" mean [to "give reason," i.e., to concede to the other]? Why are these locutions so idiomatic and thus so poorly translatable? Why do the "avoir-raison" and the "donner-raison," in these two cases, no longer belong to theoretical and speculative reason? Why is the speculation that continues to act through them no longer *speculative* in the sense of speculative or calculating reason? An affair of reason, the trap or deception is also an affair of gift, excuse, forgiveness, or non-forgiveness for a non-gift or rather for an always improbable gift.

It is as if the text did nothing but play with its title—which would be its object; it is as if the body of the titled text became the title of the title that then becomes the true body, the false-true body, so to speak, of the text, its false-true corpus, its body as ghost of a fiduciary sign, a body on credit. Everything is act of faith, phenomenon of credit or credence, of belief and conventional authority in this text which perhaps says something essential about what here links literature to belief, to credit and thus to capital, to economy and thus to politics. Authority is constituted by accreditation, both in the sense of legitimation as effect of belief or credulity, and of bank credit, of capitalized interest. This recalls a very fine saying of Montaigne's, who knew all this in advance: "Our soul moves only on credit or faith [*crédit*], being bound and constrained to the whim of others' fancies, a slave and a captive under the authority of their teaching." [17]

Accredited in this way, a "true" corpus is still, perhaps, counterfeit money; it may be a ghost or a spirit, the spirit of the body and of capital (for a title, a heading, is a capital). One might draw from this all the consequences regarding the institution of a body and a corpus and regarding the phenomena of canonization that follow. Also regarding what is called spirit. There would be no problem of the canon if this whole institution were *natural*. There is a problem because, as Montaigne says, that institution only moves "on credit" and under "the authority of teaching." In fact, if "Counterfeit Money" as a title is bifid, treacherous, and abyssal enough to say all of this and the rest without saying it (the content of the narrative, that is, the story or the narrative itself as fiction, as counterfeit money, the *I* of the narrator as fictive signature), one must, one can—*perhaps*—add to it a supplementary power of counterfeit money. What power is that?

17. "Of the Education of Children," *Essays and Selected Writings*, trans. Donald M. Frame (New York: St. Martin's Press, 1963), p. 35. The French reads: "Nostre ame ne branle qu'à crédit, liée et contrainte à l'appetit des fantasies d'autruy, serve et captivé soubs l'authorité de leur leçon."

The title, in effect, *gives one to read, gives itself as saying* or wanting to say the following (perhaps), and such would be its intention:
"Since I say and name and denominate so many things at once, since
I look as if I am entitling this while at the same time, taking back with
one hand what I give with the other, I entitle that in addition, since I
feign reference and nomination, since my reference, as fictive, is not
truly a reference, not the right one in any case, since it is indeed a
reference but remains illegitimately titled, since its referent is not necessarily what one thinks it is, well, then *I*, as title, am counterfeit
money." But obviously it doesn't say that, otherwise it would dis-
credit itself; it says it without saying it, it does not say "I," "I am" or
"I am not"; it overruns the order of assured propositions or autopo-
sitions of the type *"sum"* or *"cogito sum"*; otherwise there would no
longer be any possible counterfeit money. But at the same time, in
order for there to be counterfeit money, it must speak and it must say:
Here is what I am, I do not lie or I do not lie in saying I lie. The title
entitles itself, autonames itself but without saying so, without saying
"I," by saying it without saying it and here the *without* is irreducible.
And the whole play of the "I" here accredits its authority. To sum all
this up, we would say that counterfeit money is the title of the title,
the title without title of the title (without title). The title is the title of
the text and of its title. But it does not present its titled claims by
saying "I am (some) counterfeit money," since counterfeit money is
what it is only by not giving itself *as such* and by not appearing *as
such*, by not exhibiting its titles. And inasmuch as it obligates, it nevertheless obliges you to wonder again, at least, what is going on and
if there is money—true money, counterfeit money, counterfeit true
money and truly counterfeit money.

Another border already divided itself in indefinite abyssal supplements. The dative movement of the dedication displaced the text,
delivered it or released it from a place that is, let us recall, neither
internal to the fiction (either "Counterfeit Money" or *Paris Spleen* as
a whole) nor simply external to that fiction. Baudelaire's dedication
letter (in two versions) to "My dear friend" (Arsène Houssaye) was
clearly working in all senses on the question of the whole and the
parts, of the model (Aloysius Bertrand), and so forth. But when it
offers up for deciphering the figure of the serpent, for example ("In
the hope that there is enough life in some of these segments to please
and amuse you, I dare to dedicate the whole serpent to you"), one

may once again be tempted to read Baudelaire with Mauss. Let us note it here, in this place of transition, because the most remarkable passage in this regard makes an association in the same scene between the Serpent clan and a certain offering of tobacco. Now, in a little while we are going to read "Counterfeit Money" as a story of tobacco, among other intrigues. The passage from Mauss concerns a ceremony that is spread throughout "all the Indian civilizations of North America." The spirit, spirits, ghosts are at the party, they are the first guests at the last supper in which they take part:

> Each clan cooks food and prepares tobacco for the representatives of the other tribes, during the clan's festival. Here, for example, are excerpts from the speech made by the chief of the Serpent clan: "I greet you. It is good. How could I say otherwise? I am a poor, worthless man and you have remembered me. It is good . . . You have thought of the spirits and you have come to sit down with me . . . Soon your dishes will be filled. So I greet you once again, you humans who take the place of the spirits, etc." And when each chief has eaten, and has put offerings of tobacco into the fire, the closing formula points to the moral effect of the festival and of all the prestations: "I thank you for having come to sit down in this seat, I am grateful to you. You have encouraged me . . . The blessings of your grandfathers who have enjoyed revelations (and who are incarnate in you) are equal to those of the spirits. It is good that you have taken part in my festival. (Pp. 70–71)

How is the question of the gift and the dative posed in "Counterfeit Money"? What is it that gives the apparently finite and separable text? What is it that gives the space-time and the spacing that bears this title, "Counterfeit Money"? What is given there? What is it that finds itself *given* there? Who gives? And to whom? What and to whom?

Let us first of all not forget something trivially and massively obvious. It constitutes the elemental medium for what one is given to think here, namely, that this text—apparently finite, this bit of corpus titled "Counterfeit Money"—is for us a *given*. It is there before us who read it and who therefore begin by receiving it. If it has the structure of a given, it is not only because we are first of all in a receptive position with regard to it but because it has been given to us. From the moment he published it and even if he had not published it, from the moment he wrote it and constituted it by dedicating it to his "dear friend," the presumed signatory (Baudelaire or whoever effectively signed this text *beneath* the patronymic and accredited signature of Baudelaire—for let us not be so gullible as to believe that the effective signatory of *that* comes down to a Charles Baudelaire, any more than we believe the dedicatee goes no further than the name Arsène Houssaye), from the moment he let it constitute itself in a system of traces, he destined it, gave it, not only to another or in general to others than his "dear friend" Arsène Houssaye, but delivered it—and that was giving it—above and beyond any determined addressee, donee, or legatee (we are speaking here of an unconscious figure represented by a "dear friend" or even by a determinable, bordered configuration of public and readers). The accredited signatory delivered it up to a dissemination without return. Why without return? What history, what time, and what space are determined by such a "without return"? Whatever return it could have made toward Baudelaire or whatever return he might have counted on, the structure of trace and legacy of this text—as of anything that can be in general—surpasses the phantasm of return and marks the death of the signatory or the non-return of the legacy, the non-benefit, therefore a certain condition of the gift—in the writing itself.

That is why there is a problematic of the gift only on the basis of a consistent problematic of the trace and the text. There can never be such a thing on the basis of a metaphysics of the present, or even of the sign, signifier, signified, or value. This is one of the reasons we always set out from texts for the elaboration of this problematic, texts in the ordinary and traditional sense of written letters, or even of literature, or texts in the sense of differantial traces according to the concept we have elaborated elsewhere. And we are unable to do otherwise than *take our departure in texts insofar as they depart* (they separate from themselves and their origin, from us) *at the departure* [dès le départ]. We could not do otherwise even if we wished to do so or thought to do so. We are no longer credulous enough to believe that we are setting out from things themselves by avoiding "texts" simply by avoiding quotation or the appearance of "commentary." The most apparently direct writing, the most directly concrete, personal writing which is supposedly in direct contact with the "thing itself," this writing is "on credit": subjected to the authority of a commentary or a re-editing that it is not even capable of reading.

But whereas only a problematic of the trace or dissemination can pose the question of the gift, and forgiveness, this does not imply that writing is *generous* or that the writing subject is a *giving subject*.[18] As an identifiable, bordered, posed subject, the one who writes and his or her writing never give anything without calculating, consciously or unconsciously, its reappropriation, its exchange, or its circular return—and by definition this means reappropriation with surplus-value, a certain capitalization. We will even venture to say that this is the very definition of the *subject as such*. One cannot discern the subject except as the subject of this operation of capital. But throughout and despite this circulation and this production of surplus-value, despite this labor of the subject, there where there is trace and dissemination, if only there is any, a gift can take place, along with the excessive forgetting or the forgetful excess that, as we in-

18. Let us underscore this: to recall that only a problematic of the trace, and thus of dissemination, can allow the question of the gift and of forgiveness to arise is to displace the concept of writing. It is to signal toward something altogether other than the traditional opposition between a (living) speech and a (dead) writing. As is well known, it is on this opposition that a Greco-Christian tradition will have often ordered its interpretation of the duel between Christian and Jew.

The gift, forgiveness—if there is any—and the trace that there always is would thus be something altogether other than the themes of an opposition passively received and precipitously, compulsively credited—by a Léon Bloy, for example, when, in his customary, diabolical, and sometimes sublime ignominy, he writes:

It is through them that this algebra of turpitude called *Credit* has definitively replaced the old *Honor*, which was all chivalrous souls needed to accomplish everything.

And as if this strange people, condemned, come what may, to always being, in a fashion, the People of God, could not do anything without letting right away some reflection of its eternal history appear, the living and merciful WORD of the Christians, that used to suffice for fair transactions, was once again *sacrificed*, in all the commerce of injustice, to rigid WRITING that is incapable of forgiveness.

The infinitely decisive victory that has determined the universal debacle.

Le Salut par les Juifs (Paris: Mercure de France, 1905–6), pp. 192–93.

As if the WORD—in particular in "fair transactions"!—did not require either time, trace, or credit. As if the frontier between faith, belief, and credit were secure. *Le Salut par les Juifs* is not very far removed from the Baudelaire whom we are getting ready to read (see below, in particular p. 130). It would merit, in this specific context, a patient analysis, notably for all it has to say about the figure of the *pauper*, of the "true Pauper": Jesus Christ (p. 61). Jews are also described there as the "Creditors of an undying Promise that the Church judged to have been fulfilled . . ." (p. 84).

sisted earlier, is radically implicated in the gift. The death of the donor agency (and here we are calling death the fatality that destines a gift *not to return* to the donor agency) is not a natural accident external to the donor agency; it is only thinkable on the basis of, setting out from [*à partir du*] the gift. This does not mean simply that only death or the dead can give. No, only a "life" can give, but a life in which this economy of death presents itself and lets itself be exceeded. Neither death nor immortal life can ever give anything, only a singular *surviving* can give.[19] This is the *element* of this problematic.

The text credited to Baudelaire, and which we have barely begun to read, belongs to a scene of writing and therefore to the scene of a gift unthinkable for any subject. It is within this exceeded and excessive scene, within its destiny and its destination without identifiable addressee and without certain addressor, that our corpus is carved out. But insofar as it tells the story of a gift, this corpus is going to say "in" itself, "of" itself the exceeding that frames it and that exceeds its frame. It is going to re-mark in a supplementary *abyme* that absolute dissemination that destines the text to depart in ashes or go up in smoke.

For example, tobacco ashes and tobacco smoke. It is not insignificant that the place *from which* this scene of gift and counterfeit money *departs* is what is called in French a *bureau de tabac*, a tobacco shop. "First sentence," *incipit* of the narrative which reads as if one were continuing after an interruption, and we suddenly have the utter progress of an *infinite* leap over the abyss of two phrases that have no structural identity, the title and the beginning of the narration: "As we were leaving the tobacconist's, my friend carefully separated his change." The tobacconist's is obviously the insignia or the sign of modernity, of that "description of modern life" to which Baudelaire, in his dedication to Arsène Houssaye, says he wants to "apply" another's "procedure." But at the sign of this modernity, there is the older institution of tobacco that forms the essential decor of the scene. They have just bought some tobacco. They have just bought—offered themselves—some tobacco: The whole economy of the narrative, as well as the narrative of the economy, proceeds from a *remainder*, from

19. On this concept of surviving [*survivance*], cf. "Survivre" in *Parages* ("Living On—Borderlines" in Harold Bloom et al., eds., *Deconstruction and Criticism*, trans. James Hulbert [New York: Seabury Press, 1979]).

the change returned, from the change that remains from this purchase. *Monnaie*, money, change: in French, at least, it is the same
word (and the word is a coin, a piece of change). The word says at
once the monetary thing in general and the remainder of a monetary
operation, for example, the "monnaie qu'on rend," the change one
returns or "la petite monnaie," small change.

As for the economy of the narrative and the narrative of the
economy, we have glimpsed the reason for which the gift, if there is
any, requires and at the same time excludes the possibility of narrative. The gift is on condition of the narrative, but simultaneously on
the condition of possibility and impossibility of the narrative. The
economy of this story of counterfeit money is put in circulation *by* a
remainder but also contained *in* a remainder of change after a purchase of some tobacco. The time of the narrative begins once the
change is returned, and returned after expenditure on a luxury: an
unproductive expenditure—apparently at least—for the acquisition
of a luxury product, that is, a product of pure consumption that is
burned without leaving, apparently, any remainder. The two friends
are apparently linked, in this scene, by the common possibility of
smoking, in other words, of expending at a pure loss, for pure auto-affective pleasure, very close to the voice, this singular natural
product that is tobacco. If we yielded to the temptation, often an ir-
resistible one, of letting this reading expand without limits, we would
enter here into a discourse on tobacco—and even exclusively on tobacco and drunkenness in Baudelaire. More than one seminar would
be disseminated there in smoke. Let us contain things, for the moment, in several rings.

1. *The time of woman.* You will very quickly suspect that, if woman
seems to be absent from this narrative, her exclusion could well be
organizing the scene and marking its tempo like a clock. Without
looking any further for the moment, we might think of another incipit in *Paris Spleen* not far from "Counterfeit Money." There, as well,
everything happens "among men." And the men speak of the absent
woman. Woman is their subject. Now, this place of the among-men
is a smoking-room, and the among-men is itself defined thus: a smoking-room. Among-men, *that is to say,* a smoking-room. From the end
of the last century comes a truth uttered by a "painter of modern life,"
but a truth whose history is certainly not over, a truth stated from the
first sentence of "Portraits of Some Mistresses": "In a man's boudoir,

that is to say, in the smoking-room of an elegant gambling-house, four men were smoking and drinking."[20]

Such is the frame: a four-of-a-kind in kings, a square of kings.[21] These males are four, they are smoking, thinking about philosophy— and *consequently* about avoiding women. Second paragraph, second incipit: "One of them turned the discussion to the subject of women. It would have been more philosophical not to talk about them at all; but there are intelligent men who, after drinking, are not above commonplace conversations. In those cases, one listens to whoever is speaking as one would listen to dance music."[22] The allusion to the "after drinking" leads us back already to the economic motif of drunkenness and the superfluous, of the remainder and of superabundance as *excessive* origin and improbable possibility of the gift. "After drinking," man speaks without having anything to say, "commonplace conversations" turn the floor over to speech that is superabundant, excessive, generous, useless, redundant, luxurious. One should read here what follows as well as so many other texts that have a relation of elective affinity with this one, for example "The Pipe." Speaking in the first person, in *Les fleurs du mal*, the pipe says of the author its master that he is "a big smoker.": "Je suis la pipe d'un auteur . . . mon maître est un grand fumeur" [I am the pipe of an author . . . my master is a big smoker].

Among so many different texts on drugs and artificial paradise, we select, for reasons of pure proximity, the very brief and authoritarian "Enivrez-vous," "Get Drunk." It justifies this exhortation by the necessity of fleeing from Time. Drugs, whether hard or soft, whether in the form "of wine, poetry or virtue," are salvation from Time. For if time is given to us, it is also *counted* and our days are numbered; the "clock" is named twice in these few lines and the imperative, we would say, concerns the hour [*l'heure*]: "Il est l'heure de s'enivrer!

20. *Oeuvres complètes*, p. 345; *Paris Spleen*, p. 85.

21. On this structure, cf. "Le facteur de la vérité," *The Post Card*, notably the chapter titled "Meeting Place: The Double Square of Kings," pp. 511ff./483ff. If we take the liberty of accumulating references of this sort, it is because the reflection begun in the Seminar titled "Donner—le temps" was contemporary with and indissociable from these works, notably *The Post Card*, which, as already mentioned, refers to it in a note (see above Foreword, n. 2).

22. *Oeuvres complètes*, p. 345; *Paris Spleen*, p. 85.

Pour n'être pas les esclaves martyrisés du Temps, enivrez-vous sans cesse! De vin, de poésie ou de vertu, à votre guise" [It is time to get drunk! If you are not to be the martyred slaves of Time, be perpetually drunk! On wine, on poetry or on virtue, at your pleasure].[23] Drunkenness *gives time* but by assuring "salvation from Time." To give time would therefore come down to annuling it. Given time is time taken back. To give time is to take time and to take it back altogether, leaving, for example for Madame de Maintenon, only time enough to regret the rest. Four times time, time against time, this would be—along with smoke, money, women, and drunkenness—the subject.

2. *The "good hour" of "The Purloined Letter."* That the narrative of "Counterfeit Money" proceeds from an apparently dual situation, that it is linked to a masculine couple, that it links the two male partners between them—and to tobacco, that is, to a common consumption that goes up in smoke—that this smoke also seals their alliance, all of this forms a system of traits already inscribed in a repetition, not to say a compulsion. It cites and re-cites other narrative incipits, for example, that of Poe's "Purloined Letter." Here one would have to reread the latter text. What we find there is a model for its translator (Baudelaire) and a model that is just as recognizable as Aloysius Bertrand whom Baudelaire says he rivals. Moreover, what is at stake in this model is decisive for our problematic. As in "Counterfeit Money," it links once more the simulacrum, the process of truth and the narrative situation to the circulation of a "remnant" of money.[24] Marked by a passage that I have tried to interpret else-

23. *Oeuvres complètes,* p. 337; *Paris Spleen,* p. 74.
24. By means of a *remnant* of the paternal inheritance, apparently left out of account for the debtor, who by calculating (rigorous economy) can draw an income, a revenue from it, the surplus-value of a capital which works by itself, Dupin offers himself [*se paye*] a single superfluity, a sole luxury in which the initial luxury is relocated therefore, and which cuts across the space of the restricted economy like a gift without return. This sole luxury ("sole luxuries": the word one finds for the second time on the second line of "The Purloined Letter," but this time as a singular double luxury, the "twofold luxury of meditation and a meerschaum"), is writing: the books which will organize the meeting place and the *mise en abyme* of this entire general narration. The meeting place of the meeting between the narrator and Dupin is due to the meeting of their interest in the same book; it is never said whether they find it. Such is the literal accident: "Our first meet-

where,[25] "The Purloined Letter" also begins with this apparently dual situation (which has been shown to be in truth at least quadruple) that, beginning with the first sentence, the narrator describes thus:

> At Paris, just after dark one gusty evening in the autumn of 18--, I was enjoying the twofold luxury of meditation and a meerschaum, in company with my friend C. Auguste Dupin, in his little back library, or book-closet *au troisième, No. 33, Rue Dunôt, Faubourg St. Germain.* For one hour at least [Baudelaire translates: "Pendant une bonne heure," for a good hour], we had maintained a profound silence; while each, to any casual observer, might have seemed intently and exclusively occupied with the curling eddies of smoke that oppressed the atmosphere of the chamber.[26]

In whatever manner one reads what follows (and who knows if it has not become the subject of "commonplace conversations" among men and women in the university, at a time when almost everyone has quit smoking?), a certainty remains, which is hardly open to question: It is the promised assurance of a remainder or remnant [*reste*]. Just as in "Counterfeit Money," the whole story of "The Purloined Letter" proceeds from the surplus-value of a *remnant* or a superfluity of revenue (income or inheritance). The narrator pays for Dupin's studio while the latter, with the income from an inheritance, treats himself to books, "his sole luxury." A certain economy of labor and production *seems* at least—for it is a matter here of deception [*leurre*], simulacrum or appearance—to be exceeded by the luxury of the superfluity into which the narration enters [*s'engage*], along with the whole process of restitution and destination that follows. But we'll let the purloined letter go on its way and come back to tobacco.

---

ing was at an obscure library in the Rue Montmartre, where the accident of our both being in search of the same very rare and very remarkable volume. . . ." "Le facteur de la vérité," pp. 517–17/487–88.

As we will see, the same logic of the event, said to be of a chance "meeting" of the "accident" (*apparently* aleatory, *perhaps* unpredictable) is found at work in "Counterfeit Money." The analogy is too striking to be overlooked.

25. Ibid., pp. 511ff./483ff.

26. *The Short Fiction of Edgar Allan Poe*, eds. Stuart and Susan Levine (Indianapolis: Bobbs-Merrill, 1976), pp. 225–26.

3. *What is tobacco?*[27] *Apparently* it is the object of a pure and luxurious consumption. *It appears* that this consumption does not meet any natural need of the organism. It is a pure and luxurious consumption, gratuitous and therefore costly, an expenditure at a loss that produces a pleasure, a pleasure one *gives oneself* through the ingestive channel that is closest to auto-affection: the voice or orality. A pleasure of which nothing remains, a pleasure even the external signs of which are dissipated without leaving a trace: in smoke. If there is some gift—and especially if one *gives oneself* something, some affect or some pure pleasure—it may then have an essential relation, at least a symbolic or emblematic one, with the authorization one gives oneself to smoke. That at least is how it *appears*. But this appearance remains to be analyzed

27. Here is a question that Baudelaire might perhaps have associated with that of literature, the "new literature." In the course of an analysis of social customs that, as usual, seeks to be very historical, he describes "literary drunkenness," beginning with that of Poe, as "one of the most common and most lamentable phenomena of modern life." He finds there are "attenuating circumstances," for example, the "formless education" and the "political and literary incompetence" of women, which prevent authors from seeing in them "anything other than household utensils or luxury items." Conclusion: "One must no doubt attribute to the same transformation of social customs, which has made the literary world into a class apart, the enormous consumption of tobacco by the new literature." "Edgar Allen Poe, sa vie et ses ouvrages," *Oeuvres complètes*, vol. 2, pp. 271–72.

4

"Counterfeit Money" II:
Gift and Countergift, Excuse and Forgiveness
(Baudelaire and the Story of the Dedication)

. . . no more than the truism that there can be no counterfeit where
there is no genuine—just as there can be no badness where there is
no goodness—the terms being purely relative. But *because* there can be
no counterfeit where there is no original, does it in any manner follow
that an undemonstrated original exists? . . . . what right should we
have to talk of counterfeit at all?
   —E. A. Poe, *Marginalia*

Once, in my presence, the question was asked, What is the greatest
pleasure of love? Someone naturally responded: to receive—and someone else: to give oneself.—The latter said: pleasure of pride!—the
former: sensual delight of humility! All these filthy minds were speaking like the *Imitation of Jesus Christ*.—Finally there was an impudent
utopian who asserted that the greatest pleasure of love was to form
citizens for the fatherland.

As for me, I say: The sole and supreme pleasure of love lies in the
certainty of doing *evil*.—Both man and woman know, from birth, that
in evil is found all sensual delight.
   —Baudelaire, *Journaux intimes*, "Fusées"

One may be tempted to subtract tobacco from economy, from the circulation of labor and production, income and surplus-value, from the accumulation of capital, from money in the form of currency or non-currency. From all of that one may be tempted to subtract, purely and simply, tobacco—or rather the act of smoking and inhaling, the experience, the enjoyment and the expenditure of that which, one could say, goes up in smoke. But one can also resist this temptation as one resists an appearance. This could be shown on several registers. We will indicate only a few titles or types.

A. First of all, the *psycho-analytic* register, to use a somewhat simple designation. By way of the relation to the object one holds between one's fingers or one's lips, by way of inhalation, oral interiorization or incorporation, by way of the diverse stimuli of the central nervous system (for example, those that favor imagination, speaking or writing, that induce or proliferate substitutive operations, that reconstitute or entail the circulation of an auto-affective fantasmatics, and so forth), the demand and the enjoyment can correspond to an aim, can belong to an end-oriented system. They can accomplish real or symbolic functions. These functions are essential to the economic or even ecological balance of certain psychic organizations. There is no gratuitous expenditure, no superabundance, no overflowing of pure luxury in all this, unless one redetermines luxury so as to recognize in it an essential economic function. (Let it be said in parentheses that it is difficult to make a connection here between smoking and counterfeit money without at least evoking the case of Freud. Perhaps one day, in the wake of certain work, for example that of Nicolas Abraham and Maria Torok, we will have to map intersections that go from Freud's cigar, "the only and the best companion of his life," to his mouth cancer, and to certain stories of counterfeiters in the shadows of a family genealogy; the spectres of these forgers would have come back to haunt him in a good many ways, and from couch to couch, until one comes to a certain patient of a patient, a certain analysand of Freud's analysand—for instance the author of *Les Faux-monnayeurs*, Gide, who was, they say, in analysis with someone analyzed by Freud, Eugenia Sokolnicka. Here it would have been necessary to study *Les Faux-monnayeurs* from the perspective of its formal structure (literary, narrative, and so forth) and the relation of this structure with the story of counterfeit money.[1] Let us locate in passing here the space of a complex task: To study for example, in so-called modern literature, that is, contemporaneous with a capital—city, *polis*, metropolis—of a state and with a state of capital, the transformation of monetary forms (metallic, fiduciary—the bank note—or scriptural—the bank check), a certain rarification of payments in cash, the recourse to credit cards, the coded signature, and so forth, in short, a certain dematerialization of money, and therefore of all the scenes that depend upon it. "Counterfeit Money" and *Les Faux-monnayeurs* belong to a specific period in this history of money.)

B. Second type of analysis: *economy* in the narrow sense, the politico-economic exploitation of smoking, the production and speculation in the tobacco market and the drug market in general. The state-owned *bureau de tabac* still *represents* the modern form of this commerce, at least in the retail market and in a modern French city. So as to put the obvious economic dimension of this market in relation with the poetics of smoking that interests us at present, we will take just one example. There is, as everyone knows, a poetics, a tradition and a genre, a thematics of smoking. One day there appeared

---

1. In *Les monnayeurs du langage* (Paris: Galilée, 1984), a book that richly develops the chapter titled "Numismatiques" from his earlier book (*Economie et symbolique* [Paris: Le Seuil, 1973]), Jean-Joseph Goux proposes a reading of *Les faux-monnayeurs* and of Gide's famous *mise en abyme*. This historical reading is organized in particular around a set of distinctions that Goux credits to Gide's uncle, the economist Charles Gide: (1. gold or silver money "with full intrinsic value"; 2. representative paper money, the convertibility of which is assured by the State; 3. fiduciary paper money, with no certain guarantee; 4. conventional paper money or "fictive money," non-convertible and set at a fixed rate). Gide's novel would mark, both as a symptom and as a writing that records the event, the degradation or fictionalization of a literary language that (after World War I and the transition to non-convertible money and to a fixed rate) is no longer "comparable to gold money" (p. 29). Without questioning either the interest of this hypothesis or the necessity of trying to pinpoint the greatest possible historical differentiation, one wonders nevertheless how far one can credit the proposed break (between "gold-language" and "token-language") and its *analogy* with an "historical *rupture*" in a literary periodization ("romantic realism," Zola, Hugo, on one side, Mallarmé, Valéry, Gide, and a few others on the other side, the side of a "fundamental crisis" of "the language of literature, in its relation to being" [p. 180]). Does not this hypothesis tend to naturalize and de-fictionalize gold-money, that is, to confirm an old and stable convention, the very one that "Counterfeit Money" interrogates obliquely? And above all: where would one situate "Counterfeit Money" in this historical schema? And its author?

a sort of journal, *Poésie 1*, that presented itself as an instrument in the fight to defend poetry. Its first issue proposed an anthology of poetries of tobacco. It bore the subtitle "Poets and Tobacco" and contained some sixty classical and modern texts; but its principal title marked in an ingenuous way the extent to which the poetics of tobacco does not expend itself at a pure loss and above all does not let itself be disseminated in smoke. This title was: "La Poésie ne part pas en fumée" (Poetry does not go up in smoke). Indeed, in this case it goes up so little in smoke, it keeps itself and keeps itself so well from going up in smoke that on the back cover there is an ad for *Gitanes Internationales* and, on the title page, the editors thank the *Seita* (the French national tobacco company) for its support: "We thank the *Seita*, whose help, whose dynamism, and whose wealth of archival documentation allowed us to produce this special issue of *Poésie 1*." Even better than that, the authors of this volume wanted to respect the rules of the institution, the copyright and the legislation governing authors' royalties and those of their legatees, the *ayants droit*, as one says in French. Thus, on the second page of the volume, even before the title page, one could read the following: "Bibliographical credits: Despite our research, it may be that we were unable to identify all the *ayants droit* of the quoted poems. In that case, we ask them to contact us so that we may fill in the lacunae for which we apologize." Truly, then (this is the whole question of the legacy and the bequeathed trace), poetry does not go up in smoke—not for everyone. It happens that the publishers of this remarkable volume call themselves *Editions du Cherche-Midi* as if they wanted to pay tribute with this title to the smoker-narrator of "Counterfeit Money" who is forever occupied "à chercher midi à quatorze heures," looking for noon at two o'clock.

C. Thirdly and consequently, the reinscription of tobacco in the economic cycle of exchange—contract, gift/countergift, alliance— necessarily follows the incessant movement of *reappropriation of an excess* in relation to the system of simple natural need and to the circular equivalence between so-called natural need and the labor or production that corresponds to it. But this excess in relation to so-called natural need does not mean that the passage to the symbolic suspends the economic movement. Tobacco is a symbol of this symbolic, in other words, of the agreement [*engagement*], of the sworn faith, or the alliance that commits the two parties when they share the two fragments of a *symbolon,* when they must give, exchange, and obligate themselves one to the other. Tobacco symbolizes the symbolic: It seems to consist at once in a consumption (ingestion) and a purely sumptuary expenditure of which nothing natural remains.[2] But the fact that nothing natural remains does not mean, on the contrary, that nothing symbolic remains. The annihilation of the remainder, as ashes can sometimes testify, recalls a pact and performs the role of memory. One is never sure that this annihilation does not partake of offering and of sacrifice.[3]

Is there an essential relation between the seduction that attracts one into an alliance, desire as desire for tobacco, and a certain work of mourning linked to the incineration of the remainder? If such a relation exists, how is it to be determined? This is one of the questions that will concern us from now on. It has been taking shape for a while now. To go no further than the *incipit* and the first lines of a text, remember this opening of Molière's *Dom Juan.* Sganarelle is holding a tobacco pouch and says:

> Whatever Aristotle and all of Philosophy might say, there is nothing to equal tobacco: It is the passion of gentlemen and whoever lives without tobacco does not deserve to live. Not only does it please and purify the human brain, but it also teaches the soul virtue and with it one learns to become an

2. Since tobacco is consumed neither in the raw or "natural" state nor in the cooked state, Lévi-Strauss assigns it a "meta-" or "ultra-culinary" status, in opposition to the "infra-culinary" status of honey: "The most common method of consuming tobacco places the latter, contrary to honey, not on the *hither side* of cooking but *beyond* it. It is not consumed in the raw state, as is honey, nor exposed to fire in order to cook it, as is the case with meat. It is incinerated, so as the smoke thus released can be inhaled." *From Honey to Ashes: Introduction to a Science of Mythology, Volume Two,* trans. John and Doreen Weightman (Chicago: University of Chicago Press, 1973), pp. 17–18. The ultra-culinary gives rise to procedures that, as regards their result, are either *complementary* (the incineration of feathers and tobacco) or *supplementary* (incineration at the stake) (cf. pp. 27–29). The "pivotal role that has fallen to tobacco in the system" comes particularly from the fact that it unites contradictory values. "Only tobacco worthy of the name unites attributes that are generally incompatible" (p. 29; cf. as well p. 61). On this ambivalence, see above, chap. 2, n. 1.

3. On these problems, one must from now on refer (and I hope to do so in more detail elsewhere) to the recent and fundamental book by Jean-Luc Nancy, *Une pensée finie* (Paris: Galilée, 1991), notably to the chapters titled "L'insacrifiable" and "L'offrande sublime."

honest gentleman. Do you not see, as soon as a man takes some, how *obligingly* he acts with everyone and how *delighted* he is *to give* it away right and left wherever he may be? He does not even wait to be asked but anticipates people's wishes, because verily tobacco inspires feelings of honor and virtue in all those who take it. [Emphasis added.]

One must recall that tobacco, which had been introduced in France a century earlier, was forbidden by Louis XIII to be sold and was denounced by the pietists. The offering and the use of tobacco give access to honor and virtue by raising one above the pure and simple economic circulation of so-called natural needs and productions, above the level of the necessary. It is the moment of celebration and luxury, of gratuity as well as liberty. If one may accredit without reservation such a distinction (which, once again, we will be careful not to do here), tobacco seems to open onto the scene of desire beyond need.

So as to register his disappointment, Michel Serres briefly links this motif of tobacco in *Dom Juan* with Mauss's essay.[4] One should also note, and Serres does not, that beyond generalities on the gift, Mauss

---

4.

Now open *The Gift* and you will not fail to be disappointed. You will find there interest and compensation, alms and banquet, the supreme law that dictates the circulation of goods in the same way as that of women and promises, feasts, rites, dances and ceremonies, representations, insults and *jokes;* you will find there law and religion, esthetics and economy, magic and death, trade fair and market, in sum: *comedy*. Was it necessary to wander for three centuries over the dull azure eye of the Pacific to learn slowly from others what we already knew of ourselves, to go overseas to witness archaic scenes, the same that we represent everyday on the banks of the Seine, at the *Comédie Française,* or at the bistro across the street?" ("Le don de Dom Juan," *Critique* 250, March 1968, p. 263.)

Unless it is faked, this disappointment with *The Gift*, because it neither says nor gives anything one cannot find in one's own backyard, translates the flip side of a recognition of debt; and indeed that is the last sentence of the same paragraph: "But would we ever have been able to read Molière without Mauss?" If we had to speak of disappointment here (which we don't believe we do), ours would not concern the fact that someone or other, at home or elsewhere, had been the first to discover what there is to be said about the gift, but rather that neither Molière nor Mauss, at bottom, has ever said anything about the gift *itself*. And what we are trying to explain here is why there is *no fault* in that.

explicitly takes account of the offering of tobacco. He does so precisely after the passage on the Serpent clan that I quote once again to
underscore this time how the experiences of mourning and gift, the
evocation of food (the cooking of food and the preparation of tobacco)
and of ghosts or spirits are linked in the same time and on the same
scene:

> In the tribe of the Winnebago (the Sioux tribe), the chiefs of the
> clans very typically give speeches to their fellow chiefs from
> other tribes; these speeches are very characteristic, models of
> the etiquette widespread in all the Indian civilizations of North
> America. Each clan cooks food and prepares tobacco for the
> representatives of the other tribes, during the clan's festival.
> Here, for example, are excerpts from the speech made by the
> chief of the Serpent clan: "I greet you. It is good. How could I
> say otherwise? I am a poor, worthless man and you have re-
> membered me. It is good . . . You have thought of the spirits
> and you have come to sit down with me . . . Soon your dishes
> will be filled. So I greet you once again, you humans who take
> the place of the spirits, etc." And when each chief has eaten,
> and has put offerings of tobacco into the fire, the closing for-
> mula points to the moral effect of the festival and of all the
> prestations: "I thank you for having come to sit down in this
> seat, I am grateful to you. You have encouraged me . . . The
> blessings of your grandfathers who have enjoyed revelations
> (and who are incarnate in you) are equal to those of the spirits.
> It is good that you have taken part in my festival. (Pp. 70–71)[5]

You will no doubt find such a long detour to be excessive, especially on the subject of an elliptical allusion to the tobacconist's in the
first line of "Counterfeit Money." Why this digression? Is it because
a digression—wandering or risky promenade, apparently without
method—marks the step of the two friends in "Counterfeit Money"
and no doubt the rhythm of every incalculable scene of the gift? Or
can the digression be justified by the fact that Baudelaire often paid
attention, in other narratives, to the symbolics of tobacco or more
exactly to tobacco as symbol of the symbolic itself? If, then, smoking

5. On the invitation to the Spirits by tobacco smoke, on the Spirit as origin of tobacco, cf. Lévi-Strauss, *From Honey to Ashes,* pp. 368–69 and 438.

symbolizes in fact the symbolic, namely here alliance and contract, it does so *between men* (note that we say between men, apparently *between men*, both in the sense of humanity and of masculinity, and of a humanity better represented, as always in this exemplarist logic, by the example of men than by that of women). Since we are thinking of Mauss's Indians, who have just come on stage, feasting and at peace, we note that Baudelaire also wrote, in imitation of Longfellow ("Imité de Longfellow" is the subtitle of the poem and thereby poses the question of mimetic rivalry that we noticed with Aloysius Bertrand and Poe), "Le calumet de la paix," "The Peace Pipe" ("Debout, il alluma comme un divin fanal,/ La Pipe de la Paix . . . / Et lentement montait la divine fumée . . ." [Standing, he lit like a divine beacon,/ The Peace Pipe [. . .]/ And slowly rose the divine smoke . . .]).[6]

But let us insist on tobacco for reasons that are more strictly internal to "Counterfeit Money." You would in fact miss one of the surest means of access, if not the most visible, to the stakes of this duel if you overlooked the contract or the alliance between the narrator and the one he repeatedly calls "my friend"; if you therefore situated the center of this story, in conformity with its appearance, between the beggar and the one who gives him the counterfeit money, in other words, who *offers* or *holds out* to him money without *giving* him anything, in any case without giving him anything that is legally or legitimately *accredited*. There is here a scene of gift and forgiveness, of a gift that seems to give nothing and of a forgiveness that is finally withheld. Double annulment, double circle and double annulus of the annulment. The agonistic scene is invested with a powerful libidinal charge between the narrator and his friend, within or on the basis of a friendship, a transference, an alliance, a contract—of which tobacco seems to give the key. It does so *before all:* It seems to be there before the beginning. Before the first act, before speech, there is, there was, there will have been tobacco. That is the point of *departure*, to wit, the first partition or sharing [*partage*]; everything comes out of it, everything issues from it, everything is born of it, as from the *logos* of which it is already the origin, and one can only *depart* from there, that is, proceed from there, that is, leave it in the distance: "As we were leaving the tobacconist's . . ."

6. *Oeuvres complètes*, 1, p. 243.

A betrayal, perhaps a false witness threaten the sharing, the contract, or the sworn faith from the *first step* they take leaving the tobacconist's. Their steps, their gait, their deambulation are the rhythmed story of this threatened betrayal. Whence a reading hypothesis: What is suspected, accused, condemned is not so much the act itself, namely, the deceit that consists in tricking the beggar, even though this act in fact occupies the center of the narrative. In truth, it would be the betrayal of the narrator by his friend that remains unforgiven. More exactly, that betrayal is judged and is held to be unforgivable by the one who says "I."

But in what, then, does the betrayal consist? What is finally not forgiven? What are the reasons adduced for the judgment? This remains obscure. It is obscure not only because it is very difficult to determine, but because the very conditions of determinability cannot be given in the (formal and thematic) structure of this scene. The reasoning that culminates in non-forgiveness for a non-gift is tricky; to justify itself, it convokes a whole philosophy whose high noon (the sun without shadow) is very elliptical. It is to the narrator—and not to the beggar, a silent witness—that the "friend" has failed to give. By giving counterfeit money (assuming at least that he did what he said!), the friend would have failed to keep his promise, he would have deceived someone, abused someone's confidence in him, betrayed—but betrayed what and whom? To try to answer that question, one must take some distance from the center of a narrative whose alchemy mixes so well, for lack of meaning as Mallarmé might have said, esthetics with political economy, "credit," "capital," and "money" ("A certain deference, toward the extinct laboratory of the philosophers' elixir, would consist of taking up again, without the furnace, the manipulations, the poisons cooled down into something other than precious stones, so as to continue through sheer intelligence. Since there are only, in all, two pathways open to mental research, into which our need bifurcates—namely, esthetics on one side and also political economy—it is principally of this latter aim that alchemy was the glorious, hasty, and troubling precursor. Everything that once stood out pure, for lack of meaning, prior to the current apparition of the masses, should be restored to the social domain. The null stone, dreaming of gold, once called the philosophal: but it foreshadows, in finance, the future *credit,* preceding *capital* or reduc-

ing it to the humility of *money!* With what disorder, all about us, are
such things pursued, and how little understood!")[7]

To better introduce the libidinal drama and the apparently homo-
sexual duel that is played out not only in the story but in the narrative
of "Counterfeit Money" (given that there is no gift without the possibility *and* the impossibility of an impossible narrative)[8], to better announce the third party who haunts this duel as if begging for a place
in it, here again is the counterpoint of another narrative in this poor
man's literature. Not "Assommons les pauvres" (Beat Up the Poor),
which is too richly complex to be merely touched upon here, and not
"Le joujou du pauvre" (The Poor Child's Toy), but "Les yeux du
pauvre" (The Eyes of the Poor). We have already read it, already *seen*
it [*déjà* vu], if one may put it that way: In the third paragraph of
"Counterfeit Money," when they meet the poor man, it is his supplicating eyes, the mute and accusatory eloquence of those eyes "for the
sensitive man who knows how to read them," it is this look that
speaks the absolute demand to which the "offering of my friend," an
offering apparently without gift, feigned an answer. In "The Eyes of
the Poor," this look is multiplied by three: a father and two children,
his own children whom he is "taking out for some evening air,"
thereby fulfilling the rôle of "nursemaid." Here too, then, as in

---

7. As translated in *Dissemination;* the French text reads as follows:

Quelque déférence, mieux, envers le laboratoire éteint du grand oeuvre, con-
sisterait à reprendre, sans fourneau, les manipulations, poisons, refroidis
autrement qu'en pierreries, pour continuer par la simple intelligence. Comme il
n'existe d'ouvert à la recherche mentale que deux voies, en tout, où bifurque
notre besoin, à savoir l'esthétique d'une part et aussi l'économie politque: c'est,
de cette visée dernière, principalement, que l'alchimie fut le glorieux, hâtif et
trouble précurseur. Tout ce qui à même, pur comme faute d'un sens, avant
l'apparition, maintenant de la foule, doit être restitué au domaine social. La
pierre nulle, qui rêve l'or, dite philosophale: mais elle annonce, dans la finance,
le futur *crédit*, précédant le *capital* ou le réduisant à l'humilité de *monnaie!* Avec
quel désordre se cherche cela, autour de nous et que peu compris!

Mallarmé, "Magie," *Oeuvres complètes*, pp. 399–400; emphasis added. "The Double
Session" (in *Dissemination*) is inscribed, more exactly inserted, between two fragments
of this interrupted quotation (pp. 198, 318/172, 286) of which it proposes, in effect, in
the interval, a reading.

8. Cf. *Parages*, in particular beginning in the sub-chapter titled "La fausse monnaie," pp. 227ff.

"Counterfeit Money," there is the look of the poor; here too there is the withheld gift; here too there is the narrator with someone else; here too there is a link, the alliance between the narrator and someone other; here too there is on the part of this other a refusal to give—be it only to give attention to these looks of the poor; here too there is a refusal of forgiveness—even hatred on the part of the narrator for the other who flees from the poor man's look and rejects his demand. These are so many invariant elements, features common to both narratives. The difference, if one can put it thus, is none other than sexual difference. The other and the ally of the narrator, his symbolic partner is a woman. With this woman to whom he is bound by love, he goes into a café, another place of sumptuary consumption; and there follows the scene of which we will read only the borders, the beginning and the end. Another formal difference, besides a heterosexuality as apparent as is the homosexuality of the other narrative, is that the narrator, the one who says *I*, tells the story, to be sure—he is truly a narrator who summarizes and presents what happened—but his addressee, the addressee of the narration, the narratee, is *she* whom he loves or, if you prefer, whom he hates, and to whom this time *he addresses himself* in order to declare his hatred and his love. The form of the narrative is here the apostrophe, in the sense both of the discursive mode and of the provocative interpellation.

So! You want to know why I hate you today? It will certainly be harder for you to understand than for me to explain it to you, since you are, I do believe, the most perfect example of feminine impermeability that anyone could ever meet.

We had spent a long day together which to me had seemed short. We had duly promised each other that all our thoughts would be shared in common, and that our two souls henceforth would be but one—a dream which, after all, has nothing original about it except that, having been dreamed by everyone on earth, it has been realized by none.

That evening, a little tired, you wanted to sit down in front of a new café forming the corner of a new boulevard still littered with rubble but already gloriously displaying its unfinished splendors . . .[9]

9. *Oeuvres complètes*, pp. 317–18; *Paris Spleen*, p. 52; trans. modified.

Description of the café and its luxury by a painter of modern life, and then the old man appears (he is about forty) with his two children, a little boy and another too weak to walk. The *six eyes* stare at the two lovers. And this story of the eye also takes account of the lovers' eyes. The narrator later concludes:

Not only was I moved by this family of eyes, but I felt a little ashamed of our glasses and decanters, too big for our thirst. I turned my gaze to look into yours, dear love, to read *my* thought in them; and as I plunged my eyes into your eyes, so beautiful and so curiously soft, those green eyes inhabited by Caprice and inspired by the Moon, you said to me: "Those people are insufferable with their eyes open wide as coach doors! Couldn't you ask the proprietor to send them away?"

So you see how difficult it is to understand one another, my sweet angel, and how incommunicable thought is, even between people who love each other![10]

Let us retrace our steps. Let us go back to what links the event to the gift: No gift without the advent of an event, no event without the surprise of a gift. What happens to the beggar and to the friend of the narrator, what in effect passes or comes to pass between them seems, at first glance, to constitute the central event of the narrative. But the repercussion of this gesture *appears only in a discourse*, in the friend's triumphant *confession* when he says to the narrator: "It was the counterfeit coin." Then, in fact, all the rest is taken up with a sort of interior monologue or private deliberation by the narrator. The latter speaks in the first person. He always does so, he speaks continuously *to himself*, and sometimes he remarks it, as if speaking out loud in an inner voice, for example, when he says *to us* what he is saying *to himself*: "'What a singularly minute distribution!' I said to myself." The essential movement of the narrative as such, what makes it advance depends *first of all*, or one could say only, on what then happens to the narrator. And what happens to him is what occurs in his friendship, what befalls that friendship, so as to surprise it [*la surprendre*]. But still more precisely, the event does not boil down to what befalls the narrator and affects his friendship. It takes the form of a meditation *on the event* and a meditation that is not exempt from rea-

10. *Oeuvres complètes*, p. 319; Ibid., p. 53, trans. modified.

soning and speculation—*ad infinitum*. The narrator speculates on a speculation, on this event which, consisting in a gift (the gift of some money that *proves* [s'avère], if one can put it that way, to be counterfeit), could well be the effect of a speculation that engenders in its turn, in a capitalizing fashion, other speculative events. The event, in sum, is what urges the "I" to ask himself: "What is happening to me?" "What has just happened?" and "What is an event?" What does "to happen" [*arriver*] mean? Can one create an event? Can one *make history*, make *a story*, can one *make* in general on the basis or with the help of a simulacrum, here counterfeit money? The narrator says, *to himself*, at a certain momment, at the beginning of his speculation: "such conduct in my friend was excusable only by the desire to create an event in this poor devil's life."

But what passes and what comes to pass, through a movement of *transference*, is that the event has been created in the life of the narrator himself; it has affected the fabric of *relation* itself, relation as narrative and narration, that is clear, but first of all the relation *between* the narrator and his friend.

What happens through what comes to pass happens to the narrator and to his relation of friendship: to be unable to absolve the other, to be incapable of forgiving him, of giving him his forgiveness following the event that the other will have *perhaps* provoked by offering counterfeit money. The narrator tells us, in effect (and one must hear it in the act of narration rather than in the content of the story or the narrative, to make use still of these three categories): This is what is happening to me; this is what is happening to us, to my friend and to me. I cannot give him my forgiveness, in truth I do not owe him this forgiveness, I ought even to refuse to give it to him—and we infer from that: because by not really giving *to this poor man*, he has not given *to me*. Given what? The question is relayed by too many detours and ruses for a single and immediate response to measure up to it right away. For the moment, let us simply try to exhibit one locus of the event that risks remaining in the background of the story and even of the narrative.

The event takes place in the structured layers of the narration, in the fabric of the narrative relation that links the narrator to his friend. For even the relation as link or as religion of friendship between them also takes—between them—the manifest form of the narrative relation. If the friend had not told the narrator what had in fact happened

("'It was the counterfeit coin,' he replied calmly as though to justify himself for his prodigality"), if the friend had not recounted what had in truth happened, if he, while seeming to boast, had not confessed, told, *made* the truth, nothing would have happened to the narrator and to the narration. Whatever perverse or twisted motivation we may attribute to the friend when he tells the narrator the truth (and we will come back to this), we have every reason to think that he wanted to produce an effect on the narrator. This effect *had* [devait] to happen to the narrator or to the friendship that links him to the narrator. It was a matter of "creating an event" also on that side of things, the side of the narrator. One hardly needs to push things very far in this direction to imagine that, had he been alone with the beggar, the friend would not perhaps have offered the counterfeit money; he only did it *in the presence of the narrator* and in order to *provoke* the narrator with his confession. For a confession is at the center of this circulation or this economy, a confession without repentance and without mercy, but a confession in which the guilty one (the so-called or supposed guilty one, the accused) confides by confiding the truth in the friend-narrator. *Confiding himself* thus (in the name of truth or of friendship), he *gives* himself, to be sure, he pretends at least to give himself, to make a show of himself [*se donner en spectacle*], to present himself to view, to give himself over to judgment, but we will see that the narrator does not want to take any account of this gift and in any case he will not respond with forgiveness. If the friend sought to provoke the narrator, what did he want to push him to do? And how? Perhaps we will see, presuming, that is, that there is anything *to see* and that the *relation* (ference, reference, difference, differance, transference, or narration) is not there to say the saying inasmuch as it withholds from seeing.

So something happens, an event takes place. Where does it take place? Where does it happen? To whom does it happen? In what does it consist? That which happens here is not the content of a story, those events that a narrative relation generally reports. What happens happens to the narration, to the elements of the narration itself, beginning with the fiction of its supposed subject. One generally thinks that narrative discourse reports events that have taken place outside it and before it. Narrative relation, so one thinks, does not recount itself; it reports a content that is given outside it and before it. Here, we must keep in mind that what happens happens to the narrator and to the narration; what happens provokes the narrator and the narration; the components of the narration are that without which the event no doubt would not take place. It is *as if* the narrative condition were the cause of the recounted thing, *as if* the narrative produced the event it is supposed to report. It is on the condition of the narrative that the recounted event would have taken place, that it will have taken place. As cause and condition of the thing [*chose*], it is the narrative that *gives* the possibility of the recounted thing, the possibility of the story as story of a gift or of a forgiveness, but also and by the same token the possibility of the impossibility of gift and forgiveness: "I will never forgive him," concludes the narrator. Let us note in passing: In every situation where the possibility of narration is the condition of the story, of history [*de l'histoire*], of the historical event, one ought to be able to say that the condition of knowing or the desire to know (*ēpistemē, historia rerum gestarum, Historie*) gives rise to history itself (*res gestae, Geschehen, Geschichte*), which could complicate, if not contradict, finally, many argumentations of the Hegelian or Heideggerian type that always seem to require the inverse order (no *Historie* without *Geschichte*), although it is true they do so only after having first integrated the possibility of narration or of the relation to knowing into that of the event.

Such would be the given time, such would be the given space, such would be the strange spacing structure of "Counterfeit Money" from the moment the two friends—of whom one is the narrator—take their distance, one from the other, but first of all together from the tobacconist's. Spacing: They leave in the same step, but in a step that must also be altogether other. This step scans the time of the story, it proceeds from a given moment to a given moment.

There must be event—and therefore appeal to narrative and event of narrative—for there to be gift, and there must be gift or *phenomenon of gift* for there to be narrative and history. And this event, event of condition and condition of event, must remain in a certain way unforeseeable. The gift, like the event, as event, must *remain* unforeseeable, but remain so without keeping itself. It must let itself be structured by the aleatory; it must *appear* chancy or in any case lived as such, apprehended as the intentional correlate of a perception that is absolutely surprised by the encounter with what it perceives, beyond its horizon of anticipation—which already appears phenomenologically impossible. Whatever the case may be with this phenomenological impossibility, a gift or an event that would be foreseeable, necessary, conditioned, programmed, expected, counted on would not be lived as either a gift or as an event, as required by a necessity that is both semantic or phenomenological. That is why the condition common to the gift and the event is a certain unconditionality (*Unbedingtheit*: let us leave this German word suspended here; it says something about the thing [*Ding*] and the non-thing; we should moreover read it after Heidegger, return it to Heidegger). The event and the gift, the event as gift, the gift as event must be irruptive, unmotivated—for example, disinterested. They are decisive and they must therefore tear the fabric, interrupt the continuum of a narrative that nevertheless they call for, they must perturb the order of causalities: in an instant. They must, in an instant, at a single blow, bring into relation luck, chance, the aleatory, *tukhē*, with the freedom of the dice throw, with the donor's gift throw [*coup de don*]. The gift and the event obey nothing, except perhaps principles of disorder, that is, principles without principles. In any case, if the gift or the event, if the event of the gift must remain unexplainable by a system of efficient causes, it is the effect of nothing; it is no longer an effect at all, even if there are, as I would say in French and in both senses of the word, *des* effects *de don*, gift *effects*: for example, the aleatory events created by the gift of counterfeit money and on which, in sum, both partners are speculating.

And yet—effects of pure chance will never form a gift that has the meaning of a gift, if in the semantics of the word "gift" it seems implied that the donating agency freely has the intention to give, that it is animated by a wanting-to-give and first of all by a wanting-to-say, the intention-to-give to the gift its meaning of gift. What would a gift be in which I gave without wanting to give and without knowing that I am giving, without the explicit intention of giving, or even in spite of myself? This is the paradox in which we have been engaged from the beginning. There is no gift without the intention of giving. The gift can only have a meaning that is intentional—in the two senses of the word that refers to intention as well as to intentionality. However, everything stemming from the intentional meaning also threatens the gift with self-keeping, with being kept in its very expenditure. Whence the enigmatic difficulty lodged in this donating eventiveness [*événementialité*]. There must be chance, encounter, the involuntary, even unconsciousness or disorder, and there must be intentional freedom, and these two conditions must—miraculously, graciously—agree with each other.

This element of *tukhē* superimposes itself in "Counterfeit Money," it re-marks itself. If we believe the narrator, his friend could only have been "excusable" (the one who says "I" does not seem to distinguish thematically between excuse and forgiveness) "by the desire to create an event"; he would be excusable by the desire not only to produce an event that cannot be foreseen from its causes or conditions, out of a single stroke of luck, but to "create" an event the consequences of which are unforeseeable:

> But into my miserable brain, always concerned with looking
> for noon at two o'clock (what an exhausting faculty is nature's
> gift to me!), there suddenly came the idea that such conduct on
> my friend's part was excusable only by the desire to create an
> event in this poor devil's life, perhaps even to learn the varied
> consequences, disastrous or otherwise, that a counterfeit coin
> in the hands of a beggar might engender. Might it not multiply
> into real coins? Could it not also lead him to prison? A tavern
> keeper, a baker, for example, was perhaps going to have him
> arrested as a counterfeiter or for passing counterfeit money.
> The counterfeit coin could just as well, perhaps, be the germ of
> several days' wealth for a poor little speculator. And so my
> fancy went its course, lending wings to my friend's mind and
> drawing all possible deductions from all possible hypotheses.

While talking to himself, while reflecting—and the whole narrative is caught in the echo of this mirror—the narrator speculates on the speculation like a painter of modern life. He speculates on what can happen to capital in a capital during the age of money, more precisely, in the age of value as monetary sign: The circulation of the counterfeit money can engender, even for a "little speculator," the real interest of a true wealth. Counterfeit money can become true capital. Is not the truth of capital, then, inasmuch as it produces interest without labor, by *working all by itself* as we say, counterfeit money? Is there a real difference here between real and counterfeit money once there is capital? And credit? Everything depends on the act of faith and the credit we were talking about in the wake of Montaigne. This text by Baudelaire deals, in effect, with the relations among fiction in general, literary fiction and capitalism, such as they might be photographed acting out a scene in the heart of the modern capital.

Let us return to the place of this scene, we could say to the scene of the crime. Throughout, this narration is in fact deployed as a discourse of incrimination or recrimination. A crime must have taken place.

The *tukhē* of the gift, let us say rather the apparently aleatory event of the offering, comes to remark another *tukhē* which, preceding it, made it possible. But this condition of possibility will never be a sufficient cause. Here the condition takes the form of an event of chance meeting, the *encounter* with the poor man: "We encountered a poor man who held out his cap with a trembling hand."

> As we were leaving the tobacconist's, my friend carefully separated his change; in the left pocket of his waistcoat he slipped small gold coins; in the right, small silver coins; in his left trouser pocket, a handful of pennies and, finally, in the right he put a silver two-franc piece that he had scrutinized with particular care.
>
> "What a singularly minute distribution!" I said to myself.
>
> We encountered a poor man who held out his cap with a trembling hand.

Nothing would happen, nothing would have taken place without this "encounter," without the chance poor man, without this encounter of fortune. We are translating *tukhē* here by "fortune." This chance poor man is the fortune of the story. Apparently, nothing would have happened—neither the gesture of the gift, nor the confession, nor the argument of the refused forgiveness—without the *good fortune* that puts the beggar in the path of the friends, and friends with a fortune who have at their disposal at least the change from a purchase, a remainder of money. For obviously—and it is in order to play with it that we have translated *tukhē* by "fortune"—the stakes are those of chance, of *the luck of the draw* [*sort*] (*fors, fors fortuna*) that presides over this whole essay on gift and forgiveness, over this whole attempt at gift and forgiveness. The fate (*fors*), the lot, the lottery that preside there and form the general condition of the scene are situated no doubt even before the aleatory of the event created *perhaps* (*perhaps: fors, forte; forsan, forsit, forsitan, fortasse*) by the offering of counterfeit money, even before the aleatory of the encounter with the poor man by chance or by luck (*forte*).

Even before these two fortuitous conditions, or these conditions of fortuity, one must suppose and take into account another and altogether initial condition. It appears with the first paragraph when it is a question of these two idlers who are leaving the tobacconist's and have at their disposal enough money for all this. This first condition is the *social condition* of the two partners: It is given to them to be well-fortuned, to be sufficiently favored by fate or the luck of the draw to be able to envision giving away the surplus, the supplement or the superfluity. Like Auguste Dupin in "The Murders in the Rue Morgue" (he is "reduced" to "poverty" but lives comfortably on credit, "by courtesy of his creditors," and can even offer himself the luxury of books),[11] the two friends are not necessarily rich but they can afford the luxury of giving alms. As nothing is said about the origins of this wealth, or of the conditions of this social condition, everything happens as if it were natural, as if nature had decided this belonging to social class. Fortune is nature. It gives *gratis* to those who have the grace to receive from it this gift, it gives them a gift that gives them the wherewithal to give. This unity of nature and fortune is remarked later in the text when the narrator confesses: "But into my miserable brain, always concerned with looking for noon at two o'clock (what an exhausting *faculty* [in other words, gift: he is gifted] in nature's gift to me!), there *suddenly* came the idea that such conduct on my friend's part was excusable only by the desire to create an event . . ." (I underscore this relation between the gratuitousness of the gift and the irruptive suddenness of the idea).

It is nature, then, that has given him this gift of fortune. It has made him the gift of this gift of working in an exhausting manner to seek what cannot be found in the place where it should naturally be found. Nature has endowed him with this gift of looking for what does not naturally occur in its place. So here is a sort of counter-natural gift of nature: to look for, that is to interrogate, question, demand, desire against the natural tendency. This luck, this chance of birth, gives him by fortuitous grace the wherewithal to go apparently against nature, artificially, artificiously, laboriously, by working hard. There is a supplementary paradox to this natural gift of the counter-natural: At the end of a laborious concentration of his mind completely occupied "with looking for noon at two o'clock," an idea comes to him "suddenly." It does not come about as fruit of his labor,

11. Cf. "Le facteur de la vérité," in *The Post Card*, pp. 515ff./487ff.

but in a rather unexpected, unforeseeable manner, in a discontinuous way with the labor that has preceded it. It is given gratuitously and fortuitously, as if by chance encounter:

> But into my miserable brain, always concerned with looking for noon at two o'clock (what an exhausting faculty is nature's gift to me!), there suddenly came the idea that such conduct on my friend's part was excusable only by the desire to create an event in this poor devil's life, *perhaps* even [*fors, forte*] to learn the varied consequences, disastrous or otherwise, that a counterfeit coin in the hands of a beggar might engender.

Under the sign of this *perhaps* are then deployed all the unforeseeable consequences of the event provoked by his friend's counterfeit money

This unity of fortune and nature, of the luck of the draw (*fors*) and what gives generously *at birth, to the nascent being* (to nature, perhaps to the nation) is an alliance that dominates the whole discourse of the narrator and provokes there the most paradoxical effects. Since we are talking about paradox, let us recall here that Baudelaire had planned to entitle a story "Le paradoxe de l'aumône," (The Paradox of Alms), and that some of his editors consider this to be in fact the first title of "Counterfeit Money." All these paradoxes are programmed by the concept (the history of the concept) of nature and first of all of *phusis*. The history of this concept of nature has an essential relation to the gift. And this in two ways: Naturizing, originary, and productive *phusis*, nature can be *on the one hand* the great, generous, and genial donor to which everything returns, with the result that all of nature's others (art, law [*nomos, thesis*], freedom, society, mind, and so forth) come back to nature, are still nature *itself in differance;* and, *on the other hand,* let us say after a Cartesian epoch, nature can be the order of so-called natural necessities—in opposition, precisely, to art, law (*nomos*), freedom, society, history, mind and so forth. So the natural is once again referred to the gift but this time in the form of the given. We cannot go beyond this outline here.[12] One

---

12. This "logic" and this "aporetics" of the gift here deploy those of differance. The question of the gift was inscribed in the text that bore this title ("Différance," in *Margins,* p. 27/26). In recalling the Heideggerian remark ("the gift of presence is a property of Appropriating [*Die Gabe von Anwesen ist Eigentum des Ereignens*]," *Zeit und Sein,* p. 22), I was interested then in underscoring that "there is no essence of differance," that "it

may also ally the concept of *production* with that of *phusis*. Like that of labor or work, the concept of production can sometimes be opposed to the derived (post-"Cartesian") sense of naturality and sometimes as well to the value of gift: The product is not the given, and producing seems to exclude donation. But is not the *pheuin* of *phusis* first of all the donation of what gives birth, the originary productivity that engenders, causes to grow or increase, brings to light and flowering? Is it not what gives form and, by bringing things into the phenomenality of the light, unveils or develops the truth *of that which* it gives? Of the very thing it gives and of the fact that it gives? In this donating production, fortune (fate, chance, luck, *fors*, fortuity) and necessity are not opposed; on the contrary they are allied.

How is one to behave with regard to this originary productivity, chance and necessity of donating nature? That is the question—both a physical and an ethical question, let us say—ordered by "Counterfeit Money." The narrator brings his response to it, a possible response. But gifted by nature with the faculty of "looking for noon at two o'clock," he will also have elaborated the question. This elaboration makes sense only when referred to a scheme, or as Kant might say, to a schema that relates productive nature to moral nature by the intermediary of the gift. On the subject of the enigmatic unity of fortune (from *fors*) and productive or donating nature, let us note, without drawing any conclusions from it, that the French dictionary *Littré* refers *fors, fortuna* to *ferre* (*fero, ferre*; in Greek, *pherô*) which means to bear, produce (for example fruit or crops [*fruges*]). *Fero* also means "I report," in the sense of recount, of *relation* (*latum*, the participle of *ferre*), relation as narrative or relation as *socius*. And we need not point out that this problematic of counterfeit money carries us and carries us back incessantly to the heart of the great questions of ref-

---

(is) that which not only could never be appropriated in the *as such* of its name or its appearing, but also that which threatens the authority of the *as such* in general. . . ." Which is, in effect, what is being said here about the gift, and thus one must hesitate to say: about the gift *itself*. The "necessity of a future itinerary" was then remarked: "Differance is not a 'species' of the genus *ontological difference*. If the 'gift of presence is the property of Appropriating,' differance is not a process of propriation in any sense whatever. It is neither position (appropriation) nor negation (expropriation), but rather other. Hence it seems—but here, rather, we are marking the necessity of a future itinerary—that differance would be no more a species of the genus *Ereignis* than Being."

erence and difference. Where is the true referent of "Counterfeit Money"? What is it to refer to money or to a monetary sign? And when money gets dematerialized (checks, credit cards, coded signatures, and so forth), what becomes of the act of giving, for example to the poor man in the street? What is "credit" in this case and to cite Montaigne once again? What is faith? What is credit in literature? Can one tell the story of money? And will this story participate or not in literature of some sort? Can one quote money? Can one quote a check? What is it worth?

All these questions are enveloped in the word "fortune," that is, *fors, fortuna*. Under the heading of the aleatory that makes sense, that is, the chance with which one is not allowed to play in just any way whatsoever, here is an interesting coincidence, one might call it a homonym if this phenomenon took place simply within a single language. To limit its exegesis, I will keep as strictly as possible to the limits of Baudelaire's text. But not without having first recalled two things: *on the one hand,* the problematic that, from another point of view, we had tried to elaborate in a text that bears in French the homonymic title "Fors";[13] *on the other hand,* the fact that the event of the gift must always keep its status of incalculable or unforeseeable *exception* (without general rule, without program, and even without concept). Now, there is a French word, *fors,* which also comes from the Latin (this time from *foris,* outside, exterior to, an adverb that is itself

13. "Fors," Préface au *Verbier de l'homme aux loups,* by Nicolas Abraham and Maria Torok (Paris: Aubier-Flammarion, 1976); "Fors," Preface to *The Wolf Man's Magic Word,* trans. Barbara Johnson (Minneapolis: University of Minnesota Press, 1986). Here again, it is a matter of the limits of a problematic of appropriation—and the question of the gift will never be separated from that of mourning:

> Sealing the loss of the object, but also marking the refusal to mourn, such a maneuver is foreign to and actually opposed to the process of introjection. I pretend to keep the dead alive, intact *safe (save) inside me,* but it is only in order to refuse, in a necessarily equivocal way, to love the dead as a living part of me, dead *save in me,* through the process of introjection, as happens in so-called normal mourning. The question could of course be raised as to whether or not "normal" mourning preserves the object *as other* (a living person) dead inside me. This question—of the general appropriation or safekeeping of the other *as other*—can always be raised as the deciding factor, but does it not at the same time blur the very line it draws between introjection and incorporation, through an essential and irreducible ambiguity? Let us give this question a chance to be reposed. (Pp. 16–17/xvi–xvii; cf. passim, notably p. 26/xxii)

a homonym of the noun *foris* that signifies "door"), and which means "with the exception of," "except." It has nothing to do with the Latin word *fors* that means chance, fate, or fortune. Well, it happens that Baudelaire, in a prophetic or apocalyptic passage from *Fusées* of which we will quote only a few fragments, reserves the status of absolute *exception* not for the gift but for money. At the end of the world, which is near, when "supreme evil" will win out, a "pitiless good sense" "will condemn everything, *except* [*fors*] money." The only thing that will be saved from perdition in this sinking world, the only thing that, since it is not a thing, will keep some credit in the eyes of this implacable good sense of tomorrow, in a mechanized and "Americanized" world, says Baudelaire's anger in what he himself calls an "hors d'oeuvre," is money. What has to be condemned in the advent of industrial capitalist society is democracy and "progress." Baudelaire does not differentiate between "universal progress" and "universal ruin." And he condemns them *in the name of the spirit*, but of the spirit of evil which he opposes here to the evil of progressism or to the triumph of historical optimism in industrial (capitalist and democratic) society. Here are these fragments which we will read, up to the "smoke" of a certain "cigar," while asking ourselves how Baudelaire's admirers (and that includes all of us, doesn't it?) accept, would accept or would silence today such (spiritualist and demonic) invectives against democracy, progress and, finally, human rights.[14] The least

14. Who would dare to laugh at Baudelaire's anti-Belgian xenophobia, indeed racism? And who will rush to neutralize this genocidal passage from *Mon coeur mis à nu*: "A nice conspiracy to organize for the extermination of the Jewish Race. Jews, *Librarians* and witnesses to the *Redemption*" (*Oeuvres complètes*, p. 706)? Benjamin is ready to see in this passage a "gauloiserie" or a prank [*facétie*]: "Gauloiserie . . . Céline continued in this direction (Facetious assassins!)" (*Das Passagen-Werk*, ed. Rolf Tiedemann [Frankfurt am Main: Suhrkamp Verlag, 1982], p. 380). Which confirms that Céline was already excusable and pardonable, sheltered by literature and language, for having done and said worse things than so many others whom numerous prosecutors today do not allow to get away with anything, for reasons that can be analyzed. Claude Pichois, editor of the *Oeuvres complètes*, confesses that "this passage is not very easy to interpret." Which does not prevent him from concluding with confidence: "Any [charge of] anti-Semitism is to be dismissed." As if his hypothesis, which must be cited *in extenso*, were heterogeneous with the roots of anti-Semitism and thus as innocent in this regard as the irony with which Baudelaire is here credited (prank here, irony there). Pichois comments: "Here is how we understand it: Given that God is a scandal (end of folio XI of *Fusées*, p. 660) and thus a scandal the incarnate Redeemer, it is necessary—ironically,

significant of these sentences ought to wring cries of protest today
from all the champions of liberal democracy. (We will emphasize in
passing certain words, for reasons that seem to speak for themselves.)

What is not a prayer? Shitting is a prayer, according to what
the *democrats* say when they shit.

[. . .]

Man, that is to say everyone, is so *naturally* [Baudelaire's em-
phasis] depraved that he suffers less from the universal debase-
ment than from the establishment of a reasonable hierarchy.

The world is coming to an end. The only reason it might en-
dure is that it exists. How weak this reason is compared to all
those that announce the contrary, particularly this one: What
does the world have to do henceforth under the sun? [. . . .]
A new example and new victims of the inexorable moral laws,
we will perish by that by which we thought to live. *Mechanics*
will have *Americanized* us to such a point, progress will have
so thoroughly atrophied the *spiritual* part of us that nothing
within the sanguine, sacrilegious, or anti-natural reveries of the
utopians will be comparable to its positive results. [. . . .] But
still this will not be *the supreme evil.*

Human imagination can conceive, without too much trouble,
republics or other communal states, deserving of some glory if
they are led by sacred men, by certain aristocrats. But it is not
especially through political institutions that *universal ruin or universal progress—for the name little matters*—will become manifest.
It will be through the degradation of feelings [*des coeurs*]. Need
I say that what little remains of politics will struggle painfully
in the clutches of general animality and that those who govern
will be forced, in order to sustain themselves and to create a ghost

---

let it be said—to exterminate the Jews who were the witnesses of this Redemption.
Any anti-Semitism is to be dismissed" (p. 1511). Oh, is that so? Would the irony here
consist in proposing to exterminate only the witnesses? And there is no anti-Semitism
in that? Claude Pichois does not integrally cite the passage to which he refers. Here it
is: "God is a scandal—a scandal that pays off [*Dieu est un scandale—un scandale qui
rapporte*]" (p. 660). "Extermination of the Jewish Race": the idea, in any case, was not
so new in Europe. Nor was it the sole property of Nazi Germany.

of order, to resort to means that would send shivers down the spine of our present-day humanity, which is, however, so hard-hearted?—So the son will flee the family, not at eighteen years but at twelve, emancipated by his greedy precocity; he will flee it not to seek heroic adventures, not to deliver a beautiful maiden imprisoned in a tower, not to immortalize a garret by sublime thoughts, but to *begin a business,* to get rich, and to compete with his vile papa—founder and shareholder in a newspaper that will spread enlightenment and would make the *Siècle* of the day look like a henchman of superstition.—Then, errant women, the *déclassées,* those who have had a few lovers and whom one sometimes calls Angels, by reason of and in thanks for the thoughtlessness, which is the light of *chance,* that shines *in their logical existence, logical like evil*—so these latter, I say, will be no more than pitiless good sense [*sagesse*], a good sense that will condemn everything, *except money* [fors l'argent], everything, even the *errors of the senses!* [Baudelaire underscores these last words]. [. . . .]—These times are perhaps very near; who knows if they have not arrived and if the coarsening of our nature is not the only obstacle that prevents us from appreciating the milieu in which we breathe!

As for me who feels sometimes in myself the ridiculousness of a prophet, I know that I will never find there the charity of a physician. Lost in this ugly world, elbowed by the crowds, I am like a wearied man whose eye can see behind him, in the depths of the years, nothing but disillusion and bitterness, and before him only a storm which contains nothing new, neither lesson nor suffering. In the evening when this man *has stolen from destiny* several hours of *pleasure,* lulled in his digestion, forgetful—as far as possible—of the past, content with the present and resigned to the future, drunk on his *sang-froid* and his dandyism, proud of not being so low as those who are passing by, he says to himself, *while contemplating the smoke from his cigar:* What does it matter to me where all these souls [*consciences*] are going?

I think I have veered off into what those in the trade call a *hors-d'oeuvre.* However, I will keep these pages—because I want *to date my anger.*[15]

15. *Oeuvres complètes,* pp. 665–67.

Scansion, cadence of the events of fortune, chances, strokes of luck that rhythmically punctuate this story of gift and forgiveness, or rather this step, this *pas de don* and this *pas de pardon:*[16] Everything is done and everything happens *while walking.* We have resorted to the Greek word, indeed to the Aristotelian concept of *tukhē,* in opposition to *automaton. Tukhē* designates in general a chance when the latter derives its meaning with regard to a human finality, intention, or intentionality. Is it by chance that Aristotle chooses the example of *credit* to illustrate this difference? The creditor, going to the market in the agora, who runs into his debtor by chance and gets his debt repaid, thinks that there is *tukhē* in it, finalized chance, whereas *automaton* designates chance in general, spontaneity without intentional implications. It is true that Aristotle does not always respect this distinction.[17] We had to privilege this Aristotelian concept of *tukhē* for reasons essential to the structure of the gift and the *pas de don,* the gift step/no gift. For in that structure chance is constantly, in advance even, re-finalized, re-intentionalized and regularly reappropriated by a teleology: the desire to create an aleatory event, the benevolence of nature in the gift that the narrator has the good luck to receive from it, and so forth. And even the first event—the first stroke of luck, the encounter with the poor man—however aleatory it may be or may appear to them, takes on meaning from an expectation and a project. The friend had prepared his coup, his coup of the false gift. In the distribution, the "singularly minute distribution" he made of his change, he had first of all sought out, recognized, then separated the counterfeit coin which "he had scrutinized with particular care." So he was waiting for the *kairos,* the right occasion, the *casus,* the chance or the falling due; he was anticipating it and knew that *it would indeed be the case.* In advance, he imagined what would doubtless not fail to present itself.

16. These locutions can be translated either "step of gift" and "step of forgiveness" or "no gift" and "no forgiveness" (Trans.).

17. *Metaphysics,* A 3, 984b. On these dimensions of the aleatory, notably in certain of their effects on the Baudelairean text, we refer to "My Chances/*Mes Chances:* A Rendez-Vous with Some Epicurean Stereophonies," translated by Irene E. Harvey and Avital Ronell, in *Taking Chances: Derrida, Psychoanalysis, and Literature,* ed. Joseph H. Smith and William Kerrigan (Baltimore: The Johns Hopkins University Press, 1984); "Mes Chances: Au rendez-vous de quelques stéréophonies épicuriennes," *Confrontation* 19 (1988).

On the other hand, can one speak of chance regarding the encounter with a poor man, that is, with this absolute demand that can be read ("for a sensitive man who knows how to read them") in the "supplicating eyes" and in their "mute eloquence"? The encounter with the poor man gives rise to the narrative and perhaps, quite simply, the poor man himself represents here, by his very demand, the veritable donor. His encounter is no more a chance affair, in the sense of *automaton,* no more aleatory than the offering, let us say the real one, the one that would give authentic money and not be content to offer simulacra. This encounter is perhaps no more aleatory than the real alms is a pure gift that is exempt from the market, symbolic calculation, and sacrificial parade.

Everyone knows that the encounter with a poor man and with a poor *beggar* (since every poor man does not demand and every demand does not beg) is never absolutely aleatory in a given social space. The beggar occupies a determined place in a social, politico-economic, and symbolic topology. He does not work. *In principle,* begging produces nothing, no wealth, no surplus-value. The beggar represents a purely receptive, expending, and consuming agency, an *apparently* useless mouth. One must indeed say, as always, *apparently,* for in fact he can play a role of symbolic mediation in a sacrificial structure and thereby assure an indispensable efficacity. In any case, he has no role of productive work in the creation and circulation of wealth. He consumes and destroys surplus-values. But the fact that he does not work and does not produce does not mean he is inactive. The beggar has a regular activity, ordered by codes, rites, socio-topological necessities. Although beggars are often passersby or vagabonds, their itineraries and the places where they are tolerated, or even assembled (because other places are forbidden to them, for example, today certain middle-class buildings and streets in certain neighborhoods), severely restrict their nomadic behavior. In conformity with the policing of this very well regulated social space, the activity of beggars may be of the most intense kind, even if it remains non-laboring and seems to produce no material wealth. It is in any case regular and ordered to the point that the beggar's estate has often been considered—and sometimes designated in a barely metaphoric fashion—as a profession, a status, or a social function. Along with that of madmen and delinquents—criminals or thieves—with which it is not fortuitously associated, this social category, in its anthropology or history, delineates the pocket of an indispensable internal exclusion. According to a structure analogous to that of the *pharmakos*, of incorporation without introjection and without assimilation, the expulsion of the beggar keeps the outside within and assures an identity by exclusion, the exception made (*fors*) for an interior closure or cleft.

In France, the social corps of beggars has known all manner of transformations.[18] In its wealth and even in its superabundance, the literary treatment of the theme of alms during the Baudelairean or Mallarméan period has a strict relation with the state of the mendicant population in the cities and countrysides of a certain capitalist society at a determined stage of its industrialization. From this point of view as well, *Paris Spleen* proposes a picture of *Modern Life*, of the modern city and streets, of tobacco shops and cabarets *at the entrance to which* (*foris*) one often comes upon beggars. This is the case of "Beat Up the Poor!" which could be read as a symmetrical counterpoint to "Counterfeit Money," but also as another *story of the eye*. We will have to be satisfied with lifting a few lines from it: "As I was about to enter

18. On the transformations of this status in the eighteenth century and on what he calls "the new division" [*"le nouveau partage"*], see the analyses of Michel Foucault in his *Histoire de la folie à l'âge classique*, 2d edition (Paris: Gallimard, 1972), especially pp. 422ff. Argenson relates how, in 1750, the order was promulgated "to arrest all the beggars in the realm" while preventing them from "pouring" into Paris. Then: "In Paris, all the beggars were released after having been arrested and there followed the seditions we have seen; we are inundated with them in the streets and on the main roads" (quoted by Foucault, p. 425, in connection with the becoming-economic, even economistic, of this interpretation and of this politics of poverty; "Indigence becomes an economic thing," he writes, p. 428). One then has a proliferation of speeches and initiatives aimed at reinserting, as we say today, the "able-bodied poor" or "misfortune" into the cycle of productive work, so as to render the potential or the capital of energy profitable. Poverty becomes a capitalizable credit in the—reciprocal—service of the state and the individual, the former being thereby authorized to order the latter to work. "Mendicity is the fruit of poverty, which itself is the result of accidents occurring either in the cultivation of the land or in the production of manufacturing, or in the rise of commodity prices, in an excess of population, etc." (Brissot de Warville, quoted by Foucault, p. 428); or this: "Misfortune may be regarded as an instrument, as a power, since it does not destroy one's strength and this strength may be used to the advantage of the state, even to the advantage of the individual who is forced to make use of it" (Coqueau, quoted by Foucault, p. 433). In 1777, the Academy of Châlons-sur-Marne received more than a hundred responses to its proposed essay competition on the topic: "The causes of mendicity and the means of eradicating it."

a cabaret, a beggar held out his hat to me and looked at me with one of those unforgettable looks which, if spirit moved matter or if a magnetizer's eye ripened grapes, would overturn thrones." Next the ear relays the eye and there follows an interior meditation on the voices of the Angel, of Socrates and of his "prohibiting Demon," then of the "great affirming" Demon whispering an order in the ear of the narrator who attacks the beggar, the *eye* of *his* beggar: "Immediately I leaped upon my beggar. With a single punch, I closed one of his eyes which became, in a second, as big as a ball." The beggar then gets back up and counterattacks, aiming this time at both eyes ("the decrepit brigand hurled himself at me and proceeded to give me two black eyes . . ."). Conclusion:

> With my energetic treatment, I had thus restored his pride and his life. . . . "Sir, *you are my equal!* Please do me the honor of sharing my purse. And remember, if you are really philanthropic, when any of your colleagues asks you for alms, you must apply the theory that I have just had the *pain* of trying out on your back." [19]

The situation was different before the age of industrial capitalism, in the Middle Ages for example (think of the beggars in *Notre Dame de Paris*), in the seventeenth and eighteenth centuries. Already, however, there was apprehension concerning a socio-political and socio-professional problem. Voltaire speaks of the "edicts" that were "given out" in order to "extirpate the vile profession of beggars, a very real profession that sustains itself in spite of the laws, to the point that one may count two hundred thousand vagabond beggars in the kingdom [therefore a *census* was possible, which perhaps distinguishes the status of beggars from that of today's "homeless"]." To this repressive severity of Voltaire one could oppose a passage from *La nouvelle Héloïse:* There the state of beggar is designated as a sort of profound index of the socius, at the foundation of the social contract that should unite all men: "If one merely considers the state of the beggar to be a trade, far from having anything to fear from it, one finds there only that which nourishes in us the feelings of interest

---

19. *Oeuvres complètes*, p. 359; *Paris Spleen*, pp. 102–3, trans. modified. The poem was first published posthumously in 1869; the manuscript ends with the sentence: "What do you say to that, citizen Proudhon?"

and humanity that should unite all men" (Book V, 2). This quasi-professional regularity has always given rise to political policies. One finds another sign of that in the existence of religious orders called mendicants, mendicant monks, and so forth.

But this is not the place to go off into an endless discourse, however necessary it may be, on alms and begging. Let us retain merely a formal trait. By reason of their very marginality, by reason of their exteriority in relation to the circulation of labor and to the productions of wealth, by reason of the disorder with which they seem to interrupt the economic circle of the same, beggars can signify the absolute demand of the other, the inextinguishable appeal, the unquenchable thirst for the gift. This "thirst" is moreover suggested in the Baudelairean situations of "lack" or "addiction" (tobacco, alcohol: the narrator of "Beat Up the Poor!" goes out into the street "with a great thirst" before running into the beggar at the entrance to the "cabaret"). The regularity of this social irregularity each time reinscribes begging and alms in a sacrificial structure. Sacrifice will always be distinguished from the pure gift (if there is any). The sacrifice proposes an offering but only in the form of a destruction against which it exchanges, hopes for, or counts on a benefit, namely, a surplus-value or at least an amortization, a protection, and a security. Now, as soon as alms and begging are marked by some institutional regularity, by a place, a status, a topo-sociological assignment, a function, it is no longer *encountered* by chance. The encounter is no longer a chance meeting. In turn, alms fulfills a regulated and regulating function; it is no longer a gratuitous or gracious gift, so to speak, which is what a pure gift must be. It is neither gratuitous nor gracious. We are not distinguishing here between economy and symbolic but between the economy of so-called material wealth (production or consumption of material goods) and the so-called symbolic economy. As soon as almsgiving is regulated by institutional rituals, it is no longer a pure gift—gratuitous or gracious, purely generous. It becomes prescribed, programmed, obligated, in other words bound [liée]. And a gift must not be *bound*, in its purity, nor even *binding*, obligatory or obliging. Alms can be bound either by moral obligation or by religion, by a law—natural or positive, moral or religious; a person could be liable for alms, that is, condemned to pay alms to the benefit of the poor or the Church ("*Aumôner*"). The ecclesiastical office of the almoner is charged with the organized distribution of alms. Laws, therefore, transform the gift or rather the offering into (distributive) justice, which is economic in the strict sense or the symbolic sense; they transform alms into exchangist, even contractual circulation.

One may understand, then, why Mauss situates his remarks on alms within a long chapter, or rather a long general "Note" on *sacrifice* which is entitled "The Present Made to Humans, and the Present Made to the Gods." Within this long note (pp. 14ff.), before the "Note on Alms," one finds a whole inventory of gifts made to men in view of attracting the benevolence of nature or the gods, in order to seduce, appease, conciliate natural or supernatural powers, or contract an alliance with them. He writes:

> The purpose of sacrificial destruction is precisely that it is an act of giving that is necessarily reciprocated. All the forms of potlatch in the American Northwest and in Northeast Asia know this theme of destruction. It is not only in order to display power, wealth, and lack of self-interest that slaves are put to death, precious oils burnt, copper objects cast into the sea, and even the houses of princes set on fire. It is also in order to sacrifice to the spirits and the gods, indistinguishable from their living incarnations, who bear their titles and are their initiates and allies. (P. 16)[20]

There is also a kind of purchase from the gods, the gods who know "how to repay the price of things." In a more developed form, this notion of purchase sometimes precedes that of ordinary commerce. It is in this perspective of sacrificial commerce that Mauss situates his "note" on a kind of alms that would be part of this same process, the process of a calculated sacrifice. As marginal people excluded from the process of production and circulation of wealth, the poor come to represent the gods or the dead. They occupy the place of the dead man or the spirit, the return of the ghost, that is, of an always imminent threat. Perhaps that is what neither the narrator's mistress in "The Eyes of the Poor" can bear ("Those people are insufferable with

---

20. On the European equivalents of the potlatch, cf. Emile Benveniste, "Donner et prendre," "Don et échange," in *Le vocabulaire des institutions indo-européennes*, vol. 1, notably p. 76.

their eyes open wide as coach doors"), nor the narrator in "Beat Up the Poor!" when he punches the beggar in the eye.

A beggar always looks threatening, incriminating, accusatory, vindictive in the absolute of his very demand. This demand comes and comes back from the other. You must pay, in other words "give," so as to acquit yourself with regard to the spirit, the ghost, the god, or all that comes back. You must pay, you must *indeed* pay and pay *well* [*il faut* bien *payer*] so that it comes back without haunting you or so that it goes away, which amounts to the same thing. In any case, you must get in its good graces and make peace with it. Whence the institution of alms. Among the Hausa of the Sudan, in order to avoid the spread of fever when the guinea-corn ripens, one must give presents of this wheat to the poor. Sometimes children play the same role as the poor; they are also excluded from the process of production and commerce. "Generosity is an obligation," says Mauss, "because Nemesis [both distributive justice and the enforcing power of vengeance] avenges the poor and the gods for the superabundance of happiness and wealth of certain people" (p. 18). In these conditions, the gift obeys a regulating, distributive, compensatory principle that naturally is transmitted by very complex psycho-symbolic relays. The *Nicomachean Ethics* (Book IV) analyzes liberality, prodigality, magnanimity (*megaloprepeia*), and sometimes avarice as well in the liturgies (*letourgiai*), that is, in the payments imposed on rich citizens who must outfit a fleet, a cavalry corps, a choir or a "theory" (for Delos or Olympia). Aristotle points out that the magnanimous man does not spend for himself but for the common good. His gifts bear a certain resemblance to votive offerings, although the same gifts are not appropriate for the gods and for men, for a temple and for a tomb. There are different sorts of largesse, of gift, of present. Through all this one sees at work a whole ethic of the happy medium, of good measure, of median-ness (*mesotes*), of justice as balance. But it remains implied that giving is better than keeping or taking. The excess of liberality (prodigality) is worth more in principle than the avarice of the "cumin cutter" (*kuminopristes*) who saws a grain of cumin in two rather than give it whole. He is someone who "would shave an egg" as we say in French.

On the subject of this justice of alms, Mauss cites the Arab *sadaka* or the Hebrew *zedaqa*. The one and the other prescribe giving to the poor. After a brief allusion in his "Note on Alms" (pp. 17–18), Mauss comes back to this at length in his "Political and Economic Conclusions." Thus, as we have already seen, he accredits, under the heading of morality, the spirit of that socialism which, as a good manager of its own generosity, as a stranger to mercantilist rationalism and to individual profit, is capable finally of *giving time*, of giving in truth *its* time—a crucial distinction here since the "exchangist producer . . . wishes to be rewarded, even if only moderately, for this gift."

> The very word "interest" is itself recent, originally an accounting technique: The Latin word *interest* was written on account books against the sums of interest that had to be collected. In ancient systems of morality of the most epicurean kind it is the good and pleasurable that is sought after, and not material utility. The victory of rationalism and mercantilism was needed before the notions of profit and the individual, raised to the level of principles, were introduced. One can almost date— since Mandeville's *Fable of the Bees*—the triumph of the notion of individual interest. Only with great difficulty and the use of periphrasis can these two words be translated into Latin, Greek, or Arabic . . . .
>
> *Homo oeconomicus* is not behind but lies ahead, as does the man of morality and duty, the man of science and reason. For a very long time man was something different, and he has not been a machine for very long, complicated by a calculating machine. . . . It is perhaps good that there are other means of spending or exchanging than pure expenditure. In our view, however, it is not in the calculation of individual needs that the method for an optimum economy is to be found. I believe that we must remain something other than pure financial experts, even in so far as we wish to increase our own wealth, whilst becoming better accountants and managers. The brutish pursuit of individual ends is harmful to the ends and the peace of all, to the rhythm of their work and joys—and rebounds on the individual himself.
>
> As we have just seen, already important sectors of society, associations of our capitalist firms themselves, are seeking as bodies to group their employees together. Moreover, all syndicalist groupings, whether of employers or wage-earners, claim they are defending and representing the general interest as fer-

vently as the individual interests of their members or even their corporations. These fine speeches, it is true, are adorned with many metaphors. However, we must state that not only morality and philosophy, but even public opinion and political economy itself, are beginning to elevate themselves to this "social" level. We sense that we cannot make men work well unless they are sure of being fairly paid throughout their life for work they have fairly carried out, both for others and for themselves. The exchangist producer feels once more—he has always felt it, but this time he does so more acutely—that he is exchanging more than a product or his labor-time, but that he is giving something of himself—*his time,* his life. Thus he wishes to be rewarded, even if only moderately, for this gift. To refuse him this reward is to make him become idle or less productive.

Perhaps we may point out a conclusion that is both sociological and practical. The famous Sourate LXIV, "mutual disappointment" (the Last Judgment) given to Mahomet at Mecca, says of God:

15. Your wealth and your children are your temptation, whilst Allah holds in reserve a magnificent reward.

16. Fear Allah with all your might; listen and obey, give alms (*sadaqu*) in your own interest. He who is on guard against his avarice will be successful.

17. If you make a generous loan to Allah, He will pay you back double; he will forgive you because he is grateful and long-suffering.

18. He knows things visible and invisible, he is the one powerful and wise.

Replace the name of Allah by that of society or the occupational grouping, or put together all three names, if you are religious. Replace the concept of alms by that of cooperation, of a task done or service rendered for others. You will then have a fairly good idea of the kind of economy that is at present laboriously in gestation. We see it already functioning in certain economic groupings, and in the hearts of the masses, who often enough have a better sense of their interests and of the common interest than do their leaders.

Perhaps by studying these obscure aspects of social life, we shall succeed in throwing a little light upon the path that our nations must follow, both in their morality and in their economy. (Pp. 76–78; emphasis added)

Our insistence on this *economy of alms* will help us to recognize the system of anticipations, probabilities, and calculations that programs the aforementioned "encounter with a poor man" by the two friends. This encounter was not a pure, aleatory, or unforeseeable event. Neither the demand nor the gift it elicits can be foreign to calculation, be it a sacrificial calculation, even if the demand comes from the beyond of the system, which is what makes it at once imperious and unbearable. Its infinity provokes the calculation of a reappropriation that it simultaneously renders impossible. Even if the gift or the alms were authentic money, fully titled and guaranteed, this experience would not be pure of all calculation or all parade. It cannot relate or refer back to itself without self-gratification or self-congratulation. The word *parade* can designate at the same time the ostentation of the offering, the donating exhibition, or the triumphal show of prodigality, the parading order of the sumptuary, and, on the other side, the side that sidetracks or parries the blow [*et d'autre part, la part de ce qui pare*], it designates protection, the apotropaic, the defense that goes on the offensive. Even if it were not counterfeit money, the gift would not be pure of all parade. Will one say that this is true *a fortiori* for the offering of counterfeit money? Yes and no. What happens once the poor man is encountered, in this encounter that is not a chance or fortunate meeting?

There is *misfortune* [*de l'*infortuné] from the first moment of this encounter. What? Whose? The poor man's, of course. But also the two friends'. As we will verify more than once, all the places can and must be exchanged. The poor man is defenseless, he has nothing, he is destitute of everything. He is even speechless. The absolute demand passes by way of his mute gaze. But, by the same token, he accuses, he frightens, he begins to persecute like the law, justice, the imperious order, an order that comes from outside the economy and in face of which the two friends are in turn destitute. The poor man has nothing to give, he can demand only restitution and look implacably at those who happen by and at what is happening. The two friends are *disquieted*. "We encountered a poor man who held out his cap with a trembling hand. I know of nothing more *disquieting* than the mute eloquence of those supplicating eyes that contain at once, for the sensitive man who knows how to read them, so much humility and so much *reproach*. He finds there something close to the depth of *complicated* feeling one sees in the tear-filled eyes of a dog being beaten." The "mute" and imploring demand of this look, which is all the more imperious, imperious like the law, takes on the figure of an animal, at once too human and inhuman: the beaten dog. The poor man is a dog of society, the dog is the fraternal allegory of social poverty, of the excluded, the marginal, the "homeless"—more than ever, no doubt, in the Paris of the time. Elsewhere Baudelaire associates, in a more insistent fashion, the figures of the dog and the poor man, notably in "Les bons chiens" (The Good Dogs). This is the opportunity for the poet to define what he calls his "muse citadine," his "urban muse," his poet's inspiration as painter of modern capital and of the modern capital. This poet is that animal, such an animal, the *brother* of such an animal whose fate he shares. Baudelaire then opposes "good dogs," stray dogs, the outcasts of society, to the domestic dogs of bourgeois luxury who are the real "parasites":

> Away, academic muse! I have no need of that pedantic old prude. I invoke the friendly, urban, living muse to help me sing of good dogs, poor dogs, mangy dogs, the dogs everyone kicks aside because they are diseased and flea-bitten, *except the poor man whose companions they are, and the poet who looks upon them with a brotherly eye.*[21]

The one who speaks (the poet or the narrator of the prose poem) lines himself up, therefore, on the side of dogs and the poor. He looks *with the eye* of the dog or the poor man. So one may suppose that, in "Counterfeit Money," he is also on the side of the poor man, that is, on the other side, on the side of the other; yet it is true that his friend may have—*who knows?*—made the poor man rich (by the very play of capitalist speculation and destinerrance that can cause counterfeit money to bear fruit), and, with that, as we warned a moment ago, everything begins to change places. After having denounced purebred dogs and apartment dogs, the poet once again describes an exchange of looks with the dog. It is still a story of the eye:

21. *Oeuvres complètes*, p. 360; *Paris Spleen*, p. 104; emphasis added.

To their baskets with them, all these tiresome parasites!

Let them return to their silken and padded baskets! I sing the mangy dog, *the poor dog*, the homeless, roving dog, the circus dog, the dog whose instinct, *like that of the poor man, the bohemian, and the strolling player,* has been so wonderfully sharpened by necessity, that excellent mother and true patron of wit.

I sing the luckless dogs, whether it is those who wander alone through the winding ravines of huge cities or those who, *with their blinking and spiritual eyes,* have said to the abandoned man: *"Take me* with you, and out of our joint misery perhaps we can make a kind of happiness."[22]

We cannot devote to these "Good Dogs" the word-by-word attention they deserve. Beyond rhetoric, or rather exceeding rhetoric in the direction of that which puts this circle of its substitutions in motion, this figure of the dog appears in what might be considered a long meditation on justice, law, the law of the other insofar as it crosses the frontier of law and first of all the frontier between the human and the animal, as well as between the human and the ahuman. Let us note merely a significant paradox: The demand of the good dogs is essential because they demand that one *give* to them, to be sure, and that one give what one *has*, but that one give by *taking* them, by taking what they *are* and by taking them such as they *are*: "Take me with you . . ." Once again, it would be necessary to cross the categories of having and being, giving and taking.

The dog, the poor man, the poor dog is disquieting and complicated. These things reproach and object [*ça reproche et ça objecte*]. The demand is not only an entreaty; it is also the figure of the law. The two friends are sentenced to pay, they are indebted and guilty as soon as it looks at them, as soon as the thing, the poor thing looks at them without talking to them. They are summoned to pay and to acquit themselves. They must restitute and enter again into the symbolic circle. They are on trial, they appear before the donee's court as before the law. With the result that in the final accounting, at the end of this trial, it will be a question of their own *gratitude* with regard to whoever accepts their damage payment and acquits them of their ini-

---

22. *Oeuvres complètes*, pp. 360–61; *Paris Spleen*, p. 105, trans. modified; emphasis added.

tial guilt, the guilt of their *situation*, by permitting them to acquit themselves of their debt.

This story is thus a trial [*procès*], the process of a trial. The two friends progress, proceed, since they continue to walk and to walk the length of the story, to the step of the story which is also the time of a judicial procedure: incrimination, law, and judgment that end in a sentence. They are *before the law*. Without going back over all the structural complications that we analyzed regarding the title, the dedication, the narration, the narrative, and the story, what we are saying here of the (narrated) story is also valid for the (narrating) narrative, for narration and textual dissemination in general. We will not pause over this folding back and this reduplication, but one may constantly draw out the relation between these kinds of folded back relations, relate them to each other or fold them back on each other.[23]

Faced with the mute eloquence of this indictment and because they appear together, the two friends are summoned to acquit themselves by sacrificing, by offering or by offering *themselves*; and one of them has more to offer than the other. "Has to offer" means as well "must offer" since their *co-appearance* [*comparution*] before the law in the sense in which they have to appear before the eyes of the other that make a limitless demand as well as in the sense in which they appear *together*, they co-appear—places them in a situation of identificatory rivalry. The exhibition of the offering has to shine, it has to phenomenalize itself not for the poor man or for the law but first of all or also for the other, for the partner, and for the friend. And this because, as friends, they are not only indebted with regard to the poor man; *they owe themselves each to the other*, they are indebted one with regard to the other. The comparison of their respective offerings is thus the very element of the story—as if they were giving themselves, were making (of) themselves an offering one *to* the other or one *for* the other, as if the poor man, the law, the third party were also but the mediation as well as the condition of their exchange, in truth, of their bidding war, their competition, or their potlatch. But it is a potlatch that consists less in giving more of this or that than in giving

---

23. In French, this reads: "on peut sans cesse faire le rapport entre ces rapports de rapports, les rapporter les uns aux autres ou les uns sur les autres." The verb *rapporter* has a wide usage and several of its meanings are in play here: to bring back, to relate, to recount, to yield (profit, interest). (Trans.)

more, *absolutely*, by giving in [*en donnant raison*] to the other, by giving him the advantage, and in being right by winning out over the other [*d'avoir raison en ayant raison de l'autre*]. First remark of the narrator: "My friend's offering was considerably larger than mine, and I said to him: 'You are right; next to the pleasure of feeling surprise, there is none greater than to cause a surprise.' 'It was the counterfeit coin,' he calmly replied as though to justify himself for his prodigality."

Apparently feeling no offense that his friend has given more than he, the narrator approves of his action, *lui donne raison*, as he says, that is, tells him he is right but only by displacing the accent from what his friend has *given* onto the quantity of what he has *taken* or what he has given *himself*, namely, pleasure—the pleasure of an auto-affection, the pleasure he has given himself or to which he has treated himself, that he has bought for himself (very dearly, thinks the narrator at first: "You are right; next to the pleasure of feeling surprise, there is none greater than to cause a surprise"—in other words, your calculations are good). Concerning the pleasure that the friend has offered himself by offering something other to the other, the narrator has a thesis or an hypothesis, namely, that pleasure always has its cause in a surprise, therefore an event, the sudden coming of the new, of that which cannot be anticipated or repeated. Pleasure is always and first of all the pleasure of being surprised; and still more, before that, and more intensely, quantitatively and qualitatively, it is a pleasure caused by the fact of causing a surprise in the other, that is, of causing in the other the pleasure of being surprised: The greatest pleasure is to cause in the other the greatest pleasure after one's own. The cause of pleasure in the other is surprise, the passion of wonder, as at the origin of philosophy (the *thaumazein* as originary *pathos* of the philosopher, according to Socrates in the *Theaetetus*, since philosophy has no other cause [*arkhē;* 155d]). But the cause of the cause, in which I take the greatest pleasure, is to be the cause of the cause, the all-powerful cause of the cause in the pleasure I give *myself* by giving it to the other. An intoxicating pleasure, like tobacco or drugs, to be as close as possible to the auto-affective *causa sui*.

Naturally, auto-affection is not pure; the other always has something to do with it and, counting the time of the detour, in the course of the trial, that is to say, along the way and during the transference, all manner of catastrophes are possible. The other never lets himself or herself get caught or taken in by the auto-affective circle. For as always in this affair of the gift, it is a matter of *taking*, of taking over and bringing under control [*arraisonner*], of harpooning: of taking and before that of overtaking with surprise. As you have noticed, pleasure is *taken* [*pris*], measured in the sur-prise, and above all other pleasures, in that of the *caused* surprise. To overtake the other with surprise, be it by one's generosity and by giving too much, is to have a hold on him, as soon as he accepts the gift. The other is taken, caught in the trap: Unable to anticipate, he is delivered over to the mercy, to the *merci* of the giver; he is taken in, by the trap, overtaken, imprisoned, indeed poisoned by the very fact that something happens to him in the face of which he remains—having not been able to foresee anything—defenseless, open, exposed. He is the other's catch or take [*prise*], he has given the other a hold [*prise*]. Such violence may be considered the very condition of the gift, its constitutive impurity once the gift is engaged in a process of *circulation*, once it is promised to recognition, keeping, indebtedness, credit, but also once it *must be*, *owes itself to be* [*se* doit *d'être*] excessive and thereby surprising. *The violence appears irreducible, within the circle or outside it, whether it repeats the circle or interrupts it.* An expected, moderate, measured, or measurable gift, a gift proportionate to the benefit or to the effect one expects from it, a reasonable gift (that "good but moderate blend of reality and the ideal" that Mauss favored) would no longer be a gift; at most it would be a repayment of credit, the restricted economy of a differance, a calculable temporization or deferral. If it remains pure and without possible reappropriation, the surprise names that instant of madness that tears time apart and interrupts every calculation.

These are the structural paradoxes, the stigmata of the impossibility with which we began: So as not to take over the other, the overtaking by surprise of the pure gift should have the generosity to give nothing that surprises and appears *as* gift, *nothing that presents itself as present, nothing that is;* it should therefore be surprising enough and so thoroughly made up of a surprise that it is not even a question of getting over it, thus of a surprise surprising enough to let itself be forgotten without delay. And at stake in this forgetting that carries beyond any present is the gift as remaining [*restance*] without memory, without permanence and consistency, without substance or subsistence; at stake is this rest that is, without being (it), beyond Being, *epekeina tes ousias*. The secret of that about which one cannot speak, but which one can no longer silence.

This allows one to hear an accusation in the narrator's praise of his friend ("You are right; next to the pleasure of feeling surprise, there is none greater than to cause a surprise"). Against this implicit accusation the other will have to defend himself. The narrator accuses by telling his friend he is right, by *donnant raison*, giving us by the same token to think, if you will, that a perversity can always, even if it need not do so necessarily, secretly corrupt the "donner raison à l'autre," the "giving reason to the other." The narrator says to him in effect: Well played, you are right, you have calculated well; reason, rationality, *ratio* are on your side, as well as *logos*, which also means account, what counts and what can be counted or counted upon; you have taken the maximum pleasure (it is to be inferred that he means—and inferred by these congratulations that are intended as moral—you have done well); if you have *given* more than me, it's because you wanted *to take* the maximum. The link between morality and the arithmetic, economy, or calculation of pleasures imprints an equivocation on any praise of good intentions. In giving the reasons for giving, in saying the reason of the gift, it signs the end of the gift. The equivocal praise precipitates the gift toward its end and reveals it in its very apocalypse. The truth of the gift unveils only the non-truth of its end, the end of the gift. Times are (no longer) near, there is time no more.

That is why the friend's response is so impervious to deciphering. Even before the narrator "lends," as he puts it, "wings" to his mind in the course of countless hypotheses, the friend had furnished a response in itself difficult to decipher and one whose enigma is precisely that which leaves the field open to the "lending" of wings and to the credit of all the hypotheses: "'It was the counterfeit coin,' he calmly replied as though to justify himself for his prodigality." "As though to justify himself for his prodigality": This first hypothesis is a confession. The narrator confesses in this way that a suspicion, an accusation, or some blame was not absent from his own first remarks, from the "You are right" that obliged the other to "justify" himself. He would have to justify himself for having wanted to take too much pleasure by surprising the poor man, but also his friend the narrator—by surprising the narrator and by dominating him when he gives an "offering [that] was considerably larger." He has been doubly violent and he ought—so thinks the narrator, more or less consciously—to justify himself. (When we say that he thinks "more or less consciously," we are not probing his soul behind the surface of his utterances and would not do so even if these did not belong to a literary fiction; we are merely analyzing the semantic and intentional possibility of these utterances, such as they are readable on this very surface itself.) In any case, this shows that the pleasure taken by the friend is to be measured by what he is doing to the narrator and not just to the poor man. This, then, is the axis of the scene; it implicates the narrator and leaves no room for neutrality. That said, we have not yet—not by a long shot—come to the end of our surprises and the folds of this text. For finally, why does the friend say: "It was the counterfeit coin"? Here we can speculate and extend credit: at least three hypotheses, but in fact a series of innumerable prognostications.

1. He may say it in order to confess and in the hope of getting himself excused: not only for his prodigality, of which the other implicitly accuses him, but also for the violence he has just employed toward his friend—and that he would thereby annul. In that moment, and according to this hypothesis, he confesses, he tells the truth that he owes to his friend, he interrupts the violence between them. He had even interrupted it in advance by giving in fact, in real money, no more than his friend, by not entering into competition with him. It would have been out of friendship that he gave counterfeit money, that is, in sure and absolute terms, he gave less than the narrator. No potlatch: that is the most authentic sign of friendship. What is more, according to the hypothesis of this calculation, the confession would have been encouraged by the other's praise ("You are right . . .").

2. "It was the counterfeit coin" may also signify a surplus of naïve triumph and boastfulness close to cynicism: So, you recognize how good I am at treating myself to the greatest pleasure; well, I am even sharper than that: I bought myself the greatest pleasure at the lowest price; you give me credit, but I speculate even better than you think.

3. But these speculative hypotheses do not exclude each other; on the contrary, they superimpose themselves on each other, they accumulate like a capital of true or (perhaps) counterfeit money that may produce interest; they overdetermine each other in the ellipsis of the declaration. Each is justifiable and each has a certain right to be credited, accredited. This is the phenomenon without phenomenality of counterfeit money: The friend's response also *may be* counterfeit money. One can also credit the friend with feeling innocent of having

given a counterfeit coin—to the point that he does not hide it from the narrator—since, by means of this counterfeit coin, he withdrew from the cycle of the gift as violence toward the poor man. Since he knows, at least *one supposes* he knows, that he did not give anything to the poor man—even as he left him the chance to use the counterfeit coin by making it (perhaps) bear fruit in the capitalist system in which he operates as much as he analyzes it, about which he speculates as much as in which he speculates—he, the false-donor, is pure of any mastery that a donating consciousness might have secured for him. And he is assured this possible innocence by the aleatory nature of the capitalist machine. In this way the poor man owes him nothing. Let us go a step further: The counterfeiter will have figured out how to indebt himself infinitely, and will have given himself the chance of escaping in this way from the mastery of reappropriation. He will have figured out how to break indefinitely the circle or the symmetry. Conditions: fault, debt, duty.

And thereby another—*inverse*—hypothesis is authorized, but one which is included in the preceding one. It is the hypothesis of the worst violence: At little cost, while giving the poor man his chance, he has indebted that man who can do nothing about it, he has surprised his friend not only by the force of his calculations but also by the calm force of his confession. He has honored his contract of friendship because he has told the truth: I owe you the truth, I will tell you the truth, it was the counterfeit coin. Assuming that he did tell the truth, and the truth counts here! Assuming that there is any sense in speculating on it! For it is also possible—we will never know and there is no sense in wondering about it *in literature*—that he gave real money and then boasted to his friend that he gave a "counterfeit coin" so as to produce a certain effect, not on the beggar but on the narrator. Such a calculation would be worthy of a connoisseur of counterfeit money, that is, of a liar. It is to the narrator that he would have passed on counterfeit money by letting him *believe* that he had chosen the counterfeit coin. The narrator would still be, as we were suggesting earlier, in the position or the place of the beggar. This tells us something about literature and about the place of *belief* or of *credit* from which it is written or read. This place is the non-place of a frame (the four-sided border, the spacing out of a given moment), but it is the dislocated frame of a triptych, a scene of three plus or minus an excluded fourth term, all the positions being exchangable there to infinity, in an endless circulation as in "The Purloined Letter."[24] The counterfeit money is the purloined letter. All the same, there as here the circulation can only get going and continue endlessly on the condition of an expropriation or rather an ex-appropriation that forbids what it seems to permit: the return to self or the closing of the circle.

Why does this last hypothesis correspond to the most powerful and most interesting speculation? Nothing in what is readable for us here can exclude or limit such a speculation, as if the friend's secret were all of a sudden giving itself without giving itself. It is and always will be possible that the friend is lying, that he gave a coin of "honest and true," legally minted money while letting one of his partners, namely, the narrator or archivist, *believe* that it was counterfeit so as to produce on him the effect that we've seen. The narration is framed in such a way that, like the narrator, we are the friend's debtors, but to the paradoxical extent that we live on the very credit *we are obliged to extend to him*. Whether or not we take him at his word, we have only his word. We are at once his debtor and his creditor. To exit from this situation and this secret, the beggar, in any case a third party, would have to test the money and tell us whether or not and when (one time out of two) the friend lied, and so forth. But that is excluded, the third party is excluded by the secret of the dual scene. The two of them, and only two, are talking in a *tête-à-tête*. It is, finally, to the extent that talking always involves two, at least two (at least in the "at least" of this "at least two," the structure of which is indestructible even when it enters into the composition of vasts polylogues of 2 + n voices), to the extent, then, that *there is dialogue,* there can be lie and inviolate secret. This is why it is so important to the structure of the scene in "Counterfeit Money" that there are only two of them talking, that the dialogue is reported by the account of only one of them (as in "The Purloined Letter"), that the beggar is mute and that the secret (which is perhaps not shared, which is shared in the mode of non-sharing) between the two friends is sheltered by the *localized* secret of their stroll *tête-à-tête*. Let us not forget that in the cycle to which "The Purloined Letter" belongs as well, before it is at all question of the secret *content* of the story (the story of the purloined letter itself), the staging of the narration places the narrator and his friend in "solitary confinement," so to speak, in a secret lo-

24. Cf. "Le facteur de la vérité," notably pp. 519–20/490–92.

cation ["*au secret*"]. The narrator recalls: "Indeed the locality of our retirement had been carefully kept a secret from my own former associates."[25] But what are we saying when we say that a character in fiction forever takes a secret with him? And that the possibility of this secret is readable without the secret ever being accessible? That the readability of the text is structured by the unreadability of the secret, that is, by the inaccessibility of a certain intentional meaning or of a wanting-to-say in the consciousness of the characters and *a fortiori* in that of the author who remains, *in this regard*, in a situation analogous to that of the reader? Baudelaire does not know, cannot know, and does not have to know, anymore than we do, what can be going "through the mind" of the friend, and whether the latter finally wanted to give true or counterfeit money, or even wanted to give anything at all. Assuming that he even knew it himself—and *one can only assume it*.

The *interest* of "Counterfeit Money," like any analogous text in general, comes from the enigma constructed out of this crypt which gives to be read that which will remain *eternally* unreadable, *absolutely* indecipherable, even refusing itself to any promise of deciphering or hermeneutic. *Even if we assume that he himself knew* in a decidable manner and that there is therefore some hidden truth (and this is yet a different order of question), there is no sense in expecting or hoping to know one day what the friend did, wanted to do, wanted to say in

---

25. This secret is deepened still further by reason of Dupin's preference for darkness, a preference that the narrator, through identification, ends up sharing, to the point that both of them begin to behave like strange counterfeiters. They go so far, in fact, as to "counterfeit" not the day, presence, phenomenality, or indeed the truth, but, on the contrary, the night, the "presence" of the night, the truth of the non-truth, assuming that here night is the contrary of this necessarily invisible condition of phenomenality, presence, and truth that is day itself. One can "make the truth" ["*faire la vérité*"] (the expression is Saint Augustine's) only to the extent that the possibility remains forever open of "counterfeiting" it [*la "contrefaire"*]. If one can imagine what such a counterfeiting might mean, as well as the singular possibility of *counterfeiting the presence of the night*, one would then no longer be very far from what "to give time" or "to kill time" might mean, beyond common sense. "It was a freak of fancy in my friend (for what else shall I call it?) to be enamored of the Night for her own sake; and into this *bizarrerie*, as into all his others, I quietly fell; giving myself up to his wild whims with perfect abandon. The sable divinity would not herself dwell with us always; but we could counterfeit her presence" ("The Murders in the Rue Morgue," p. 179). On this subject, see "Le facteur de la vérité," p. 518/490.

truth, and whether or not he wanted to give in the "authentic" sense of these terms.

Here we touch on a structure of the secret about which literary fiction tells us the essential or which tells us, in return, the essential concerning the possibility of a literary fiction. If the secret remains undetectable, unbreakable, in this case, if we have no chance of ever knowing whether counterfeit money was actually given to the beggar, it is first of all because there is no sense in wondering what actually happened, what was the true intention of the narrator's friend and the meaning hidden "behind" his utterances. No more, incidentally, than behind the utterances of the narrator. As these fictional characters have no consistency, no depth beyond their literary phenomenon, the absolute inviolability of the secret they carry depends first of all on the essential superficiality of their phenomenality, on the *too-obvious* of that which they present to view. This inviolability depends on nothing other than the altogether bare device of being-two-to-speak [*l'être-deux-à-parler*] and it is the possibility of non-truth in which every possible truth is held or is made. It thus says the (non-) truth of literature, let us say the secret *of* literature: what literary fiction tells us about the secret, of the (non-) truth of the secret, but also a secret whose possibility assures the possibility of literature. Of the secret kept both as *thing* or as *being*, as *thing thought*, and as *technique*. And thus of the secret beyond the reserve of these three determinations and of the very truth of these truths. What we are saying here about literature could also be said of the money that, in this case, it talks about and makes into its theme: As long as the monetary *specie* [espèce] functions, as long as one can reckon with its phenomenality, as long as one can *count with and on cash money* to produce effects (effects of alms, then perhaps effects of purchase and speculation of the sort the narrator himself imagines when he speculates on the possible speculations of the other on the basis of counterfeit money), as long as money passes for (real) money, it is simply not different from the money that, perhaps, it counterfeits. There is in any case no possible sense, no possible place, no possible mark for this difference, at least when the situation is framed thus, that is, in the contextual frame of this convention or of this institution. But beyond this frame, assuring thereby finite possibilities of decision and judgment, other contexts are delimited and opened up in their turn. They are more powerful but they are not infinitely powerful, and they inscribe effects of reference, of reality, and of truth in conventional or institutional devices [*dispositifs*]. In structures of belief, of credit, of the supposition of knowledge. As there is no limit to this embedding of one into the other, the opposition of the conventional to the natural finds itself discredited there, let us say more rigorously, it finds itself limited in its indispensable credit, in the speculation that it will always have to authorize.

This would confirm, in any case, that everything was being played out *for* the narrator, in the sense in which it encloses him in his *pour-soi*, for-itself, but also in the sense in which the friend would not have done any of this if it had not been *for* his friend the narrator, *to* his friend the narrator. A terrible scene of friendship (*O philoi, oudeis philos*):[26] Everything happens to the narrator, everything is dedicated to him. In its dative dimension, the time of the story is given to the narrator, oriented toward him, which situation is not lacking in *interest:* The narrator recounts a story whose meaning is dedicated to him. And that he therefore has, by his situation, the greatest difficulty deciphering. The time given has thus simultaneously been refused, denied to him (there is only denegation and potentially denegating sentences in this situation). Given and denied, time will have been killed, and what we are talking about in this transfer of credit is a murder. The narrative gives and kills time. But nothing has yet begun. We have already observed that, in this ruthless rivalry (war without gift or forgiveness, merciless war) around the "It was the counterfeit coin," they exchange only one sentence apiece and in fact the second, the friend's sentence, is already but the citational echo of the narrator's sentence. And by means of this citational exchange they each acknowledge that the other is right [*ils se donnent raison l'un à l'autre*]. Both of them are right [*ont raison*]. The narrator says to his friend: "You are right [*Vous avez raison*]; next to the pleasure of feeling

---

26. "Oh friends, there is no friend." This is the famous saying attributed to Aristotle by Diogenes Laertes and quoted, in almost a proverbial fashion, by so many philosophers and writers, from Montaigne to Blanchot, Kant to Nietzsche. Its philological and grammatical deciphering already poses difficult problems, not to mention the other paradoxes of this utterance (apostrophe or aphorism). I devoted a seminar to them in 1987–88. The minimal outline of a work in progress may be found in "The Politics of Friendship," *Journal of Philosophy,* 11 (Nov. 1988).

surprise, there is none greater than to cause a surprise," then after the response "It was the counterfeit coin" has plunged the narrator into the speculative or specular phantasm of a reverie occupied with looking for noon at two o'clock, the friend "suddenly shattered my reverie by repeating my own words: 'Yes, you are right [*vous avez raison*]; there is no sweeter pleasure than to surprise a man by giving him more than he hopes for.'" Through this specular reversal ["you are right"/"you are right"), he says to him in effect: Yes, yes—yes, you are right (when you said why I was right and so you are right to say I am right); there is no "sweeter" (sweeter, *plus doux*, instead of greater, *plus grand*) pleasure than to surprise by giving him more than he hopes for (and therefore by giving period if the gift must always give more than one expects). So they tell each other they are right to tell each other they are right. They say to each other they are right, they confirm that they are right. Literally, in the French (and one has to be attentive to the literal here because it is insistent: one reads twice "Vous avez raison") and in the letter (*avoir raison* in the sense of to be right or correct and not only to be rational or reasonable), this could mean several things:

1. We are right [*Nous avons raison*] and this confirms that we have reason, we are men, reasonable beings, we belong to the species of the *animal rationale* (*logon ekhon*).

2. We know how to count, we know how to keep accounts (*logon, rationem*), we know how, following the principle of reason, to explain, to make or render accounts (*rationem reddere, logon didonai*), and to recount this story of counting and currency; we are men of knowledge and calculation, but also good narrators, even good authors of literature, and so forth; But to concede that the other is right [*donner raison à l'autre*] is not only to observe that he is right or that reason is on his side; it is also, on a level that is no longer simply theoretical, constative, or descriptive, to acknowledge [*lui donner acte de*] his justice, no less than his exactness, and often to confess one's own wrong rather than one's error. Or if one does, then, recognize one's own error, while the other has managed to avoid it, then to concede he is right [*lui "donner raison"*] implies a moral, and not simply theoretical, judgment.

3. Our calculation has prevailed, *nous avons eu raison de*, literally we have had reason of, meaning we have carried off the day, we have

won, we have controlled [*arraisonné*] by reasoning, controlled the other, the poor man or you yourself, my friend. Which is to say, also the reader caught in the game of interest: you, we, I who am speaking to you.

Now, at this precise moment, at the moment this specularity triumphs, at the moment a certain circle enjoins them to give each other reason in winning out over the other [*se donner raison l'un l'autre en ayant raison de l'autre*], the rupture takes place and the breaking of the contract and the acknowledgment of this cancellation. An interruption opens, in truth it recalls to its opening the space of an absolute heterogeneity and an infinite secret between the two, *between all the two's of the world.* This is what we are going to see, so to speak: If they have told each other they are right, if they have given each other reason, it is for having given or forgiven *nothing,* as if the gift or the forgiveness were always *destined* not to have reason, to be wrong, as if one had to choose between reason and gift (or forgiveness). The gift would be that which does not obey the principle of reason: It is, it ought to be, it owes itself to be without reason, without wherefore, and without foundation. The gift, if there is any, does not even belong to practical reason. It should remain a stranger to morality, to the will, perhaps to freedom, at least to that freedom that is associated with the will of a subject. It should remain a stranger to the law or to the "il faut" (you must, you have to) of this practical reason. It *should* surpass *duty* itself: duty beyond duty [*Il devrait passer le devoir même: devoir au-delà du devoir*]. If you give because you must give, then you no longer give. This does not necessarily mean that *every* law and *every* "you must" is thereby excluded from the gift (if there is any), but you must then think a law or a "you must" that are not determinable by some practical reason. A law or a "you must" without duty, in effect, if that is possible. If one pursues the consequence of these strange propositions, and if one holds that the gift shares with the event in general all these conditions (being outside-the-law, unforeseeability, "surprise," the absence of anticipation or horizon, the excess with regard to all reason, either speculative or practical, and so forth), one would have to conclude that nothing ever happens by reason or by *practical* reason. In any case, no event could be testified to. But it is the question of the witness that is posed to us every time a "duel" marks the inviolate secret of a scene.

What in fact happens here between our two friends? The narrator seeks first of all to make *excusable* that which his friend has just confessed to him, perhaps triumphantly. One could speculate *ad infinitum* about the narrator's interrupted "reverie" on this subject, and on the word "reverie" at this point. For this reverie is deployed as an interminable speculation in itself. Only an external accident or the intrusion of another could put a stop to it. One could speculate *ad infinitum* on what happens between the two "Buts" ("But in my miserable brain, always concerned with looking for noon at two o'clock [. . . .] But the latter suddenly shattered my reverie by repeating my own words . . ."). The reverie is interrupted only by the echo, coming from the other, of the words that the dreamer himself had addressed to the other: "by repeating my own words." For lack of time (there is not time, it takes time, time is lacking, one has to stop, one has to select), let us retain only a few motifs:

1. The desire to "create an event" by the offering of counterfeit money can only *excuse*, can only render a criminal enjoyment excusable if there were *desire* to create an event. In itself, this desire would be good, it would be the desire to give that on which to live, very simply, *to give more (with which) to live* [donner plus à vivre], indeed to give life (". . . such conduct on my friend's part was excusable only by the desire to create an event *in* this poor devil's *life*" [emphasis added])

2. The chance of this event is not limited to the immediate experience of it by the poor surprised devil. It integrates the possible, aleatory, incalculable consequences of counterfeit money. We were saying that one can give only in the measure of the incalculable; therefore, only an hypothesis of counterfeit money would make the gift possible. No one ever gives true money, that is, money whose effects one assumes to be calculable, money with which one can count and reckon and recount in advance the events one counts on from it. Unless this opposition between true and counterfeit money loses here all its pertinence—which would be one of the things demonstrated by this literary experiment, by this language as always possibly counterfeit money. Now, according to the figures of conception, engendering, and germination, these aleatory consequences are of the genetic type (let us underscore: ". . . the varied consequences, disastrous or otherwise, that a counterfeit coin in the hands of a beggar might *en-*

gender" and then further on "The counterfeit coin could just as well, perhaps, be the *germ* of several days' wealth for a poor little speculator"). The speculation of the narrator who speculates on the probable speculation of his friend on the subject of the possible speculation of the poor devil passes by way of counterfeit money as ovular or seminal capital engendering true money. In principle, without assignable limit. What takes shape here is the infinity or rather the indefiniteness of the "bad infinite" that characterizes the monetary thing (true or counterfeit money) and everything it touches, everything it contaminates (that is, by definition, everything). What takes shape here is the quasi-automaticity of its accumulation and thus of the desire it calls forth or engenders. This is no doubt what Aristotle had in mind when he distinguished between chrematistics and economy. The first, which consists of acquiring goods by means of commerce, therefore by monetary circulation or exchange, has no limit in principle. Economy, on the other hand, that is, the management of the *oikos*, of the home, the family, or the hearth, is limited to the goods necessary to life. It preserves itself from the illusion, that is, from the chrematistic speculation that confuses wealth with money.[27] Of course, for Aristotle, it is a matter of an ideal and desirable limit, a limit between the limit and the unlimited, between the true and finite good (the economic) and the illusory and indefinite good (the chrematistic). Here, this limit gets blurred since the contamination we are talking about affects *a priori* family goods. By the same token, it affects the limit between the supposed finiteness of need and the presumed infinity of desire, the transcendence of need by desire. As soon as there is monetary sign—and first of all sign—that is, differance and credit, the *oikos* is opened and cannot dominate its limit. On the threshhold of itself, the family no longer knows its bounds. This is at the same time its originary ruin and the chance for any kind of hospitality. It is, like counterfeit money, the chance for the gift itself. The chance for the event. Nothing can happen without the family and without economy, to be

27. Cf. Aristotle, *Politics*, 1257b, 1258a. (I thank Egide Berns for having recalled this passage to my attention.) Mauss makes a brief allusion to it from a somewhat different point of view (p. 71). Cf. as well Marc Shell, *The Economy of Literature* (Baltimore: The Johns Hopkins University Press, 1978), p. 92. And of course Marx, *A Contribution to the Critique of Political Economy*, ed. Maurice Dobb (New York: International Publishers, 1970), pp. 117 and 137.

sure, but neither can anything happen in the family: in the family, that is, in the sealed enclosure, which is moreover unimaginable, of the restricted, absolutely restricted economy, without the least chrematistic vertigo. When one says that nothing can happen without a certain chrematistics, that nothing happens when a certain chrematistics is dispensed with or bypassed, perhaps one loses sight of Aristotle. This is not certain. But in any case one recalls, in passing, that if *khrema* signals in the direction of the monetary sign, of goods, fortune, and wealth, it also signifies, and this is even its first meaning in ordinary language, the thing and the event, the thing one is concerned with and the event that happens, everything of which "it is the case," in a word: the *occurrence*. To put it quickly: With "Counterfeit Money," we are at the heart of a literary experience or experiment with all the semantic and ultra-semantic resources, the truthless truth, the lawless law, the dutyless duty that are concentrated and lost in the enigma of *khrē*, of *khrema*, of *khraomai*, of *to khreon*, and their whole family. *one must, to need, to lack, to desire, to be indigent or poor,* and then *owe, ought, duty, necessity, obligation, need, utility, interest, thing, event, fatality, destiny, demand, desire, prayer,* and so forth.[28]

28. Here it would be necessary to reread Heidegger's "Anaximander Fragment" (1946, in *Holzwege* [Frankfurt am Main: Klostermann, 1950]; in Heidegger, *Early Greek Thinking: The Dawn of Western Philosophy*, trans. David Krell and Frank A. Capuzzi [San Francisco: Harper & Row, 1975]), in particular its last pages which are devoted to the *to khreon* that, before anything else, before any other translation (for example, "necessity") would name, according to Heidegger, the presencing of what is present [*das Anwesen des Anwesenden*] (p. 334; trans. p. 52). Let us simply recall for the moment that, in a very internal fashion, the motifs that are so important to us here—gift, hand, logos—are crossed and interwoven there. One finds there already the formula whose Lacanian uses we analyzed above (chap. 1, n. 2): "to give what one does not have."

1. The *gift:* Meditating on a certain *didonai diken* of Anaximander, Heidegger writes:

What does 'give' mean here? [*Was heisst hier geben?*] How should whatever lingers awhile, whatever comes to presence in disjunction, be able to give jointure? [*Wie soll das Je-Weilige, das in der Un-Fuge west, Fuge geben können?*] Can it give what it doesn't have? [*Kann es geben, was es nicht hat?*] If it gives anything at all, doesn't it give jointure away? Where and how does that which is present for the time being give jointure? . . . How should what is present as such [*Anwesendes als solches*] give the jointure of its presencing? The giving designated here can only consist in its manner of presencing [*in der Weise des Anwesens*]. Giving is not only giving-away [*Geben ist nicht nur Weggeben*]; originally, giving has the sense of acceding or giving-to [*das Geben im Sinne des Zugebens*]. Such

When one asks: *ti to khrema,* it is as if one were asking the question at the birth of all questions that may be determined by all possible contexts: What is it? What is happening? What is the matter? What must I do? What does that mean? Why? In view of what? Of what, of what?

The genetic vocabulary ("the varied consequences . . . that a coun-

---

giving lets something belong to another which properly belongs to him [*Solches Geben lässt einem anderen das gehören, was als Gehöriges ihm eignet*]. . . . The *didonai* designates this 'letting belong to' [*dieses Gehörenlassen*]. (P. 329; trans. pp. 43–44)

An analysis of the same type may be found in a seminar on Heraclitus and I will come back to this in a forthcoming text ("*Geschlecht* IV: Philopolemology, Heidegger's Ear").

2. The *hand:*

We are accustomed to translate the word *khreon* by "necessity." By that we mean what is compelling—that which inescapably must be [*das unentrinnbare Müssen*]. Yet we err if we adhere to this derived meaning exclusively. *Khreon* is derived from *khrao, khraomai.* It suggests *e kheir,* the hand; *khrao* means: I get involved with something [*ich be-handle etwas*], I reach for it, extend my hand to it [*lange danach, gehe es an und gehe ihm an die Hand*]. At the same time *khrao* means to place in someone's hands or hand over [*in die Hand geben*], thus to deliver, to let something belong to someone [*einhändigen und so aushändigen, überlassen einem Gehören*]. But such delivery is of a kind which keeps this transfer in hand [*dass es das Überlassen in der Hand behält*], and with it what is transferred. (P. 337; trans. pp. 51–52)

I have approached this passage from another point of view, but one which is also related to the experience of the gift, between the hand and the gift, in "*Geschlecht* II: La main de Heidegger" in *Psyché* ("*Geschlecht* II: Heidegger's Hand," trans. John P. Leavey, Jr., in *Deconstruction and Philosophy: The Texts of Jacques Derrida,* ed. John Sallis [Chicago: University of Chicago Press, 1987]). I noted that, at least in the texts I was then referring to (the Seminar on Parmenides [1942–43] and *What Is Called Thinking?* [1951–52]), Heidegger made no "allusion, for example in the Kantian style, to the play of difference between right and left, to the mirror, or to the pair of gloves" (p. 182). I ought to have specified that, as has been pointed out to me since, Heidegger had made more than just an allusion to this, as is well known, in ¶ 23 of *Sein und Zeit,* p. 109.

To sharpen, in this context, the question of the gift and the hand in relation to the monetary thing (and it is no doubt significant that Heidegger speaks so little of this thing), we may at least wonder what kind of constraint is put on the narrative of "Counterfeit Money" by the fact that the money must indeed be "given" from hand to hand. What happens when money is dematerialized enough that it no longer circulates in the form of cash, from hand to hand? What would counterfeit money be without the hand? And alms in the age of the credit card or the coded signature?

3. The *logos:* At the point at which Heidegger appeals to the single name, the "unique word" for Being, he is led to announce a sort of equivalence between *to khreon* and *logos:*

terfeit coin in the hands of a beggar might *engender*," "the *germ* of several days' wealth"), just as well as this unlivable distinction between economy and chrematistics, could lead us back from Aristotle to Plato. In a word, recall that the Good in the *Republic* takes on the features of the father, but also of Capital giving rise to offspring or interest (*tokon te kai ekgonon autou tou agathou*).[29] What it gives in giving life or in giving to be seen in the light is given from a place that remains, without Being, beyond presence, beyond Being in its presence (*epekeina tes ousias*). In "Counterfeit Money," on the other hand, it is a matter of (perhaps legitimate, one will never know) children or (perhaps real and good) interest produced not from an Idea, or even from the Idea of the Good, from true Capital, or from the true Father, not even from a copy of the idea, from an icon or an idol, for example a (monetary, conventional, and artificial) sign, but from a simulacrum, from a copy of a copy (*phantasma*). The phantasm is recognized as having the power, at least the power and the possibility—without any controlling certitude, without any possible assurance—of producing, engendering, giving. This phantasm, namely, the very place

---

The relation to what is present that rules in the essence of presencing itself is a unique one, altogether incomparable to any other relation. It belongs to the uniqueness of Being itself. Therefore, in order to name the essential nature of Being, language would have to find a single word, the unique word [*das einzige Wort*]. From this we can gather how daring every thoughtful word addressed to Being is [*das dem Sein zugesprochen wird*]. Nevertheless such daring is not impossible, since Being speaks always and everywhere throughout language. The difficulty lies not so much in finding in thought the word for Being [*das Wort des Seins*] as in retaining purely in genuine thinking the word found [*rein im eigentlichen Denken einzubehalten*]. (P. 52)

This movement, about which I formerly confessed a certain perplexity (cf. the conclusion of "Différance," in *Margins*, p. 29/27), continues so far as to *gather* in the same gathering [*Versammlung*] to khreon, the logos of Heraclitus, the En and the Moira (the division of the given share [*das Erteilen des Anteils*]) of Parmenides (pp. 55–56).

29. *The Republic*, VI, 506e. I approached this problematic, in particular from the point of view of merchandise, of money, and counterfeit money, in "Plato's Pharmacy," Part 2: "The Father of Logos," in *Dissemination*, pp. 91–94/81–84. "'Have a care, says Socrates [*Republic*, 507a], lest I deceive you with a false reckoning of the interest [*kibdelon apodidous ton logon tou tokou.*' *Kibdeleuma* is fraudulent merchandise. The corresponding verb (*kibdeleuo*) signifies 'to tamper with money or merchandise, and, by extension, to be of bad faith'" (p. 94/83; on gold and political economy, cf. as well pp. 294ff./262ff.)

of any chrematistics, is moreover itself produced by the narrator's "fancy" ("And so my fancy [*fantaisie*] went its course . . ."). But let us not put too much faith in the series "produce, engender, give," or even in the ineradicable axiomatics that associates gift with the generosity, with genial power, and thus with the natural and originary power of engendering. Would a gift that proceeds from a natural power, from an originary aptitude for giving, be a gift? Simultaneously, we come around to dissociating the gift from generosity in a paradox the full rigor of which must be assumed. If it is not to follow a program, even a program inscribed in the *phusis*, a gift must not be generous. Generosity must not be its motive or its essential character. One may give *with* generosity but not *out of* generosity, not so as to obey this originary or natural drive called generosity, the need or desire to give, regardless of the translations or symptoms one may decipher in it. (This proposition would be of a Kantian type if the naturalness that has to be broken off here by the gift were merely the naturalness or the causality of the *sensible* world; but we are talking here about *phusis* in general.) The gift, if there is any, must go against nature or occur without nature; it must break off at the same blow, at the same instant with all originarity, with all originary authenticity. And, therefore, also with its contrary: artifice, and so on. It is in this direction that we would have a few reservations to indicate regarding the most essential Heideggerian motifs, whether it is a matter there of determining what is originarily proper to Being, time, the gift, or of acceding to the most "originary" gift.[30]

We will not leave this culture in its seedling state—and it is the culture of nature itself, culture as originary nature—without having evoked, in passing (while inscribing there the same potential questions), the solar, revolutionary and superabundant motif, the generosity (in mourning that it cannot be in mourning and that it lacks for nothing) of the Zarathustrian high noon—from Nietzsche to Bataille and beyond.

3. All of this, so as to make him excusable, the narrator *lends* to his friend ("And so my fancy went its course, lending wings to my friend's mind and drawing all possible deductions from all possible hypotheses"). He lends to his friend, he credits him with all these

30. Cf. above pp. 21–22 and chap. 4, n. 18.

calculations, he advances him all these dice throws that imply a wish for a gift at the heart of a calculation. But his friend does not show himself worthy of this loan, he reveals himself to be powerless to honor the credit that has been advanced to him on the basis or on the reserve funds of a friendship contract. That at least is what the narrator says he thinks and it is (perhaps) for this reason that the other will not be forgiven. He will not be forgiven because he has not given what was expected of him; he has not even returned what was thus lent to him. But what proves that he does not deserve this forgiveness? And does one have to deserve forgiveness? One may deserve an excuse, but ought not forgiveness be accorded without regard to worthiness? Ought not a true forgiveness (a forgiveness in authentic money) absolve the fault or the crime even as the fault and the crime remain what they are? The most twisted knots of this casuistry are multiplied and capitalized in the last paragraph and the ending of the story. It continues the story of the eye that we have been following for a long time. It is at the moment he looks his friend in the eyes, in the white of the eyes, that the narrator sees, *believes* he sees the truth of what the other had wanted to do, his "aim." But perhaps this moment marks the very blindness out of which arises the speculative discourse of the narrator. In catching the other's gaze, one sees either *seeing* eyes or *seen* eyes, therefore visible. When one sees the other see, and thus the seeing eyes of the other, these seeing eyes are no longer simply seen. Inversely, if they are seen, visible, and not seeing, they become invisible as seeing eyes and secrete, in this regard, or encircle the spectator's blindness. Likewise, when one sees the eyes, when they become visible as such, one no longer sees them see, one no longer sees them seeing. Whence the act of memory and, once again, the act of faith, of credit, of belief, even of credulity that is inscribed in the most immediate intuition of the crossed gaze. When the narrator says that he looks his friend "squarely in the eyes," in the white of the eyes ["*dans le blanc des yeux*"], when he says he saw that "his eyes shone with unquestionable candor" and that he "clearly" saw this or that, he confesses his own candor, and that he *believes* he saw, *on credit or from memory*, what he says he saw, what he says he was "appalled to see." The place of the narrator is the place of credulity itself. It is also the place from which the moral judgment is proffered. And this judgment is without appeal.

I looked him squarely in the *eyes* and I was appalled to see that *his eyes shone* with unquestionable *candor*. I then *saw clearly* that his aim had been to do a good deed while at the same time making a good deal; to earn forty cents and the heart of God; to win paradise *economically*; in short, to pick up *gratis* the certificate of a charitable man. I could have *almost forgiven* him the desire for the *criminal enjoyment* of which a moment before I assumed him capable; I would have found something bizarre, singular in his amusing himself by compromising the poor; but *I will never forgive him the ineptitude of his calculation*. To be mean is never excusable, but there is some merit in knowing that one is; the most *irreparable* of vices is to do *evil out of stupidity*. (Emphasis added)

That's the end, it's too late, there is no longer time: the narrator has said his last word. Without appeal. The absence of appeal, in the sense of the judicial sentence but also in the more general sense of the appeal to the other—that is the narrator's sententious signature. Sententious by situation, exuding that stupidity of which he speaks and which he believes he can condemn but which will always hang in the air around a sentence and a judgment, the narrator has the last word, of course, always, and that is perhaps the gravest lesson of this literature. Neither the beggar nor the friend, neither the absolute plaintiff nor the accused are given the right to speak or a time to speak proportionate to their right. Nothing authorizes them to file an appeal.

Let us give ourselves one more time. Let us chance a step beyond, and for a moment pass the friends in their stroll as they come out of the tobacconist's. We will not hide the fact that, even as we read, comment, reflect, interpret, it is a matter here of writing another story whose fictional structure cannot be radically annulled. We will treat, then, by paralipsis everything that could be the object of an infinite speculation. For what does the narrator not forgive his friend? Candor? Ineptitude? Stupidity? He does not refuse him forgiveness for the crime he has committed, for the enjoyment he has sought, for the double calculation by means of which he aimed to play and win on both scores. He would have "almost" forgiven him, he says, but not altogether (are there degrees of forgiveness?) for this criminal enjoyment; he would have deemed there was a certain merit in knowing oneself to be mean, as if knowing the harm one does were already to confess it to oneself and therefore to repent. The unforgivable, the irreparable, the irremediable, that for which one cannot be acquitted is to do evil "out of stupidity." This paradox deserves a closer look. The narrator does not reproach his friend for meanness or *diabolism*—that's what Kant would have called it—which consists in doing deliberately, consciously, evil for evil's sake, in elevating opposition to the law to the rank of motive (a possibility that Kant excludes for man).[31] He does not even reproach him essentially for having an evil

31. On these Kantian distinctions, cf. in particular *Religion within the Limits of Reason Alone* (1793; trans. Theodore M. Greene and Hoyt H. Hudson [New York: Harper & Row, 1960]). Since the "stupidity" ["*bêtise*"] of which the narrator accuses his friend is certainly not to be confused with bestiality, it is worth recalling here how Kant situated man and radical evil in man: *between bestiality and diabolism*. Man's natural tendency toward evil is "radical" since it corrupts maxims at their very foundation and therefore prevents an eradication of that evil by means of other maxims. The order of the senses alone cannot explain this evil since sensibility deprives man of freedom and forbids one to speak of evil in this regard. By itself, sensibility would make of man an animal. But for all that, man cannot make of transgression a principle or a moral motive: he would be, in that case, a diabolical being. Now, so Kant thinks or asserts, it is *a fact* that he is not such a being. Kant's whole argumentation seems to proceed from the *credit* granted this supposed *fact*. Since freedom remains the condition of evil, since it distinguishes here man from animal, let us not forget, in the context that is ours here, the terms in which Kant defines such a freedom. Because speculative philosophy must leave indeterminate the law of a causality called freedom, the law of causality "by freedom" (*durch Freiheit*), the determination of freedom by the moral law can never be shown or demonstrated; it remains, from the theoretical point of view, negative. It remains the correlate of a belief, a credit, even, says Kant, of a "letter of credit" (*Creditiv*): "This kind of letter of credit [*diese Art von Creditiv*] for the moral law, namely, that it is itself demonstrated to be the principle of the deduction of freedom as a causality of pure reason, is a sufficient substitute for any a priori justification, since theoretical reason had to assume [*anzunehmen*] at least the possibility of freedom in order to fill one of its own needs [*Bedürfnis*] ("Of the Deduction of the Principles of Pure Practical Reason," *The Critique of Practical Reason*, trans. Lewis White Beck [New York: Macmillan, 1985], p. 49). The figure of faith or belief that grounds practical reason is here presented in a fiduciary, banking, or monetary rhetoric (Beck translates *Creditiv* by "this sort of credential"), which must be seen in what is, finally, its infinity or unconditionality. What then happens to rhetoric? That which links infinity, unconditionality—and the rhetoric they govern here—to belief or to credit is also what forbids separating the order of practical reason from chrematistics such as we interpreted it above.

As for the median position of man and even of radical evil, as for this absolutely

intention or an ill will, a radical evil, a natural tendency about which Kant would say that it has perverted an essentially good will that is exposed to the frailty of human nature.

No, the narrator reproaches his friend for the limits of his intelligence and of his intellectual consciousness rather than for the limits

---

original position between the animal and the devil, this is indeed practical reason according to Kant, that is, what links it to a fundamental anthropologism. "Counterfeit Money" does not necessarily fit this description. Nor the flower of evil, nor Baudelaire in general. What is perhaps suggested there to us is evil (unforgivable evil, and therefore the only one that calls for forgiveness) in the species of a diabolical "bêtise," in other words, that satanic *cruelty* that Kant does not want to acknowledge. Since we have underscored frequently the competitive proximity between Baudelaire and Poe, since one cannot, once again, dispense with reading here Benjamin's *Charles Baudelaire: A Lyric Poet in the Era of High Capitalism* (trans. Harry Zohn [London: Verso, 1973]), let us recall what he says in "Der Flaneur": "Baudelaire wrote no detective story because, given the structure of his instincts [*Triebstruktur*], it was impossible for him to identify with the detective. In him, the calculating, constructive element was on the side of the asocial and had an integral part of cruelty [*Grausamkeit*]. Baudelaire was too good a reader of the Marquis de Sade to be able to compete with Poe" (p. 43). To support his assertion, which supposes perhaps a bit too hastily the absence of Sadian cruelty in Poe, Benjamin goes to a quotation from Baudelaire to justify the necessity of returning to Sade in order to account for evil: "One must always return to Sade, that is, to *Natural man*, in order to explain evil" (Baudelaire's note is taken from a "List of titles and outlines for novels and stories," *Oeuvres complètes*, 1, p. 595). Another note by Baudelaire on Sade seems to me worth quoting at this point. Its logic appears to be the same regarding the relation between evil and knowledge, evil and self-consciousness, as that of the narrator when he says, "To be mean is never excusable, but there is some merit in knowing that one is; the most irreparable of vices is to do evil out of stupidity." In a note titled "On *Les liaisons dangereuses*," Baudelaire defines satanism by ingenuousness, unconsciousness, the ignorance or misunderstanding of self, unless the "make-oneself-ingenuous" or the "becoming-ingenuous" is a supplementary diabolical simulacrum or the excess of zeal of a bottomless perversity. As always, Baudelaire's remark remains historical. It is also a diagnosis of modern times, even of modern literature: "In reality, satanism has won. Satan has made himself into the *ingénu*. Evil that knew itself was less hideous and closer to recovery than evil that is ignorant of itself. G. Sand inferior to Sade" (*Oeuvres complètes*, 2, p. 68). The same notes on this "essentially French book" attribute the "prize for perversity" to woman while to Chateaubriand is attributed a "sinister and satanic" character, a "light-hearted satanism," and Sand is pursued unrelentingly. Quoting a letter from Merteuil to Valmont ("My head alone was in ferment. I did not desire sexual pleasure; I *wanted* TO KNOW"), Baudelaire adds: "(Georges Sand and the others)," and underlies once "I wanted" and twice "to know."

If now one considers seriously what Benjamin presumes about the "structure" of

of his moral conscience. In general, you do not accuse someone, you do not refuse to forgive someone for such reasons. Intellectual limits are generally considered to be an innate given of nature, a gift made at birth. So, then, what does he have trouble forgiving? What does he mean by the words: "to do evil out of stupidity"? Necessarily something moral and intentional, something in any case on the order of desire, if not of the will, and which would be lodged in stupidity: something on the order of the chrematistic rather than of economy, to make use once again of this untenable but convenient distinction.

Stupidity [bêtise] is not, in principle, the character of a beast, une bête. In French, no one says of a bête that it is bête. There are stupid beasts [des bêtes bêtes], for example the "bad dogs" of the bourgeois which, as we have seen, Baudelaire's analogy or anthropomorphism opposes to the "good dogs," to the poor, to poets, and so forth. But the stupidity of these beasts is a human stupidity. Nothing is less stupid, less beast-like than "dogs being beaten" and whose "tear-filled eyes" speak the infinite demand: In this story of the eye, the truth of the gift—as of the eye— would be (un)veiled by the veil of tears rather than by sight. Bêtise, stupidity, is here, in the eyes of the narrator at least, proper to man, to a rational animal that does not want to use its reason, that cannot will [ne peut pas vouloir] to use it or that does not want to be able [ne veut pas pouvoir] to use it: like a man who, as Kant would say, does not have the power or the strength to want to accede to Enlightenment, that is, to human adulthood.

Baudelaire's "drives" that would have prevented him from identifying with a detective, if one judged it possible *never* to identify with a detective (which, of course, is open to doubt), if one took the figure of the detective to be determinable, determined, one figure among others without confusing it with any position of quest or inquest in view of the truth to be established, judgment to be formed, account to be rendered, story to be continued, inquisition, search, interrogation, inquiry, or investigation to be conducted to its term, in a word, *knowledge*, then in fact one must recall that on two occasions an identification must be suspended: the identification, which in a certain manner is structural, of Baudelaire with the narrator or with the friend (both of them seem to "play" at detective); then the identification of these characters with the detective they seem to play. They are not literally detectives, in particular because one of them, the narrator, seeks above all to reach a moral judgment, however non-moral may be his investment in it; and because the other, the friend, is more concerned with deceiving justice or in any case with never permitting a truth, conclusion, and a judgment to be established.

This man would be *responsible* for his irresponsibility and for not yet being adult although he is or already can be adult. He would not have had the courage to dare to use his own understanding, first of all in order to understand the motto of Enlightenment: *Sapere aude!*

The friend's stupidity, in the narrator's eyes, stems from the fact that he does not want to understand and not only from his not being able to understand. He could understand, he *ought* to understand, he ought to have understood. However cynical or calculating he might have been in seeking the economical compromise, however deceitful, tricky, or semi-clever, however reprehensible and criminal his calculation might have been, it would have been *almost* forgivable if the friend had at least done what he could, what he *ought to have been able to* or *could have ought to* [devait pouvoir *ou* pouvait devoir] in order to have an awareness and a comprehension of it: therefore, already the beginning of remorse. This supposes that between awareness and confession there is a necessary connection, and that confession belongs to the order of known truth or—theoretical or practical— reason, all of which we have every reason to doubt. Confession does not consist essentially in making the other aware of something. One can inform the other of a crime one has committed without that act thereby *consisting* of an avowal or a confession. The intentional meaning of confession supposes, therefore, that one does not confess in order to inform, to give information or teach a lesson, to make *known*. Consequence: The eidetic purity of confession stands out better when the other is already in a position to know what I confess. That is why Saint Augustine wonders so often why he confesses to God who knows everything.

The friend did not do what he ought to have done in order *to know* that he was mean, to make it known, and to confess it to himself. And it is this trial procedure that must be read, this accusation that must be heard beneath the word *stupidity* since it is said to be irreparable as the cause of evil, of the "evil out of stupidity." Stupidity is not a state, a character, a genetic limit, a natural, native, innate given, a verifiable impotence. Stupidity, in this context, has the sense of a certain *rapport*, it is a certain relation, a certain behavior *with regard to* an intellectual power, or more generally a hermeneutic power inscribed in us by nature like genetic capital portioned out to everyone at birth, a kind of universal good sense or *ingenium* that should always be available.

The stupid perversion of the friend, the "evil out of stupidity," did not consist in *doing evil* or in not understanding, but in doing evil while not doing all he ought to have been able to do in order to understand the evil he was doing, but that he was doing by not doing everything that he ought to have been able to do in order to understand the evil he was doing, but that he was doing by that very fact. In this circle—or rather in the tail-biting figure of this text or this morsel of text, of this serpent morsel—it is finally for his failure to honor the contract that bound him to the gift of nature that the friend is accused. Nature made him the gift, as it does to everyone, in the present or on credit, of a present: the capital of a faculty of understanding. It thus put him in debt with true money, a natural and therefore non-monetary money which is absolutely originary and authentic. The friend's fault, his irreparable fault called "evil out of stupidity," is to have shown that he was not worthy of the gift that nature had given him: He has failed to honor the contract binding him naturally to nature; he has not acquitted himself of his debt—of a natural debt, thus a debt without debt or an infinite debt.

It is almost as if the other had not honored the credit that his friend the narrator had opened for him by "lending wings" to his mind. He lent him wings, the other did not return them. Remains this enigma: The narrator *occupies here the place of nature,* he has represented himself by nature or he represents it; he takes himself for (the) nature (of his friend). Since the narrator *represents* as well the origin of literature by coming here, through an "I" or a play or simulacrum, in the place of the "true" signatory, Baudelaire, we are perhaps witnessing something that *resembles the birth* of literature. In stricter terms (and the difference matters): Not the (natural) birth of literature, not its origin, but the moment of a naturalization of literature, of an interpretation of literature and of a literature of fiction *as nature,* an interpretation (perhaps) as fictive as the counterfeit money that it uses. For by putting on stage a naturalist and sententious narrator, by exhibiting the fiction of a naturalization of literature, Baudelaire, who is neither a detective nor the narrator (although he is perhaps an amateur of money, that is, a connoisseur of counterfeit money, that is, an expert regarding indiscernability in this domain), inscribes perhaps this naturalization in an institution called literature. Perhaps, then, he reminds us of the institutionality of this institution, but of an institution that can only consist in passing itself off as natural. He invites us

perhaps to suspend, at the end of a question, the old opposition between nature and institution, *phusis* and *thesis*, *phusis* and *nomos*, nature and convention, knowledge and credit (faith), nature and all its
others.

We are still saying *perhaps*. For the secret remains guarded as to what
Baudelaire, the narrator, or the friend meant to say or to do, assuming
that they themselves knew; we cannot be sure of this even in the case
of the friend who is the one who, we suppose, alone or better than
anyone, seems to know if he gave—and why—true or counterfeit
money. Yet, besides the fact that he may himself have been mistaken
in a thousand different ways, he places himself or rather he must
stand *in any case* in a position of non-knowing with regard to the
beggar's possible speculation, that is, with regard to the effects of
what he has given, and therefore with regard to the question of
knowing what he in truth gave and thus whether he in truth gave.
Such a secret enters literature, it is constituted by the possibility of
the literary institution and revealed by that institution in its possibility of secret only to the extent to which it loses all interiority, all thick-
ness, all depth. It is kept absolutely unbreakable, inviolate only to
the extent to which it is formed by a non-psychological structure.
This structure is not subjective or subjectible, even though it is responsible for the most radical effects of subjectivity or of subjectivation. It is superficial, without substance, infinitely private because
public through and through. It is spread on the surface of the page,
as obvious as a purloined letter, a post card, a bank note, a check, a
"letter of credit"—or "a silver two-franc piece."

There is no nature, only effects of nature: denaturation or naturalization. Nature, the meaning of nature, is reconstituted after the fact
on the basis of a simulacrum (for example, literature) that it is thought
to cause. For the nature that the narrator represents here, and that he
therefore also discounts and recounts, is a nature that does not so
much give as lend. And that lends more than it gives. It *extends credit*.
And when it offers someone the "exhausting faculty of looking for
noon at two o'clock," it is so that, in his turn, he may fly or steal—
fair's fair, tit for tat [*donnant, donnant*]—"lending wings to the mind."

Let us think about it. Remember Icarus—toward the sun, under
the eye of noon. Would that story, among others, be the whole story,
all of history? In any case, and at least, a certain history of philosophy.

Icarus, an Icarus complains moreover that he is not able to sign. He will not give his name, not even to the sepulture to which others would like to consign him. Unable even to give his name, to give himself a name, to give a name to his end, how could he ever claim to give? To know how to give? To know he is giving anything whatsoever? He has no sepulture and therefore no proper name: precisely because he writes, and thereby sinks, not to the bottom but into the abyss. Icarus does not sign; he complains [*se plaint*] that he cannot even pity *himself* [se *plaindre* lui-même]. A gift is not signed; it does not calculate even with a time that would do it justice. A rare thing today, and Baudelaire's "modernity," in its striking insolence, recalls us to it: He doesn't believe in the sublime either, he extends it no credit. The sublime: speculation, counterfeit money that one would like to substitute, after "careful separation," for the hopeless, cruel, prostituting, killing "love of beauty." Icarus dies for having "embraced the clouds" there where "The lovers of prostitutes/ Are happy, relaxed and satisfied" ["*Les amants de prostituées/ Sont heureux, dispos et repus*"].

Therefore we could, looking for noon at two o'clock, read again, and this will be the end, the downfall [*la chute*], "Les plaintes d'un Icare" (The Complaints of an Icarus), the end, the falling off— precisely—of the poem, its absolute humility, and just the lowest possible:

[. .]
mes yeux consumés ne voient
Que des souvenirs de soleil.

[. . .]
Sous je ne sais quel oeil de feu
Je sens mon aile qui se casse;

Et brûlé par l'amour du beau,
Je n'aurai pas l'honneur sublime
De donner mon nom à l'abîme
Qui me servira de tombeau.

[. . .]
my consumed eyes see only
Souvenirs of the sun.

[. . .]
Beneath some unknown eye of fire
I feel my wing breaking;

And burned by the love of beauty,
I will not have the sublime honor
Of giving my name to the abyss
That will serve as my tomb.[32]

32. *Oeuvres complètes*, 1, p. 143. This poem, which was added in the edition of 1868, has been interpreted from different, but it seems to me not contradictory, points of view by Benjamin (in *Baudelaire*, p. 82) and by Michel Deguy in one of his admirable readings of Baudelaire: "Le corps de Jeanne (Remarques sur le corps poétique des *Fleurs du Mal*)," *Poétique* 3 (1970), p. 338. Michel Deguy is also the poet of *Donnant Donnant* (Paris: Gallimard, 1981):

> *Donnant*
> > *Donnant est la formule*
> > > *l'échange sans marché où la valeur d'usage*
> > *ne serait que de l'échange du don où le commun n'est pas même*
> > *cherché, foison des incomparables sans mesure prise en commun,*
> > *un troc où la fleur d'ail se change en ce qui n'est pas de refus*
> >
> > > *Que désirez-vous donner*
> > > *C'est le geste qui compte*

Giving / Giving is the formula / the exchange without market where use value would only be that of the exchange of the gift in which the common is not even sought, abundance of incomparables without measure taken in common, a barter where the garlic flower changes into what is not refused / What do you desire to give / It's the gesture that counts (Paris: Gallimard, 1981), p. 57.